What people are saying about …

EQUAL

'It's hard to imagine a theme more timely for the global church today, nor a message more necessary than Katia Adams' cry for true equality between the sexes. I particularly appreciate the way she addresses the controversial Pauline texts, demonstrating that this is a matter of biblical integrity and prophetic authority as well as cultural pragmatism. Having returned to faith in Jesus under the apostolic ministry of Jackie Pullinger, I long to see women rise up to exercise spiritual authority alongside men, so that the church of Jesus Christ can bring a message of reconciliation and hope to every part of our broken world.'

Pete Greig, 24-7 Prayer International
and Emmaus Rd, Guildford

'A hope-filled and inspiring vision for mutuality in ministry! What I love about this book is that it engages so well not only with the biblical material but also, and as importantly, with the heart of the One who inspired and gave us the Word.'

Paul Harcourt, National Leader,
New Wine England

'Katia is a brilliant woman. She is intelligent, she is passionate, she is an incredible communicator and she loves Jesus. In this book you can see each of these things. You can feel her love for Jesus and her passion for the Bible. She jumps intelligently and compassionately into a debate which has over the years produced conflict and hurt; few issues have been more divisive in the church over the past generation than the role of women in the church and the home. I have many good and godly friends on both sides of this debate. Katia Adams offers a remarkably fresh take on many of the most controversial NT passages with a gentleness that is commendable. She introduces the reader to key areas of the debate, explaining exegetical arguments with a noteworthy level of simplicity and clarity, and a commendable fairness to differing points of view. Wherever one lands with regard to the topics covered in these pages, they are well worth reading, and Katia's is an important voice in the conversation.'

Debby Wright, Senior Pastor, Trent Vineyard; National Director, Vineyard Churches UK & Ireland

'I have deep admiration and respect for people who delve into topics many people choose to avoid. In this book *Equal*, Katia does an incredible job of unpacking and laying out a compelling dialogue around the gender roles within the Christian framework. What you hold in your hands is thought-provoking and will make you take a look at your own perceptions of men and women and their roles. I encourage you to read this book with a desire to be challenged and to learn; it will undoubtedly have an impact on your life.'

Eric Johnson, Bethel Church

'I'm grateful to Katia for providing a thoughtful approach to what the Bible has to say on this important topic. As I read this book I was reminded of the gospel's liberating power for women and men and its call for us to relate together in honouring, respectful and empowering ways.'

David Stroud, Senior Leader, Christ Church London; Cofounder, Everything Conference

'Katia Adams' book *Equal* will rock your world! Katia is a humble, Spirit-filled, accomplished intellectual who is extremely skilled in communicating her academic, revelatory, and biblical discoveries on this subject. She also lays out comparative interpretations from other scholars so you can personally assess the subject with objectivity. As you read this book, I predict that you will be both challenged and elated. This very topic is on the heart of God for this hour—*Equal* has been inspired by the Spirit of God for "such a time as this"! I highly recommend this wonderful work—it is brilliant!'

Dr. Patricia King, Founder, Patricia King Ministries; Author, Television Producer and Host

'Katia Adams is a phenomenal Bible teacher. Her passion for Jesus, commitment to the kingdom cause and deep love of the Scriptures beautifully position her to tackle one of the critical issues of our time. In reading *Equal* I was expecting a brilliant overview of the subject with some thoughts as to how we might build church cultures that celebrate equality and liberate women (and men). What I wasn't expecting was to also delve deep into some of trickiest passages of the New Testament, to wrestle with the text, to have my mind blown, to be both challenged and confronted in my thinking, and then invited to see familiar texts in a new light and through a new lens. I'm unbelievably grateful that Katia has written something that brings together the best of current scholarship on this subject, and has then condensed and distilled it to make it accessible to a wider audience. The argument is so well structured, so persuasive, so compelling, and phenomenally inspiring. I absolutely loved it. For those that care about liberating both men and women to lead and make their full contribution to Christ's body, I couldn't recommend this book more highly.'

Pete Hughes, Leader, KXC London

'Katia has captured profound insight and accessible application in a bold and compassionate way. This book is a brave engagement with some of the big issues of our cultural moment. These pages hold challenge and inspiration as they tackle complexity head on.'

Rev Pete Wynter, HTB Leadership Pastor
and Director of the HTB Leadership
College London, Founder of Onelife

'Katia Adams has written a helpful and important contribution to the "women in ministry and leadership" debate—the deeper issue being the liberation that Jesus and His kingdom enacted and inaugurated for women, from centuries of male dominance. This book shows how radical the gospel was in its historical context, and how equally relevant it is today in addressing the value and authority of men and women. Katia writes well, argues clearly, showing the various interpretations of the key texts under discussion, then proposes responsible, alternative ways of understanding them in their historical context, and applies the meaning to our current (church) context. However, it's not just a biblical exercise: she writes from personal experience—often deeply painful—in exercising her ministry and leadership with growing conviction and courage, as a woman. This is well worth reading; it will inform and challenge your thinking and living, your church leading and practice.'

Alexander F. Venter, Author, Pastor,
Teacher, Leadership Consultant

'From God's original intent for men and women, to Jesus' radical shattering of the proverbial glass ceiling of first-century Middle Eastern culture, to Paul's letters and female heroes of the early church, Katia Adams offers compelling and brilliant research on what the Bible teaches about gender equality. Far from staying in the comfort of academia, *Equal* is a call to action for us, the church, to come back to the front of culture shaping and relevance, leading the conversation about the Gender Divide. It offers very practical suggestions to level the playing field not only in the secular world but in pastoral leadership too. On a personal level, it expanded my biblical understanding of the matter and will direct my work towards championing gender parity in our society. I could not imagine heaven being gender biased, now I am convinced of it, thanks to Katia's work.'

Sophie le Ray, CEO Naseba, Founder of WIL
(Women In Leadership) Economic Forum

'Katia Adams has written a well-informed and readable resource that will equip the church with a helpful theological vision for understanding the biblical basis for women in ministry. Indebted to many technical works, her book provides a bridge between the academic world and the church. Here is a passionate and faithful reading of the Scriptures that will serve the next generation well.'

Dr. Sean du Toit, Alphacrucis,
New Zealand

'*Equal* makes a strong biblical case for the full equality of men and women. Katia is both firm in her conviction, and honouring to those who read Scripture differently. Whatever your position on this important topic, I'm sure you'll find much to agree with and plenty to be challenged by.'

Liam Thatcher, Teaching Pastor,
Christ Church London, Blogger,
leavenonearth.wordpress.com

'*Equal* is probably one of the most fresh doctrinal challenges that has come out in our generation about the gender issues that have plagued the church. It is filled with brilliant ideas from its author, Katia Adams, who has not only done all the heavy lifting on the subject of women in the Bible and their role, but has proposed some new conclusions that have the potential to change the very foundation of how we do Christianity. Men, you need to read it for your wives, mothers, sisters, daughters so that you have full faith for who they are meant to be according to God's beautiful design. Women, you need to read it so that you can accurately become all that God has for you. This is not a women's ministry book. This is a global identity message that will give us weapons in our hands to combat bad theology that is holding people captive all over the earth. I give this book the highest praise I could give the subject; it will reform your Christian perspective.'

Shawn Bolz, Author of *Translating God,*
Through the Eyes of Love, and *Keys to Heaven's*
Economy; Host of podcast *Exploring the*
Prophetic, www.bolzministries.com

EQUAL

EQUAL

What the Bible
Says about
Women, Men,
and Authority

KATIA ADAMS

DAVID **C** COOK™

transforming lives together

EQUAL
Published by David C Cook
4050 Lee Vance Drive
Colorado Springs, CO 80918 U.S.A.

Integrity Music Limited, a Division of David C Cook
Brighton, East Sussex BN1 2RE, England

The graphic circle C logo is a registered trademark of David C Cook.

Bible credits are listed at the end of the book. The author has
added italics to Scripture quotations for emphasis.

ISBN 978-0-8307-8065-5
eISBN 978-0-8307-8066-2

The Team: Ian Matthews, Jo Stockdale, Amy Konyndyk, Nick Lee, Susan Murdock
Cover Design: Pete Barnsley (CreativeHoot.com)

Printed in the United Kingdom
First Edition 2019

1 2 3 4 5 6 7 8 9 10

062819

For Evangeline Hope: You are a sign and a wonder,
a herald of the King. You have been given a voice
that is clear and strong to proclaim the excellencies of
the One who made you. My prayer is that you will
never be asked to justify what He in His vast wisdom
has put in you, and that what is being fought for in
my generation will be established in yours so that
this book will only be of historical interest to you.

Dedicated to Maggie Yeghnazar and Bubbles
Adams: Two courageous women whose voices
have shaped and inspired many destinies.

CONTENTS

ACKNOWLEDGEMENTS

This book is the fruit of an incredible community of family and friends who have supported me, prayed for me, and cheered me on. I am so grateful for each person who asked me how the book was going, who prayed for me, and who sent me much needed encouragement. From the bottom of my heart, thank you. I cannot name every one of you who have played a significant role, but a few people do need particular mention:

Adam Bright: You asked me when I was going to write my book long before I had ever thought of writing one. Your persistence in nudging me towards this project proved to be one of my greatest motivators. Thank you for believing in me and what I have to say enough to keep asking.

Ash Anandani, Pat Baloyi, Juliet Henderson, Warren Lewin: You all prophesied this book. Thank you for hearing from the Father for me. In moments of discouragement when I was convinced I did not have what it takes, you spoke otherwise and opened my eyes to the Father's assessment of me and this project. I cannot thank you enough. This book exists because of your faithfulness to share what you heard and saw.

Mark and Bev Landreth-Smith, Ruth and Greg Haslam, Paul and Ally Rogers, Stu and Livy Gibbs, Mick Taylor, Andrew Wilson: Though we may not fully agree on what I argue in this book, each of you in different seasons of my life were incredibly influential in calling out and nurturing the teaching gift in me. You encouraged me and made room for me generously and graciously, and in so doing you impacted me and shaped me profoundly. Thank you for seeing me and being willing to take a chance on me.

Sean du Toit: I have had the honour of discussing some of the truths in this book with you. Thank you for being generous with your time and knowledge. I am so grateful for how open you were with what you have paid a price for.

The Frequentsee Team: Each of you is an answer to prayer, and Julian and I are so grateful that God brought you across our path and gave us the immense joy of partnering with you. Thank you for all your hard work to make this project come to life. This book is a testimony to what you are believing for and giving yourselves to.

The Harvest Church Family: Thank you for being a safe space for Julian and me and our children. Thank you for loving us and honouring us and supporting us. Thank you for never complaining about the inconvenience of having us around but only celebrating the blessing. You have been such a gift from God to us, and we are so grateful.

My parents and siblings: Thank you for praying for me and cheering me on. Your encouragement means so much to me.

Vanessa Feola, Jeshua Glanzmann, Derek Morphew, Lana Silk, Alexander Venter, Tanya Walker: Thanks to each of you for helping refine early drafts of this book. Thank you for being willing to give your time to make this so much better.

The David C Cook publishing family and, in particular, Ian Matthews, Jo Stockdale, and Jack Campbell: Thank you for believing in this book and in me. Thank you for the hours of work you invested to make this come alive. Working with you has been a joy.

My wonderful Julian: I don't think I can write anything to express fully how much your role has been in the writing of this book. You have championed me tirelessly at great cost to yourself and have never been concerned to 'protect' your platform but have rather made every effort to catapult me into places of influence. No one will know the sacrifices you have made to make this book a reality and to support me to be who God made me to be, but I know that any fruit of this book, as well as any ministry I do, is credited to your account as much as it is to mine. I love you and thank Jesus for you.

INTRODUCTION

Questions around masculinity, femininity, and equality are by no means limited to a theological forum but have become commonplace in the world that we live in. You would have to live in total isolation in order to avoid a barrage of conversations around these ideas in one way or another today. Discussions on what it means to be men and women and whether both genders should be treated completely equally are not simply theoretical ones but have very practical implications for how we live our everyday lives.

For the past twenty years I have been in and around the 'Christian ministry' world in one way or another, and have become very familiar with the breadth and force of arguments around gender roles in the church. I have experienced first-hand both the beauty of godly community walking together in love despite disagreement, and the pain of community using disagreement over theological issues as boundary lines for who is allowed in and who is to be kept out. I did not approach this project lightly. I am aware that entering into dialogue on gender roles is not for the faint-hearted.

In all honesty, I never wanted to write this book. Those who reach out to get involved in this debate end up with their fingers burnt. What I wanted to do was to study from Scripture, and learn from the wisdom of profound theologians, and ask the Holy Spirit to lead me to settle the matter in my own heart. Once that was done, my intention was to throw myself into the calling that God had spoken over me without fear or hesitation—whichever side I landed on. The last few years have been a wonderful, life-giving journey in that, so much so that on a personal level this debate feels all but irrelevant to me now.

But then, two years ago, I read a book called *Half the Sky*[1] that woke me up to what is happening to women all over the world, and I felt God speak to me about coming out of the cave of my own comfort and speaking out about what I believe to be God's heart for women and for gender roles. I was provoked to overcome my own reticence and to publicly tackle some of the most contested scriptures and themes on gender.

With every generation that Christians continue in debate on this, the world suffers immensely. Brokenness and oppression to women are left largely unchecked by a church that is not clear within itself about God's heart towards women. There is a whole world that is waiting for Christians to stand up and lend their voice to bringing freedom and equality to both men and women.

And so, this book is my contribution, even in the smallest way, to a debate that needs to come to a resolution if the church is going to rise up and be all that it was created to be. I believe that we are living in times that are going to determine the experience of what it means to be men and women for many generations to come. It is the church's privilege to lead the way in that conversation rather than to be on the back foot, arguing within itself, and creating a vacuum that the world will fill with its own ideas.

Although my writing pulls no punches, one thing has been my overarching aim as I've read and researched and written countless drafts: to listen to Jesus and obey His command to walk in love. Please forgive me if at any point I have fallen short of this ideal. Sometimes I think we can be so focussed on proclaiming truth and upholding it, that we unwittingly sacrifice a more foundational and essential Christian requirement—to love one another. If we speak the truth but don't do it in love, then our effort and contribution are worthless (1 Cor. 13).

I have often wondered why Jesus didn't make a topic like this— one that potentially holds at stake the freedom and fruitfulness of half His body—completely and utterly obvious one way or another. Why not make this so airtight in His Word that no one would ever debate God's intention for gender roles? I wonder if the Bible turns out to be less explicit than we would like on this and many other issues in order to teach us to love walking in love more than we love walking in being right. I believe that God's wisdom in allowing us to journey to come to a conclusion is that it is the journey that teaches us how to love one another despite disagreement. And so my prayer is that as you read this book, no matter which side of the argument you see yourself on, you would feel honoured and loved even if at times you find yourself considerably challenged.

One more word of explanation before we delve into the study together. For the purpose of clarity I have referred to the two opposing sides of the gender debate as 'egalitarians' and 'complementarians'. Largely speaking, egalitarians do not believe that there are any authoritative differences between men and women, and complementarians do. I do not use these terms because they are a perfect portrayal of all those within the debate, but because it is necessary to use some brief and recognisable way to identify the different sides of the conversation. I am aware that there is a wide range of beliefs within both groups. Please forgive me if you do not like the terminology, or do not find yourself perfectly fitting into either category.

All that's left for me to say is that it has been an immense privilege for me to have the opportunity to bring my voice to such a crucial conversation. With all the books available on the topic, I am honoured that you would take the time to read my thoughts. I pray you will find the words here both thought provoking and life giving. Thank you.

FROM EDEN TO ETERNITY

Not long ago, I was driving my car when this 'random' thought dropped into my mind: 'Christians are abdicating their mandate, and it's time for that to stop.' I wasn't completely sure what the thought meant, but I knew that God was stirring something up in me. The following chapter came out of my trying to figure out what He was speaking about that day.

The Mandate

Right at the start of history, God had a world-shaping destiny in mind for humanity. The book of Genesis tells us that, having created human beings (both male and female), God commanded them to 'subdue and rule' (Gen. 1:28 NIV). Their role in creation was to take the lead, to influence, and to transform. It was not a suggestion, but a mandate. A mandate that was given to them both with no question as to whether they had what was needed to carry it out. They were

made in the very image of God and carried His stamp of authority—
of course they had what was required for the task.

This was God's mandate for humans at the beginning of time,
and remarkably, it's His mandate for humans still. Even with all that's
happened in history, God's purpose for His people hasn't changed. His
intention is the same: that the whole earth would be covered with the
reality of His kingdom. For those who are in Christ, the words that
God spoke over Adam and Eve rest on us now, and the provision of all
that we need for the task has been put in us by His grace (2 Pet. 1:3).

Some, however, have unwittingly abdicated this call to lead and
have veered away from the mandate that was over humanity right
from its conception.

For some of us, this is motivated by feelings of insecurity and
inadequacy to bring transformation. We have not fully recognised
who God has made us to be and just how much power is coursing
through us now that we are in Jesus. As a result, we have shrunk back
rather than stood tall, knowing who we are and who we belong to.

For others, there has been a misunderstanding of what the church
exists for, and a hesitancy to participate too much in a world that we
are not from. It is as if we have got so preoccupied in keeping ourselves separate from the world that we have given up a core purpose
of our existence: to engage with the world so that we can transform
it with His kingdom. Hence, at times, our churches have served as
bunkers, protecting us from the outside, rather than as springboards,
propelling us to impart the life of heaven's family on the earth.

But, regardless of our reticence, you and I have been put on
this planet to dispense kingdom life wherever we go. For this to
become our reality, a radical renewing of our minds is needed. A

transformation of how we see ourselves and the world He placed us in and a re-education about how kingdom and church work together. Once we align ourselves with His understanding around our identity and authority on the earth, then we will be ready to start taking up the full mantle of what we were created for.

There is another reason for abdication that needs to be addressed. One that on the surface would seem to impact only women, however, on closer inspection, affects the entire body with devastating effect. It is the question of whether God really created *women* to rule and what that looks like in practice.

The reality is that, in many church circles today, we have become so confused on gender roles and what the Bible is trying to tell us about women in leadership that we have encouraged our women to abdicate their purpose as revealed in Genesis 1:28. We have instructed generations of Eves to abdicate their God-given mandate to rule, in favour of an alternate church-given mandate to follow and serve Adam as *he* rules. And the results of this are catastrophic.

Not only does this significantly impact the women in the church, but if it is true that God saw that it was 'not good' for Adam to be alone and that he would need a suitable counterpart to achieve all that he was made for, then undermining women's roles in the body of Christ has severe repercussions for our men too. In that case, renewing our minds around God's intention when He made Eve is neither a women's issue nor following a feminist agenda. It is crucial to the destiny of men for women to understand who they really are (and vice versa).

When we see through this lens in the discussion on gender roles, the reality of why there is such a spiritual dynamic around this becomes apparent. The enemy knows that undermining women is an efficient way of incapacitating the whole body of Christ. No wonder this is such a war-ridden issue.

So, we're going to take some time to look at the first few chapters of Genesis together and come to grips with what happened both in creation and in the fall. Understanding God's intention in the beginning will set us up well to think through God's intention in redeeming the earth.

Genesis 1: Creation through a Wide-Angle Lens

The creation account of mankind in Genesis comes in two forms. First, there is the overarching story found in chapter 1 and then a zooming in and slowing down over details in chapter 2. Both have much to teach us about God's intention for men and women.

In Genesis 1, we see a culminating moment in creation when God, having created all living creatures according to *their* kinds, begins to create humanity according to *His* kind, according to His image, and filled with His breath. He created humanity—both male and female—in His likeness and commanded them both to be fruitful and multiply, to fill the earth and subdue it. And He gave them rulership over (very specifically, nothing was left to misinterpretation here) fish of the sea, birds of the air, and every living thing that moves over the earth—including livestock and creeping things (Gen. 1:26–28). He gave them *both* the instructions. Notice how it would have been impossible for Adam to walk out this mandate on his own? Given the inclusion of 'fruitfulness and multiplication' in this mandate, there is no doubt that God was addressing the command to both male and female (how else was Adam to achieve multiplication exactly?). This was in no way a one-man mandate, but right from the beginning a male and female job. Not just the multiplication bit but all of it, a job that required both male and female at the helm.

At the beginning of history, God created a man and a woman and told them both why they had been put on the planet. For both of them the job description was the same: fruitfulness, multiplication, subduing, ruling. No role was reserved for one over the other. Both were created with equal value in the image of God, both were created with equal authority given by God (rulership), and both were created with equal opportunities to fulfil the purposes of God (no role in the mandate was off-limits for either gender).

Notice that their equality didn't mean uniformity—they had been created male and female, and hence there was an inherent diversity in *expression* as they fulfilled their roles. Eve was to rule as the female image bearer. Adam was to rule as the male image bearer. Not one with greater authority over the other (for then they would not both in fact be ruling) but as two equal, wonderful sides of the same coin—ruling together but radiating the multifaceted nature of the Godhead in their different expressions. What a beautiful start to human history.

What we see in Genesis 1 makes the fact that God created Adam and Eve in two separate stages all the more intriguing. Given that the very purpose God had in mind for humanity required for there to be both male and female, we know that God must have always planned to make both Adam and Eve. Far from being an afterthought, Eve was a necessary part of reflecting the image of God and carrying out

His plan for humanity right from the beginning. The pertinent question for us, then, is why did God choose to create humanity in two different moments? Why create Eve after creating Adam? What was He trying to show Adam about Eve, and Eve about Adam? What was He wanting to show us about men and women? We can categorically say from chapter 1 (especially with verse 26 revealing forethought and planning) that Eve was not part of a spontaneously evolving plan after Adam's creation, but an inherent part of the original plan alongside His creation. So why take the time to do it as God did? This is an important question to address, and we'll look at it in some depth in a moment as we look at Genesis 2.

But let's pause just for a moment before we head there to notice something right here in the Genesis 1 narrative: there is no suggestion of male superiority. No suggestion that only the being fruitful and multiplying roles were for both male and female but that the subduing and ruling roles were specifically with the male Adam in mind. You would think that, if there was such a crucial caveat to this mandate in the heart of God, it would have been communicated clearly, especially as He is taking great pains to be so specific about the nature of the rulership remit that is given to mankind (to the point of including creepy crawlies!). Gilbert Bilezikian highlights this point beautifully:

> Because of his creator rights, God allocates spheres of authority. He assigns limits to the firmament, to the water, to the earth ... He prescribes in detail human rulership over the fish of the sea, over the birds of the air, over every living thing that moves over the earth

including cattle and creeping things, and over all the earth (vv. 26, 28). The whole created universe—from the stars in space to the fish in the sea—is carefully organized in a hierarchy meticulously defined in Genesis 1. And yet there is not the slightest indication that such a hierarchy existed between Adam and Eve. It is inconceivable that the very statement that delineates the organizational structure of creation would omit a reference to lines of authority between man and woman had such a thing existed. Man and woman are not negligible or incidental happenings in the story of creation. They constitute the climactic creative achievement of God. Consequently, the definition of authority structures between man and woman would have been at least as important as the mention of their authority over 'every creeping thing that creeps upon the earth' (v. 26). This is all the more so since the Biblical text describes hierarchical organization as an element intrinsic to creation. But nowhere is it stated that man was intended to rule over woman within God's creation design. The fact that not a single reference, not a hint, not a whisper is made regarding authority roles between man and woman in a text otherwise permeated with hierarchical organization indicates that their relationship was one of nonhierarchical mutuality. Considerations of supremacy or leadership of one over the other were alien to the text and may not be imposed on it without violating God's original design for human relations.[1]

The thrust of Genesis 1 is thoroughly egalitarian. But is that true of the whole creation narrative? Let's look at Genesis 2 to see whether there is any difference there.

Genesis 2: Creation Zoomed In

Genesis 2 reveals some details that bring fascinating insight into how God brought His creative plan about. On His foundational purpose laid out in Genesis 1:26, God chose to create mankind in two separate stages.

First, He made Adam from the ground (Adam—which in the Hebrew means 'man'—is wordplay on the Hebrew word 'ground', *adamah*). And then God made this proclamation that it was 'not good' for Adam to be alone (Gen. 2:18)—the only time this declaration was made over His creation.

We then read that God brought the animals to Adam to see what he would name them. Initially, we may assume that this was simply God giving Adam an opportunity to steward and rule creation as he had been designed to. But, on closer inspection, we find the true purpose of this exercise revealed at the end of Genesis 2:20 where we are told, 'But for Adam there was not found a helper fit for him.' This was not about Adam flexing his muscles of authority but rather a 'helper-finding' mission. 'In naming the animals, that is, in the process of determining their definition and their function in relation to himself, Adam discovered his own uniqueness as a human being.'[2] The reality is that the premise of searching out a companion was somewhat of a charade considering God knew all along that no suitable helper would be found. But it was a crucial process intended to open Adam's eyes to that fact.

Thus, naming the animals wasn't just a random occurrence at this point in creation. Nor was it done alone with Adam as a means of reserving an authoritative action just for him (the text never mentions authority at all); rather, it was the process by which Adam was to experience a searching-out of his perfect counterpart and to come to the realisation that creation, as good as it was, was insufficient to meet this need. God knew right from the beginning that the search would never come up with a suitable helper. The result wasn't a surprise to God, but it was an essential education for Adam. Adam's realisation of his uniqueness—and his need for someone just like him—is highlighted after Eve's creation, when he exclaims, 'This *at last* is bone of my bones and flesh of my flesh' (Gen. 2:23).

Adam's experience as he operated alone in naming all the animals made him recognise that nothing in creation was suitable to come alongside him in community. At no stage in the narrative is there any mention that the purpose for this was to communicate to him (and us) that there was greater authority, leadership, or rulership reserved for him. These words, or anything that would infer as such, are notably absent from the Genesis text in referring to Adam's experience from being made first. Hence, Richard Hess concludes, 'The man and the woman were created sequentially in Genesis 2 in order to demonstrate the need they have for each other, not to justify an implicit hierarchy.'[3]

Despite the absence of hierarchical words in the story, there are some (Hurley, Grudem, Piper amongst others) who assert that

Adam being created before Eve *is* nevertheless proof of Adam having authoritative supremacy over Eve. The argument tends to centre on a few ideas from elsewhere in Scripture:

1. Primogeniture: This describes the legal right of the firstborn son to receive a double inheritance in property. The logic here is that this birthright, formally instated in Mosaic law (Deut. 21:15–17), shows that the one who comes first is elevated to a superior position. But there are a few significant problems with appealing to primogeniture to argue Adam's supremacy over Eve. First, the issue of the birthright was about children, not spouses. Second, it was a system that is not about male/female relations as it only noted sons in their sequence. Third, it was not a system that bestowed greater authority but more property. Finally, it was a system that was regularly ignored, particularly at God's urging (see Jacob and Esau, Jacob's twelve sons, Ephraim and Manasseh, Solomon and Adonijah). To appeal to this loosely observed, male-sibling-only, Mosaic law to interpret the creation story is certainly an uncomfortable stretch.

2. 1 Timothy 2:13: The argument posited is that Paul refers to the sequence of creation in order to justify why women should not teach or have authority. Therefore, it is said, we can see that the sequence of creation gives men greater authority. The problem with this argument is it states as fact that which is only one possibility. It is only one interpretation of 1 Timothy 2:11–14 that shows that Paul's appeal to creation sequence was about inherent authority. The Timothy text never states that, and so 'to read it this way is to import an idea alien to Paul's thinking.'[4] In fact, as we will go on to see in this book, there are other ways to interpret 1 Timothy 2 that are true to the text and context but do not implant hierarchy of authority into the verses. It is

not good logic to feed one possible interpretation of 1 Timothy 2 with one possible interpretation of Genesis (and vice versa) and to state that these scriptures thus prove that our view is correct.

3. Christ as firstborn: This argument centres around how the New Testament shows that Christ as the firstborn of creation has supremacy and, therefore, Adam as firstborn has supremacy over Eve. Quite apart from the difficulty of applying Christological theology to Adam's position, the problem here is that there seems to be some misunderstanding in the proponents of this view about what Christ being firstborn actually means for the church. The New Testament refers to Christ as firstborn *of* not *over* creation. It is not a hierarchical title denoting His rulership over His people. The point, rather, is that Jesus is the 'firstborn among many' (Rom. 8:29)—Christ has broken the way open for us to become children of God *alongside Him* (and co-heirs with Him no less!) (see Rom. 8:29; Col. 1:15, 18–22). Attempting to underline a hierarchy between Jesus and the people of God in order to justify Adam having superior authority over Eve sadly undermines just how radical and lavish what God has done for His people is. The point is that God *could* have made us servants or slaves in a hierarchical framework, but He raised us up and seated us with Him in a place of equality with the Son of God Himself. To sacrifice this profound truth in order to justify male/female hierarchy in a text in Genesis that does not warrant it is a grievous error.[5]

A further problem with insisting that 'first' must mean 'superior in authority' is that complementarians would not follow that logic when we look at the 'firsts' recorded in the New Testament. The first recorded evangelist is a woman (John 4). The first to see Jesus after the resurrection is Mary. 'And "the dead in Christ" should be leaders of Christ's future kingdom, since they are to be raised "first" when Christ returns, and only "after that" the living (1 Thess. 4:16–17).'[6]

On further study, therefore, it becomes evident that those who wish to argue an innate hierarchy in creation's sequence are stretching the Genesis text in order to justify a position held otherwise. On this, Craig Blomberg's admission is telling: 'I concede that these chapters [Genesis 1–2], taken on their own, might not necessarily lead to a complementarian position.'[7]

On a different note, outside of the theological arguments for or against Adam's superior authority based on creation order, there seems to be a much simpler argument based on logic. If creation order is the basis on which authority is given, then surely the animals must have had greater authority than either Adam or Eve, seeing as they preceded them both. Clearly, this line of argument has a major flaw in it in that, if anything, creation gets more authoritative the further on in order, not less. Now whilst I would not use this to advocate a view that Eve was superior to Adam, neither do I think it's justified to use order of creation to argue for the opposite.

Taking all of these thoughts into account, my conclusion on the sequence of creation is that far from being intended to bring some sort of revelation of authoritative hierarchy, the two-stage creation order was intended to bring a revelation of the unique community that men and women have need of in each other.

Genesis 2: Focus on Eve

Having looked in some detail at the question of why God created male and female in sequence, let's now return to the flow of the story. There are some unique moments in God's creation of Eve that don't happen anywhere else in creation and, therefore, hold great significance.

Firstly, God didn't make Eve from the ground. He'd made 'every beast of the field and every bird of the heavens' (Gen. 2:19) from the ground and had made Adam of 'dust from the ground' (Gen. 2:7). But not Eve. There are great pains taken in the narrative, culminating in Adam's exclamation when he meets Eve, to show that Eve was not simply another creature created from the dust but was made of *exactly the same substance* as Adam. God took from Adam and fashioned Eve. She was his perfect counterpart. For the first time in creation, God chose to create a living being from a different substance than everything else. Why? Why use Adam as material for Eve rather than the dust? Surely there can be no other reason than to ensure that they both carried the same substance. They were two sides of exactly the same coin. Two expressions of one substance carrying together all that was needed to fulfil their two-(hu)man mandate. The significance then of Genesis 2:24 is not simply about sexual union in marriage but of putting the two pieces of male and female back together again in the ultimate expression of oneness. Interestingly, Genesis 2:24 is not quite what we'd expect if the context was one of male superiority, for it is not the woman who leaves her family to join her husband but the man who leaves his family to join his wife.

For some, the word 'helper' (*ēzer*) in describing Eve has proven to be a bit of a stumbling block to seeing her as Adam's equal. We have read it to mean 'deputy' or 'subordinate' called upon only should Adam choose to call for assistance. This could not be further from the truth. 'Many have pointed to the fatal flaw in this line of thinking. All of the other occurrences of *'ēzer* in the OT have to do with the assistance that one of strength offers to one in need (i.e., help from God, the king, an ally, or an army). There is no exception. More, fifteen of the nineteen references speak of the help that God alone can provide.'[8] If it is a word most often used of God, *'ēzer* can hardly be read as a word inferring a subordinate! We must reassess how we view the word 'helper', for subordination or the idea of being a 'deputy' are not inherent components of the text.

When God forms Eve, He brings her to Adam without any instruction to name her. 'The naming formula used for the animals ([Gen.] 2:20) has a clear literary parallel with Eve—but only after the fall ([Gen.] 3:20), in contrast to the differently worded phrase before-hand ([Gen.] 2:23).'[9] The charade is now over and God simply presents this perfect partner without question. And when Adam meets her, he immediately recognises her. Finally! Here is a helper that fits him perfectly because she is from him and of the same substance as him! The term 'woman' (Hebrew word *ishah*) is a further means of highlighting Eve being made from Adam's substance with its wordplay on the Hebrew word for 'man' (*ish*) (the wordplay on 'Adam' already having been used with *adamah*, meaning 'ground'). The beginning of Adam's poem recognises the woman's equality, 'bone of my bones and flesh of my flesh' (Gen. 2:23), and that reality is further underlined by the careful structuring of Adam's words: 'the second part of Genesis 2:23 is a chiasm (concentric structure) in which the words for "woman" and "man" are positioned at the centre, suggesting a corresponding and equal relationship to one another.'[10]

And so, the details of the overarching theme of the creation of humanity come into full focus. God completes His two-stage creation of mankind, and it is as if all of creation celebrates this birth of male and female in the image of God—alongside each another to multiply, fill, subdue, and rule.

So what went wrong? And why are we experiencing male/female relationships that in many ways seem alien to what was outlined in Genesis 1 and 2? Enter, Genesis 3: the fall of humanity and the subsequent curse.

Genesis 3: The Breaking of the World

We know the story tragically well. The serpent came and spoke to Eve. With carefully worded half-truths, suspicions, and promises, he won Eve's heart and ultimately she believed him (Gen. 3:13). Although we don't see Adam taking an active role in the narrative, we find out as the story progresses that he was with Eve throughout (Gen. 3:6). It's interesting that while Eve was deceived by the serpent's words, we are not told that about Adam. The more carefully you read over the story and note Paul's writing in 1 Timothy 2, the more it would seem that Adam was not so much deceived by what the serpent said but wilfully chose Eve's instruction over God's (Gen. 3:17; 1 Tim. 2:14). Regardless of their motivations, there are some points to note here.

Some have used the fact that Eve was deceived as support for the fact that she was inferior to Adam. I'm not sure if this is the most obvious interpretation. Perhaps the fact that Adam had greater experience of God (having been made first) and the fact that the original prohibition had been communicated to Adam when he was alone (Gen. 2:16–17) made Eve more vulnerable? It is noteworthy that Eve's knowledge of the prohibition is not precise (compare Gen. 2:16–17 with Gen. 3:1–3).

The effect of the deception, as we know so well, is that Eve and then Adam gave in to the temptation before them, and the course of history was forever altered as a result. They tried to hide because they were ashamed of their nakedness (Gen. 3:7, 10), when questioned by God they both shifted blame (Gen. 3:12–13), and there was what is now an all-too-familiar power shift declared in the curse where male and female were no longer on equal footing, but he would rule over her and her desire would be for her husband (a word that not only means desiring to be with him but has the sense of wanting to overcome him—see how the word is used in Genesis 4:7) (Gen. 3:16).

As we read the words of the curse spoken over Adam and Eve, we see something that is much closer to what we experience today. Considering the fact that the cross and resurrection broke the curse and restored us to a place of wholeness, this is a very sad assessment if it is true of the church today. In the fall, harmony, equality, safety, and unity were replaced with shame, blame shifting, division, and power play. This is the first hint we get of male superiority in authority—and it is not good. After the fall, we see Adam naming the woman Eve (Gen. 3:20).

The story is a devastating one and would be utterly hopeless without the redemptive purposes of God being woven in even in the midst of the brokenness. Even whilst pronouncing the curse, God spoke the solution: 'I will put enmity between you and the woman, and between your offspring and her offspring; he shall bruise your head, and you shall bruise his heel' (Gen. 3:15), words that gave a glimpse of One who would come against the serpent. Of course, we know these words speak of Jesus. That He is the One who has brought complete resolution to all that was lost in the garden in the cross and resurrection. We're told that Jesus broke the curse (Gal. 3), took on our sin and brokenness at the cross (Isa. 53), and disarmed the enemy there (Col. 2). The resurrection brings with it a 'new creation' reality—beautifully inaugurated in a garden like Eden but this one with an empty tomb as Jesus brings the first revelation of all that has changed in a conversation with a woman. What was lost in one garden is restored in another. Not only in terms of breaking the curse of sin and death but also in restoring what was intended from the beginning—for male and female to stand *alongside* one another, not *over* one another.

Looking Forward

Of course, there is so much more that could be said on these first three chapters in Genesis. However, I hope what I have done, albeit briefly, is demonstrate the clear mandate to rule that was God's original purpose for both genders and how male authority over women only came into being as a result of utter brokenness. It is tragic that, in the face of this narrative, we would propagate and protect male superiority in authority as if it was God's perfect plan all along.

As those who are in Christ, we don't need to live under the curse anymore. We don't need to follow the pattern of power dynamics at play there. We have been redeemed and restored and have the privilege of living out the harmony and equality (with the full depth of that word—not just a theoretical badge of value) that Adam and Eve were intended for.

We have seen this demonstrated as we've looked back at creation, but we can see glimpses of this further as we look forward to eternity. In the New Testament, we see again God's desire for men and women standing alongside each other—together in equality to rule and reign. Men and women are co-heirs with Christ (Rom. 8:17), seated with Him (Eph. 2:6), and reigning with Him (Rev. 5:10); our position, inheritance, and authority are not based on our gender but on our union with Christ (Gal. 3:28). Verses that communicate the position men and women have in Christ (inaugurated in the new covenant and continuing on into eternity) are notable for their lack of one thing: gender-based hierarchy.

Concluding Thoughts

I wonder why, when God created men and women to rule together from Eden to eternity, we would think that His intention for our present age is any different? Why would we believe that God would introduce hierarchy as His intention now when hierarchy is not His intention in Eden or in the kingdom fully come? The trouble with this kind of thinking is that it leads to an abdication of God's mandate where women choose to, or are convinced to, give up on why they were put on the earth in order to fall in line with how the church has interpreted a handful of verses. That's a scary thought.

An important part of the gender debate is that we recognise that 'freedom' or 'equality for women' is not a new idea that the world has thought up today. Rather, freedom and equality for women (and men) is God's idea right from the beginning, and in resisting it, we are not coming against external cultural forces, but rather the original design from God Himself.

A few months ago, I felt God speaking to me from some verses in Isaiah 61.

> The Spirit of the Sovereign LORD is on me,
>> because the LORD has anointed me
>> to proclaim good news to the poor.
> He has sent me to bind up the broken-hearted,
>> to proclaim freedom for the captives
>> and release from darkness for the prisoners,
> to proclaim the year of the LORD's favour
>> and the day of vengeance of our God,
> to comfort all who mourn,
>> and provide for those who grieve in Zion—
> to bestow on them a crown of beauty
>> instead of ashes,
> the oil of joy
>> instead of mourning,
> and a garment of praise
>> instead of a spirit of despair.
> They will be called oaks of righteousness,
>> a planting of the LORD
>> for the display of his splendour.
>
> They will rebuild the ancient ruins
>> and restore the places long devastated;
> they will renew the ruined cities
>> that have been devastated for generations.
>> (Isa. 61:1–4 NIV)

We see in Luke 4 how Jesus came and fulfilled the first few verses of this prophecy—how He came as the ultimate expression of favour to humanity. But what caught my attention from these verses is where the prophecy changes from 'He' to 'They'. '*They* will be called oaks of righteousness …' and so on. What Jesus came to do, we as His people continue to do as we are planted as oaks of righteousness to display who He is. The verse that God began to highlight to me as I marvelled at this text is verse 4—a verse that calls every believer to rebuild that which has been broken, even for many, many generations.

In Genesis 1, something beautiful was created. In Genesis 3 that beauty was shattered and stands as an ancient ruin. Clearly, gender roles are only one part of what lies in ruins. But it is a part. In Isaiah we see a picture of a people who will rebuild and restore that which has been broken. The church is not called to stay in Genesis 3 with regards to gender roles. We have been empowered to rebuild the Genesis 1 blueprint (with an even greater eternal trajectory), so that what God had always planned will be restored—men and women ruling alongside one another to see His glory cover the earth.

JESUS AND WOMEN

The more I get to know Jesus, the more I encounter a God who has no interest in making Himself what we expect. He simply will not play neatly within our preordained boundary lines. One area where this is clearly seen is Jesus' interactions with women in the narrative of the gospels. Even 2,000 years later, I wonder how many of us would end up offended with Jesus if He walked into our churches today and radically included women in the manner that He did in first-century Palestine.

Some of us have read the gospels through a twenty-first-century lens and so have concluded that, whilst Jesus was undoubtedly kind to women, to say that He was revolutionary is a stretch. But that thinking reflects a misunderstanding of just how patriarchal, even to the point of misogyny, the culture of Jesus' day was. The first-century rabbi Eliezer stated, 'Rather should the words of the Torah be burned than entrusted to a woman ... Whoever teaches his daughter the Torah is like one who teaches her lasciviousness.'[1] And this kind of thinking was hardly isolated. 'In fact, the Talmud states: "Let a curse come upon the man who must needs have his wife or children say

grace for him ..." Moreover, in the daily prayers of Jews there was a
threefold thanksgiving: "Praised be God that he has not created me a
gentile; praised be God that he has not created me a woman; praised
be God that he has not created me an ignorant man."[2] Kenneth
Bailey, one of the most respected scholars on the cultural context
of Scripture, cites Ben Sirach, an early second-century scholar, to
highlight the misogynistic attitudes towards women in the ancient
Middle East: 'Do not sit down with the women; for moth comes
out of clothes, and a woman's spite out of a woman. A man's spite
is preferable to a woman's kindness; women give rise to shame and
reproach (Sir 42:12–14).'[3] Bailey notes, 'to Ben Sirach a daughter
was a total loss and a constant potential source of shame ...'[4]

Faced with these glimpses into ancient Middle Eastern attitudes,
we have no choice but to view Jesus' interactions with women as
totally revolutionary—and offensive. Gushee and Stassen note this
as they point out, 'In the practice of his ministry, at great risk to his
own reputation, Jesus shattered numbers of taboos related to male-
female contact and association.'[5] Far from the shunning of women
that Sirach or Eliezer thought appropriate, Jesus addressed them
personally and taught them theology. He taught equality of marriage rights between husbands and wives. He allowed women to be
with Him, learn from Him, and be like Him. He entrusted the most
pivotal moment of His ministry to the testimony of a woman. These
were not just sweet acts of kindness from a hippyish representative of
love who was unaware of just how radical He was being, but deeply
offensive actions from a God of supreme authority. In Jesus, we
encounter a God who is radical and disruptive as He wilfully ignores
and disturbs the cultural order of His day.

Some of us may be comfortable with the idea of Jesus as a revolutionary; however, I wonder how many of us give Him enough credit as an intellectual who was not careless in His radical behaviour but was thoughtful, detailed, and intentional. Many of us are cautious to form theological conclusions from the gospel narratives. It is as if we believe that it is possible to pay Jesus' words and actions more attention than He realised we would or intended us to. As if He was not meticulous in the words He chose or the things He did. We often use other areas of Scripture, most commonly the epistles, to validate theology that we encounter in the gospel narratives. In this way, the 'anecdotal' gospels become second to the 'intellectual' epistles, particularly those written by Paul, when it comes to theological study.

Hence, many fall into defining Jesus' life through the lens of Paul's teaching, rather than defining Paul's teaching through the lens of Jesus' life. Our approach to Scripture indicates that we believe that Jesus came to give us a touchy-feely picture of what God is like, but, if we want theological facts, we need to look elsewhere—to Paul—to inform us. It is as if we have forgotten that the flesh-and-blood Jesus (the very same that we see in the gospels) is the One who taught Paul theology in the first place (Gal. 1:12). We vastly underestimate the Jesus of the gospels if we see Him playing an intellectual second fiddle to Paul.

Bailey writes of his own journey in this regard:

> I discovered a deep unexamined assumption in my
> own tradition about the mind of Jesus. I discovered
> that I had been unconsciously trained to admire
> everything about Jesus except his intellectual

astuteness ... Paul was the theologian and Jesus was
the supreme ethical example of that theology ...
But this equation of *Paul = serious theologian; Jesus
= storyteller/example of love* I was obliged to reex-
amine ... For if Jesus is an uneducated young man
who tells stories primarily for children and simple
fisher folk, then one set of perceptions apply as we
examine his teachings. But if he is the first *mind* of
the NT (Paul being the second), and if Jesus' teachings are to be considered as serious theology, offered
primarily to intellectuals, then a quite different set
of assumptions and perceptions come into play for
the interpreter.[6]

Jesus walking the earth was not merely an expression of love but
was God in His fullness using words and actions to carefully and
precisely teach us theology. He was neither careless nor a simpleton.

In view of this, we are wise to allow Jesus' teaching and interactions with women to inform our understanding of gender roles. He
has something to teach us on the subject. We must not simply pay
lip service to what we see of Jesus in the gospels, promptly ignoring
what He demonstrated, as we read Paul's teaching in a handful of
verses. We must work out a way of reconciling Jesus' example with
the tricky verses from Paul's teaching—but not automatically allow
one to overshadow or trivialise the other.

When we see Jesus, we encounter a wonderful breath of fresh air
in the midst of continuing controversy and debate in the Christian
community. Jesus teaches us that God is interested in lifting up,

empowering, and liberating women. There is no reinforcing of glass ceilings but rather a careful intentionality in shattering them. If the gospels were the only snapshot of God that we had, it would be difficult to argue for a gender-based hierarchy in the church. That reality should make us wonder if we're interpreting the minority verses from Paul correctly, especially in view of the fact that the majority of verses from Paul are also in complete agreement with the model we see in the gospels.

But before we delve into some of the magnificent encounters between women and Jesus, I want to address the one sticking point that is sometimes used to nullify claims that Jesus was radically 'pro-women'. The question often raised is, if God really thought of women as equal in authority to men, why did Jesus not appoint women in the twelve disciples? Surely this points to the fact that Jesus recognised equal value in both genders but neither recognised equal authority nor sanctioned equal opportunity to serve? Yes, Jesus wanted to see women empowered, but His choice of a male-only discipleship presumably shows that Jesus reserved top-level leadership and authority exclusively for men. This is an excellent point. Except for a few glaring problems.

Firstly, if we use the Twelve as proof of what sort of person Jesus thinks has authority to be in leadership, then we have to face up to a Christian faith that is not only gender biased but also racially biased. For not only did Jesus exclusively pick men to be His disciples, He also exclusively picked Jews. If the Twelve are to be taken as prescriptive of future church leaders, then we have no choice but to assert that Jews have more authority than Gentiles to be leaders.[7] If that is the case, most of the church leaders I know are in rebellion to what Jesus prescribed because they are not Jewish but have accepted roles of church leadership. Clearly, there is a fundamental flaw in using the culturally appropriate gender and race of the disciples to draw conclusions on who Jesus thinks is qualified to lead for all time. Some have tried to explain the Jewishness of the disciples as entirely necessary given the culture of the day and Jesus' primary call to Israel, whilst simultaneously trying to assert that choosing women would have been perfectly reasonable in both of those contexts.[8] Such an argument is baffling and requires a wilful disregard for what is known about attitudes towards women in first-century Palestine. If Jesus wanted to minister to Israel in the choosing of disciples as a rabbi, it would have been unthinkable to choose Gentiles or women in that group. Arguments to the contrary are utterly misleading.

Secondly, Jesus' choosing of the Twelve was to represent the twelve tribes of Israel and the twelve patriarchs, symbolic of the establishing of 'the newly constituted Israel under the new covenant in Christ.'[9] For this symbolism to be meaningful, 'the Twelve could not have been other than Jewish free males.'[10] To take the choosing of the Twelve as indicative of gender, race, or social status requirements in church leadership where the symbolism of the tribes is no longer necessary is clearly stretching the point beyond its intention.

Thirdly, Jesus' choosing of His disciples represented the start of His public rabbinic ministry. Rabbis discipled Jewish men. If Jesus had drawn a group of women and Gentiles in order to assume a rabbinic role (which would have been totally paradoxical), His ministry would never have made it out of the starting blocks. This is not to say that Jesus was afraid to be revolutionary (far from it) or that He would not bring radical provocation to the boundary lines of culture (to the contrary!), but rather that He exercised profound wisdom in how He brought about revolution. He was wise enough to establish a recognisable platform from which to bring total transformation.

Fourthly, whilst women weren't in the Twelve, they were allowed to take the posture of discipleship (Luke 10:38–42) and indeed were counted as disciples (Matt. 12:48–50). They provided for Jesus' ministry and travelled with Him alongside the Twelve (Luke 8:1–3). Women ministered to Him (Mark 15:41), anointed Him (John 12:1–8), were sent out by Him as witnesses (Matt. 28:10), and were part of the core group of 120 in the upper room waiting for the promised Holy Spirit to empower them to be witnesses of Christ to the ends of the earth (Acts 1:14). Jesus used women and tasks associated with women's roles in His parables (e.g., Luke 18:1–8) and even used the picture of a woman to represent God in His parable of the lost coin (Luke 15:8–10). Women were consistently included in every aspect alongside men (and at crucial points even *before* the involvement of men) throughout Jesus' ministry. Bailey notes, 'In Luke's Gospel I have identified twenty-seven cases in the text of the pairing of men and women. These begin with the angel who appears to the man Zechariah (Lk 1:5–20) and to Mary (Lk 1:26–36). It ends with the presentations of men and women in the passion narratives.'[11] Luke clearly went to great lengths to communicate the equality of standing between men and women in the ministry of Jesus. In view of all of this, to argue that Jesus considered women to have less authority than men requires us to turn a blind eye to the narrative that the gospel writers sought to present.

The Twelve were never intended as some kind of exclusive club that would be the 'high point' of Christianity but were chosen as a multiplying platform for the church that was to come (see Matt. 28:16–20; Eph. 2:20–22; Eph. 4:11–13). We have absolutely no indication from Jesus' teaching (or elsewhere in Scripture for that matter) that the twelve apostles were only to see that multiplication exclusively in men.

So, if Jesus choosing twelve Jewish men isn't proof of God's view on gender (in the same way that it isn't a comment on race or social status), what else can we look at from Jesus' life to inform us with regards to God's view of gender roles? We have already seen how Jesus had great respect towards women and included them just as He did men throughout the gospels. Let us now focus on some of the most significant interactions between Jesus and women.

Breaking Ceilings: Perfume at the Feet of Jesus

John 12:1–8 is a remarkable, uncomfortable encounter. It recounts a moment that would have scandalised all who were there. It is significant for many reasons, but one that is most pertinent to us is that a woman anointing Jesus 'was a priestly action that Jesus accepted as such.'[12] This was not just a random act. She assumed the role of ministering to Him, and He received it.

Can you imagine the gossip that would surround that moment? A woman broke into the male-only section of the party. She let down her hair (which was a sign of singular devotion that was not appropriate in public—a private act from wives to their husbands). She touched the rabbi. She anointed the rabbi—how dare she? And He *allowed* it. Can you imagine the outrage? Who did she think she was to do such a thing, and why on earth would a respectable rabbi allow it?

Too often we relegate what happened solely to an act of abandoned worship—which, of course, it was—but we fail to see the authority exercised in that moment of anointing Jesus. It may escape our attention, but it wouldn't have escaped theirs.

Breaking Ceilings: Mary and Martha

We know the story so well: Jesus and His disciples were at Lazarus, Martha, and Mary's house. Martha was busy with all that hosting the rabbi would entail. Mary, on the other hand, was sitting at the feet of Jesus listening to Him. Martha looked to Jesus to pull her sister back in line, but unbelievably, Jesus refused and supported Mary's decision.

Okay, so what was really going on here? Was this about two sisters fighting about who was doing the chores, or is there more going on?

To understand the radical transaction that takes place in this brief story, we have to understand ancient Middle Eastern culture. Jewish men and women did not socialise together in a mixed crowd. The men stayed with the men and the women stayed with the women. There were clearly defined roles in this deeply patriarchal society—the women busied themselves with the cooking and preparing and the serving, and the men would busy themselves with important conversation and listening to the rabbi's teaching. The two worlds were not meant to cross. There was a very firmly placed limit over women's heads about what they were allowed to do—and learning from rabbis was not included in the list of appropriate behaviour for Jewish girls.

But Mary had other ideas. She wasn't going to be left out. She wanted the same access to Jesus that the men had, so she 'sat at His feet.' This isn't a statement of Mary's proximity to Jesus but rather Mary's posture toward Jesus—to 'sit at someone's feet' was to assume the posture of discipleship (see Paul with Gamaliel in Acts 22:3).[13] Essentially, Mary was volunteering herself as a disciple in that moment. It was scandalous, but tame in comparison to what Jesus did. He not only *allowed* it, but worse, He *commended* it. He refused the pleas to rebuke Mary for taking a role that would be traditionally reserved for men but rather celebrated her for it. 'Mary thus became a disciple of Rabbi Jesus.'[14]

The problem, of course, was that discipleship was not just about learning. It was about learning *in order to become like the rabbi Himself.* Discipleship was not about theoretical education but rather a very practical apprenticeship. You didn't become a disciple simply in order to increase your knowledge. The purpose of discipleship was clear—to do what the rabbi does. Even to teach as the rabbi teaches. Once we realise that, it's easy to see why what Mary did—and what Jesus endorsed—was so revolutionary.

Breaking Ceilings: Teaching on Adultery

In Mark 10, we see Jesus being questioned by the Pharisees—nothing too remarkable about that. But what He does to put women on equal footing with men *is* nothing short of remarkable. The Pharisees asked Jesus the question, 'Is it lawful for a man to divorce his wife?' (v. 2). Note the gender bias present in the question. 'In Jewish law divorce was a male privilege'[15] (see Deut. 24:1–4). In first-century Palestine, only men were allowed to initiate divorce and that on the basis of the slightest of issues, including if the wife 'spoiled her husband's dinner, talked too loudly, or wasn't pretty enough. She was considered to be one of her husband's possessions, of the same status as his oxen and his home, according to the rabbinical interpretation of the tenth commandment.'[16]

Without getting drawn into the question of divorce in church community, let me highlight Jesus' radical answer in terms of addressing their gender bias: 'And he said to them, "Whoever divorces his wife and marries another commits adultery against her, and if she divorces her husband and marries another, she commits adultery"' (Mark 10:11–12).

In His answer, Jesus introduces a completely alien idea to His ancient Middle Eastern context: wives have the same rights as their husbands and are held to account in the same way. This idea may not seem like a profound revelation today, but in Jesus' day this was a radical idea. The rights of wives were irrelevant in first-century Palestine. What I love about the interaction here is that the question brought to Jesus was about divorce, and Jesus could have easily answered it without getting into the hidden premise of male superiority. But Jesus was not interested in maintaining patriarchal assumptions on marriage. Into His answer on divorce, He weaves His opinion on gender.

Breaking Ceilings: The Samaritan Woman

In John 4, we read of an unusual encounter. Jesus breaks some of the most rigid societal rules for Jewish men. He speaks to a woman alone, and not just any woman but a Samaritan woman at that. It is significant that the setting of the story is at noon. In the gospel of John, stories set in the day are full of blessed encounters: healings, the feeding of the five thousand, and Jesus' affirmation that He is the 'light of the world' who banishes darkness. By contrast, night is the setting for betrayal (Judas), doubt (Nicodemus), and denial (Peter). 'Under the bright noonday sun, the Samaritan woman comes, hears, believes and becomes the first woman preacher in Christian history ... The *nighttime* story of Nicodemus, the scholar of Jerusalem who wavers, and the *noontime* account of a simple Samaritan woman who believes are side by side in the text. This is not an accident.'[17]

The fact that the conversation happened is itself completely radical. 'In public rabbis did not talk to female members of their own families,'[18] much less to female strangers. The fact that this *woman* is also a *Samaritan* is a double offence that Jesus walks into quite intentionally. He then asks her for a drink, meaning that He willingly humbles Himself into a position of needing her help and 'defiles' himself by sharing her jar, making the interaction all the more unbelievable. We don't have to look at many resources outside of John 4 to know that what Jesus was doing would be seen as offensive—John puts it in the chapter plainly for us (verse 9 telling us that Jewish men would not associate with Samaritans, much less ask them for a drink, and verse 27 showing us the bewilderment of the disciples at seeing what Jesus was doing).

As Jesus engages with this woman, notice how He's not just treating her with the patronising kindness of a superior. For her, the question of gender is an issue but it is not for Him. We see Him completely disregarding her question, highlighting their gender as well as racial difference (v. 9). Furthermore, in His instruction to go, call her husband, and bring Him back, Jesus is showing a disregard for the cultural reality of a woman's place to follow, not lead, a man.[19] Instead of treating her as an inferior because of her gender, Jesus draws her into some serious theological discourse culminating in His revelation to her (the first recorded instance we have) that He is indeed the Messiah. This was no patronising conversation from a superior man to an inferior woman, but a radical discussion based on the countercultural assumptions that the woman had both the intellect and the value to warrant such theological discourse. Significantly, John's recording of this interaction places this story as the first in the series of 'I AM' statements that John frames his entire book with. Clearly, the significance of the interaction was not lost on the apostle.

As amazing as all this is, however, it's not so much the conversation I'm most in awe of, but what it results in. Jesus knew exactly what He was doing when He put Himself in the way of this woman and initiated conversation with her. His choice to reveal Himself as Messiah to her was not random but intentional. He knew the power His words would carry. The encounter results in such transformation that this ostracised woman who avoided contact with others (as seen in her unusual choice to come to the well alone and in the heat of the day) becomes 'an evangelist to her own people.'[20] Unlike other encounters (see Jesus with the leper in Mark 1:43, and with His own disciples in Matthew 16:20), there is no suggestion that Jesus tried to hold her back or silence her from sharing what she'd heard. This woman is released from her shame right into public ministry.

It's incredibly significant. Before Jesus ever sent out the Twelve or the seventy-two, He essentially sent out a Samaritan woman. Doesn't get much more revolutionary than that.

Breaking Ceilings: Mary Magdalene

Either Jesus just kept stumbling into moments where He challenged the understanding of a woman's role in society, or He was intentionally choosing for that to be the case. My guess is that it is the latter.

Just think of all the 'firsts' that Jesus chose to designate to a woman. The first news of the incarnation (Luke 1:32–35). The revelation of God's incredible act in the incarnation was brought to a teenage girl even though it would have been much more culturally appropriate to go to either her father or her fiancé. But the announcement was made to her and 'not her father, the high priest, the ruler of the synagogue, a male prophet—and not even the man to whom she was betrothed …'[21] Following that first, there's the first Samaritan convert (John 4:7–42); the first Gentile convert (Matt. 15:21–28); the first resurrection teaching (John 11:23–27); all culminating in the first witness to the resurrection (Matt. 28:9; John 20:16). Some complementarians insist that biblical order signals a hierarchy of authority. In that case, I wonder what they make of all of these firsts.

At first light on the morning of Jesus' greatest victory, before He had even ascended to His Father, He chose to reveal the reality of His resurrection to a woman. A *woman*. A woman whose testimony would not hold up in a court of law. A woman who would never be given the time of day. A woman whom His male disciples would not believe (and would be subsequently rebuked for—see Mark 16:14).

Why did He do it? Why would He jeopardise the reliability of the testimony of His resurrection by putting it in the hands of a woman? As Tom Wright notes, 'Mary Magdalene and the others are the apostles to the apostles … If an apostle is a witness to the resurrection, there were women who deserved that title before any of the men.'[22] Jesus reveals himself to Mary and, in so doing, breaks a ceiling that some in the church have been trying to put back together ever since.

It would seem that perhaps Jesus is not as convinced as some are of the lesser authority that women have. I have heard my husband say, 'What was lost in a garden was restored in a garden.' Here, in the inauguration of a new creation, in the setting of the garden of an empty tomb, Jesus restores the place of women as He entrusts a woman to be the first witness of the greatest act in all of history. A woman failed in what was entrusted to her (and her husband) in the first garden. But here, in a new garden and a new creation, a woman is entrusted again with what is most precious.

However we want to interpret it, in bringing primary revelation of the resurrection to Mary, Jesus appoints a woman in a place of undeniable authority and dignity as He sends her (the literal definition of being an apostle) to share the news with His disciples. And let us note here that this is no commission to women's ministry—Mary's testimony was not only to be shared with women; it was intended to be shared with the men as well (John 20:17).

But Is It Significant?

Because of how many of us are conditioned to justify Jesus' life through a lens of Paul's teaching, we are often tempted to somehow soften the nature of Jesus' encounters with women in order to uphold a certain interpretation of Paul's teaching on gender roles. To this end, some argue that Jesus' interactions with women weren't revolutionary, despite the fact that the best scholars on cultural context insist that Jesus' interactions as described above were radical to the point of complete offence.

It would seem that some are more comfortable with softening the radical nature of Jesus' interactions than with softening their own interpretation of a minority of Paul's teachings. I wonder why that is the case?

In His everyday life, Jesus systematically broke down a staunchly patriarchal system and opened the doors for women to enter into male-only roles. Jesus' treatment of women was so staggering that it created a different way of men and women worshipping. Where once there would have been clear gender separation in Jewish worship, we see in Acts 1 men and women praying and worshipping together as they wait for an encounter with the Holy Spirit. His careful, meticulous approach to changing the cultural understanding of women's roles resulted in the early church taking a very different stance with regards to gender roles than what had gone before.

The very fact that there were women from Jewish backgrounds who were prominent in ministry in the early church shows us that Jesus' example and revelation to His people revolutionised the role of women in ministry. Where there once was a very clear male-only leadership, women were being raised up who were influential and instrumental in church growth (a quick glance at Romans 16 will show us just how significant the role of women had become). The inclusion of women in the persecution of the early church is also significant.

It's interesting that at the crucifixion the women were able to come and go and see what was happening without fear of the authorities. They were not regarded as a threat and did not expect to be so regarded ... It's fascinating, then, that when we turn to Acts and the persecution that arose against the Church not least at the time of Stephen, we find that women are being targeted equally alongside the men ... Bailey points out that on the basis of his cultural parallels that this only makes sense if the women too are seen as leaders, influential figures within the community.[23]

Jesus broke the ceilings that had been over women for generations. He addressed women as equals to men and was not interested in allowing religious traditions to dictate the freedom of half of His body. Is it possible that He was too simple to know, or too careless to care, that He was disrupting rules long held in place? Why is it that there is such a push to put back into the box the women whom He set free? He liberated women around Him. He didn't patronise them but treated women as equals as He empowered them. As His people, I hope the same can be said of us.

1 CORINTHIANS 11: HIERARCHY BY DESIGN?

Let us turn our attention to the book of 1 Corinthians. It is a fascinating letter written by Paul and Sosthenes (1:1) to the community in Corinth (1:2). In reading the letter, we not only face the usual challenges of hermeneutics given the difference of time, context, culture, and language, but we are met with a further, arguably more significant, difficulty. The problem is that 1 Corinthians is our doorway into a conversation that is well underway. It is not the first letter written in the series—it is simply the first letter of the series that we have access to. What we read in 1 Corinthians is the third letter in an ongoing conversation. This makes the deciphering of this letter all the more problematic for us as modern-day readers. It's like walking into a movie halfway through and trying to make sense of the plot and the characters despite the fact that we have missed much of the preliminaries necessary to fully understand what is going on. Nevertheless, there is so much richness in 1 Corinthians as we give ourselves to grappling with the text. Thankfully, there are sections that are relatively straightforward where there are enough contextual clues embedded in the text for us to piece together what has been going on. But, inevitably, there are other segments that are not quite so easy to navigate and, hence, cause much debate amongst scholars today. Unfortunately for us, two of the most debated sections are pertinent to the topic of gender roles. The disagreements over these two texts are not simply due to the sensitivity of the subject of gender but are more so because of the complexity of the ideas and seeming inconsistencies present in the text. In this chapter, we will focus our attention on the first of these difficult sections.

1 Corinthians: Context

Corinth was one of the most significant cities in ancient Greece with a multicultural population of Greeks, Romans, and Jews. The church community that Paul and Sosthenes addressed in the letter of 1 Corinthians was one that they were very familiar with. Sosthenes was once the ruler of the synagogue in Corinth (Acts 18:17), and we know that Paul spent more than eighteen months living in Corinth and preaching the gospel to both Jews and Gentiles (Acts 18:11). Unfortunately, after leaving Corinth, Paul started hearing reports about the community that gave him cause for concern, prompting his first letter (which we don't have), which included teaching against the sexual immorality that was impacting the community (1 Cor. 5:9). The worrying reports continued, however, with news reaching him from 'Chloe's people' that quarrelling and division were taking root in the church (1 Cor. 1:11). The community was not a picture of great health. Having received their reply to his initial letter (see 1 Cor. 7:1), Paul proceeded with a second letter filled with encouragements, instructions, and a fair number of rebukes. As we read through 1 Corinthians, we can trace an outline of some of the issues that were going on: quarrelling and division (1 Cor. 1), sexual immorality (1 Cor. 5), lawsuits between members of the community (1 Cor. 6), idolatry (1 Cor. 10), disagreements over how men and women were to behave (1 Cor. 11; 14), ungodliness and selfishness in the context of communion (1 Cor. 11), confusion about the use of spiritual gifts (1 Cor. 12), disruptions in worship (1 Cor. 14), false teaching around the resurrection (1 Cor. 15). Hardly a stellar report. No wonder the church needed Paul's correction!

Woven within the letter are three sets of instructions that specifically address how men and women are to relate in the community. The first of these instructions is found in Paul's teaching on marriage in 1 Corinthians 7, and we will look at that in due course when we study Ephesians 5 together. There are two further sets of instructions relevant to gender roles. These are both found in a prolonged section of teaching on worship in 1 Corinthians 11–14, and we will turn our attention to the first of these instructions now.

1 Corinthians 11

> Now I commend you because you remember me in everything and maintain the traditions even as I delivered them to you. But I want you to understand that the head of every man is Christ, the head of a wife is her husband, and the head of Christ is God. Every man who prays or prophesies with his head covered dishonours his head, but every wife

who prays or prophesies with her head uncovered dishonours her head, since it is the same as if her head were shaven. For if a wife will not cover her head, then she should cut her hair short. But since it is disgraceful for a wife to cut off her hair or shave her head, let her cover her head. For a man ought not to cover his head, since he is the image and glory of God, but woman is the glory of man. For man was not made from woman, but woman from man. Neither was man created for woman, but woman for man. That is why a wife ought to have a symbol of authority on her head, because of the angels. Nevertheless, in the Lord woman is not independent of man nor man of woman; for as woman was made from man, so man is now born of woman. And all things are from God. Judge for yourselves: is it proper for a wife to pray to God with her head uncovered? Does not nature itself teach you that if a man wears long hair it is a disgrace for him, but if a woman has long hair, it is her glory? For her hair is given to her for a covering. If anyone is inclined to be contentious, we have no such practice, nor do the churches of God. (1 Cor. 11:2–16)

We should approach 1 Corinthians 11:2–16 tentatively because scholars are virtually unanimous in expressing that this section poses many difficulties and has not yet been satisfactorily interpreted. 'Whatever else may characterize this text, its multiple exegetical problems seem unparalleled.'[1] This should make us extremely wary to build theological principles on the basis of these verses. There is such a wide array of interpretations offered that reading commentaries on this chapter can prove quite dizzying.

It is not difficult to see why there is so much controversy over this text. Paul's terminology is difficult to understand. How are we to understand 'head' in verse 3? Who is 'man' referring to in verse 3 when we read 'the head of every man is Christ' (all men or only redeemed men)? Is the whole passage talking about men and women in general or wives and husbands specifically (both are possible in the Greek)? Is the discussion on head coverings a reference to hairstyles or to an actual covering (and if this is the case, what kind of covering)? What is the symbol of authority that Paul refers to in verse 10, and is it a symbol of the woman's own authority or a symbol of authority exerted over her? What does the reference to angels mean in verse 10? Each of these questions leads to multiple possible answers. In addition to the complexity of deciphering Paul's meaning in language, we have the added challenge of interpreting Paul's seeming double mindedness in the text. Verses 3–10 communicate something quite different to verses 11–16 with regards to how men and women should relate. How do we resolve the different views given in this section? And why is he so adamant in his views on cultural customs in the first place? To top it all off, how do we reconcile the representation of the Genesis account in verse 7, which is different to what Genesis itself states? Given the questions that arise as we read this passage, it is little wonder that there is so much difficulty in coming to a consensus on Paul's meaning.

In exploring this passage, I will not attempt to answer all of the questions mentioned above. There are many thorough (and differing!)

scholarly works if one wants to search out answers at length. For our purposes here, it is enough to point out the existence of these significant questions in order to highlight the difficulties we face in approaching this passage of Scripture and, hence, the caution required in claiming anything definitive for gender roles from this text.

For the purposes of our study, we will grapple with only the most pertinent questions raised for gender roles and then tentatively explore a possible interpretation that may answer more of the complexities of this passage than most. In approaching theological study, scholars agree that the wisest approach is to allow more straightforward passages to interpret complex ones. Therefore, whilst my aim is to offer a plausible interpretation of 1 Corinthians 11:2–16 which has been put forth by a number of scholars, I would still be reticent to use this text as a lens to justify gender roles in the church. There are clearer texts to turn to for that.

Having laid out reasons for caution as we move forward, let us now go ahead and look at some of the questions that arise from the text. In our initial discussion we will assume, as most readers do, that the text portrays solely Paul's views and that the problem group in this passage was primarily the women who were misusing their newfound freedom to overthrow respectable customs of the day.[2]

Headship

> Now I commend you because you remember me
> in everything and maintain the traditions even as
> I delivered them to you. But I want you to under-
> stand that the head of every man is Christ, the head

of a wife is her husband, and the head of Christ is
God. (1 Cor. 11:2–3)

The conversation is introduced with a commendation to the community for maintaining Paul's teaching. 'It was good rhetorical practice to start with a subject in which one could "commend" or "praise" the audience'[3] (v. 2). But even in the context of this encouragement, we can see that all was not well, hence Paul's next sentence, 'But I want you to understand' (v. 3). Thus, having opened the section with a commendation, Paul moves on to bring clarity and correction.

He starts with the idea of headship. It is this subject that raises the first question that is pertinent for us: what is it that Paul meant by the word 'head' used repeatedly in verse 3? The sentence consists of three couplets, each illustrating a relationship of headship: the head of every man is Christ, the head of a woman (or wife) is a man (or husband), and the head of Christ is God. In each couplet, the word 'head' is the Greek word *kephalē*. This is a word that has sparked much debate due to its range of possible meanings, which include a literal meaning of the anatomical head or metaphorical meanings of ruler, leader, source, preeminent, or one in authority. For many readers, there is a temptation to lean towards an interpretation of authority or leadership when we see the word 'head' because that is the meaning that is most often associated with a reference to 'head' in English (and indeed many other languages). But we must be careful that we do not import into the Greek text a meaning simply because it is the most natural association in our own language. Philip Payne highlights this difficulty: 'One reason for the popularity of this interpretation [interpreting *kephalē* as one in authority] is that in English, German and Hebrew (and numerous other languages) the most common metaphorical meaning of "head" is "leader".[4] But this was not the case in ancient Greek. 'The Greek OT (LXX) shows that most of its translators did not regard "head" (κεφαλή) as an appropriate word to convey "leader".'[5] Payne goes on to demonstrate that when the Hebrew Old Testament was translated into Greek, wherever the Greek translators saw the word 'head' in the text, if it's usage was literal, they overwhelmingly chose the word *kephalē* as their translation. In contrast, whenever the word 'head' was used metaphorically in the Hebrew text to convey a meaning of leadership, the Greek translators overwhelmingly chose to use words other than *kephalē* for the Greek translation. And so, let us bear in mind a Greek mindset, quite different to our own, when we read the word 'head' as written in 1 Corinthians 11.

In addition to the Greek understanding of the word, let us take note of the structure of verse 3. The progression of the verse is intriguing. If Paul was meaning 'head' to signify a clear hierarchy of authority or leadership within the couplets, it would have made sense for him to open the sentence with the Christ/God couplet (as that is the pairing with the highest authority) and then to progress further down a hierarchical ladder with the other two couplets.[6] But Paul did not follow a logical progression if hierarchy was what he wanted to communicate. The positioning of the Christ/God couplet therefore suggests that authoritative hierarchy is *not* the point of this sentence. In contrast, if 'source' is how we read 'head', then Paul *has* put the couplets in logical order—an order that is *chronological*, not *hierarchical*: 'Man came from Christ's creative work, woman came from "the man," Christ came from God in the incarnation.'[7]

Furthermore, the Christ/God couplet in itself gives us an additional means of assessing appropriate ways of interpreting 'head' in verse 3. It is extremely unlikely that Paul intended for us to read a different meaning of 'head' in each couplet and, therefore, the Christ/God couplet brings clarity to what headship will mean in the others. Early church fathers—the earliest commentators on 1 Corinthians 11:3—identified this reality and, therefore, leant towards a Greek understanding of *kephalē* rather than one of leadership or authority. Chrysostom was opposed to any reading that might imply subordination of the Son or subordination of women.[8] Gordon Fee quotes Cyril of Alexandria, 'Thus we can say that "the head of every man is Christ." For he was made by *[dia]* him … as God; "but the head of the woman is the man," because she was taken out of his flesh … Likewise "the head of Christ is God," because he is of him *[ex autou]* by nature.'[9]

We have looked at a few different angles by which to assess the meaning of 'head' in verse 3. The support for a reading of 'head' as 'source' is significant and explains why 'the majority view in recent scholarship has shifted to understand "head" (κεφαλή) in this passage to mean "source" rather than "authority".'[10] Having discussed this at some length, let us now look at a few more questions raised by 1 Corinthians 11 which are relevant to our discussion.

Hairstyle or Head Covering?

> Every man who prays or prophesies with his head covered dishonours his head, but every wife who prays or prophesies with her head uncovered

> dishonours her head, since it is the same as if her
> head were shaven. For if a wife will not cover her
> head, then she should cut her hair short. But since
> it is disgraceful for a wife to cut off her hair or shave
> her head, let her cover her head. (1 Cor. 11:4–6)

Having laid the foundations of headship, Paul moves on to focus on the idea of how the incorrect behaviour of men and women may lead to the dishonour of their corresponding metaphorical heads mentioned in verse 3. There is some scholarly debate over the exact meaning of the Greek text in verses 4 and 5. The literal translation of what most texts translate 'head covering' is 'having down the head'[11] and, hence, some scholars argue that this text is not about head coverings at all but actually about hairstyles. We will explore the strengths and weaknesses of both options here.

1. Hairstyle

If we are to take 'having down from the head' literally, then it is plausible that Paul's instructions were based on concerns over men having long hair and women letting their hair hang down. Payne argues for this reading, pointing out that long hair was generally associated with homosexuality or effeminate behaviour in men and hence would have been seen as disgraceful. In addition, he states that virtually all portraiture that we have of Greco-Roman women from the time of Paul's letter depict respectable women with their hair done up, not hanging down loose.[12] A reading of hairstyles is given further weight given Paul's own reference to hair length a little further in the text in verse 14. Additionally, verses like 1 Timothy 2:9 certainly seem to suggest that women's hairstyles were very much on display in the church community rather than covered up by veils when in public gatherings.

There are a few difficulties, however, with reading this 1 Corinthians text as relating to hairstyles. Firstly, there is the Jewish tradition of Nazirite vows for us to consider. Nazirite men would not cut their hair as a demonstration of their devotion to God. It is difficult to see why Paul would so thoroughly denounce that behaviour as disgraceful or shameful. Secondly, we see in Acts 18:18 that Paul himself followed the custom of growing his hair whilst under a vow (and if we follow the timeline of Acts, this would most likely have been the case whilst Paul was in Corinth). It is difficult then to see how Paul would bring such opposing teaching to something we know he did.

2. Head Covering

On the other side of the coin, there are those who argue that an actual veil or shawl must be what Paul is talking about (especially given the weaknesses associated with the hairstyle argument). But this view is not without difficulty either. If a veil or shawl is really what is being discussed, which cultural custom (Jew, Greek, or Roman) was it to reflect? We know that the Corinthian community was not made up only of Greeks but was multicultural. The difficulty is that the three cultures represented did not have the same customs with regards to head coverings, and so what would have been 'shameful' in one culture would not have been so in another. We are faced with 'the almost impossible task of identifying which cultural practices he [Paul] is referring to that would be universally shaming for both men and women in relation to head coverings.'[13] The customs for women were different in the three different communities. Jewish women were required to cover their heads whenever they were in public, Greek women did not cover their heads even while in prayer, and Roman women assumed the same practice as Roman men by covering their heads during religious sacrifices.[14] Additionally, we have good evidence that, contrary to Paul's appeal to culture to show that it was shameful for men to cover their heads in prayer, 'Liturgical head coverings for men were common practice in Roman, Greek, and Jewish culture.'[15] Clearly, we have a problem here.

What then are we to conclude? Both readings have significant problems that make it difficult for us to see how Paul would teach either option with any conviction. We are at somewhat of an impasse here with one option making Paul seem oddly arbitrary in the picking of one cultural custom over another (and contradicting the majority custom with regards to men), and with the other option demonstrating that Paul lacked consistency given his own actions with growing his hair long. There *is* a way we can resolve the difficulties here, but we will hold off on discussing that for a moment whilst we continue assessing questions that the text raises for us.

Why Is This So Important to Paul?

> For if a wife will not cover her head, then she
> should cut her hair short. But since it is disgraceful
> for a wife to cut off her hair or shave her head, let
> her cover her head. (1 Cor. 11:6)

It is often assumed that the problem in this community was that women were pushing the boundaries of convention having found freedom in the grace that they'd encountered.[16] It is suggested that, regardless of which custom Paul wanted upheld (hairstyle or head covering), the need for this teaching had arisen because the women had become rather unruly in the community. Rather than using their freedom wisely, they were abusing that freedom and so dishonouring the men around them. Paul's intention here is to curb behaviour that will be seen as shameful. He spends some time building his argument and recommends a strict consequence for women who will not follow his teaching: they should shave their heads. Citing Wallace, Payne points out, 'This is not just hypothetical. These imperatives are "stronger than a mere option, engaging the volition and placing a requirement on the individual."'[17] Shaving a woman's head was a deeply humiliating punishment. 'In Paul's day, if a woman was convicted of adultery, the hair of her head was shamefully cut off as punishment … Accordingly, 1 Corinthians 11:6 calls on such a woman [one who will not adhere to the instructions in the chapter] to accept the punishment of a convicted adulteress.'[18]

The narrative of unruly women who were abusing their freedom and needed to be brought back in line is a compelling one (not least of all because it has been offered by many scholars over the years). But we have to ask some questions here as there are a few challenges to face.

Firstly, let us ask why Paul would feel so deeply (to the point of totally humiliating women who were disobedient) about protecting a custom that was not uniformly followed in the city in question. As discussed previously, there was no consistent custom with head coverings or hairstyles that fully matches Paul's instructions to the men and women. The text assumes a universal shame/honour principle at work but, as we have seen, that was not the case. It is strange for Paul to make such strong assertions appealing to cultural norms that would not have made sense to all of his readers. Secondly, let us consider why Paul specified such a humiliating punishment for the women who disobeyed his instructions. Not only does the punishment seem unusually harsh, but it is difficult to fathom because there is no corresponding punishment suggested for men if they disobeyed the instructions. No matter what our views are on Paul's attitude to women in leadership, surely we do not believe that he was intentionally misogynistic in isolating women for punishments and turning a blind eye to men who might fall into error? That sort of attitude is one we would expect of the Pharisees (the story from John 8 of the woman caught in adultery comes to mind—where was the man she was caught with?) but doesn't seem consistent with an apostle of Christ. This is most especially true when the very thing being pronounced as 'shameful'—a woman uncovering her hair and allowing it to hang loose—is played out exactly in the woman with the alabaster jar in an act of worship to Jesus and, far from rebuking her, Jesus commends her for her abandoned act of love. Something here does not add up.

Unfortunately, if we assume that this text fully represents Paul's views, then answers are not easy to come by, for indeed the women are singled out more harshly than the men, and we do not know why. As I've hinted previously, there is another way to read this section of Scripture that offers a possible solution for us, but we will look at one more question from the text before we turn our attention to that interpretation.

Genesis Reference

Paul roots his instruction on head coverings in the creation account of Genesis. Oddly, the reference to Genesis in 1 Corinthians 11:7 does not match the creation account found in Genesis 1 and 2 but gives an alternative version of events. Not only does it change 'image and likeness' from Genesis 1:26 to 'image and glory' but, in direct contradiction to Genesis 1:27, it asserts that only man was made in the image of God and that woman instead was created in the image of man. Which account are we to believe? When we look at Genesis 1 and 2, both male and female were made in the image of God, and though woman was made from man, we are never told that she was made in his image. Furthermore, in 1 Corinthians 11 we find the one-sided statement that 'woman was made from man, man was not made from woman' which totally disregards Genesis 4's assertion that man came from the woman 'with the help of the Lord.'[19] What are we to make of this? To further complicate issues, 1 Corinthians 11:12 then seems to change direction somewhat and reminds us of the mutuality of creation and ends up echoing the sentiment of Genesis 4. Which of these accounts are we to put weight on? We may try to argue that Paul is bringing some clarification or further detail to the Genesis account, but that is difficult to argue given the clear contradiction of the accounts. Again we find ourselves struggling to makes sense of the argument in 1 Corinthians 11—not only because of its inconsistency with scripture elsewhere but with its own inconsistency between verse 7 and verse 12.

Is 1 Corinthians 11:2–16 Double Minded?

It's as if two voices are speaking in this passage. Scholars acknowledge that there is somewhat of a tension between the first and second halves of this text. Perhaps Paul is bringing balance in the second half to the somewhat hierarchical teaching he's brought in the first half? Certainly the second part of the text affirms the equality of both genders in a way that is conspicuously different to the first part of the text. We are reminded again that 1 Corinthians 11 is not the best scripture to lean on for gender roles as it seems to argue for both sides of the debate in different moments. If the whole text is a reflection of Paul's views on gender roles, then it is impossible to come to a conclusion either way.

But there is another way to read this passage. Though it has been suggested by scholars before, it has most recently been reintroduced by Lucy Peppiatt. This interpretation is different to the broad brush-strokes of others because:

> a. It does not assume that the women were the problem group in the community in Corinth.
>
> b. It does not assume the whole section of 1 Corinthians 11:2–16 to be reflective of Paul's views alone, but suggests that there are two voices interlaced in the text: Paul's own voice and the voice of the Corinthian community, which Paul is quoting.

There are compelling reasons to read 1 Corinthians 11:2–16 in this way. Let us look at some of those reasons together now.

1. The Use of Rhetoric in Ancient Greek Debate

The use of rhetoric and carefully crafted indirect arguments were an integral part of ancient Greek debate. Within Greek philosophical traditions, the use of arguments that employed the opposition's thoughts in order to then prove those very thoughts erroneous is well documented. This was a way of argumentation that was seen not only as less aggressive than direct confrontation but also as a better means of winning the hearts of the hearers. Douglas Campbell highlights this fact: 'Good philosophers functioned as midwives, bringing truth to birth in their interlocutors [listeners] from *their own* assumptions, teasing out a correct understanding by a process of cross examination ... (in particular, interlocutors could be confronted with the contradictions in their own positions and forced to abandon at least one half of such dilemmas ...).'[20] He goes on to say, 'Even that construct [the argument belonging to the audience] is permitted to speak.'[21] Hence, those who suggest that Paul may be employing such a method of argumentation here are not suggesting something that would have been at all out of the ordinary in Paul's day. Rather, they are identifying a well-recognised method of argument by some of the best minds in ancient Greece.

2. Paul's Acknowledged Use of Rhetorical Argument Elsewhere

It is widely acknowledged by Bible scholars today that Paul *did* employ such a means of argument elsewhere in 1 Corinthians (and so too in his other letters), e.g., 1 Corinthians 1:12; 3:4; 6:12–13; 7:1; 8:1,

4; 10:23.[22] Whilst it is true that these examples are shorter than the
rhetorical argument proposed in 1 Corinthians 11:2–16, the fact that
it is virtually universally accepted that Paul *did* use this method of
argument at least allows us to consider the possibility that he may
have chosen to use it in 1 Corinthians 11. It is important to note
that several of the currently recognised rhetorical instances mentioned
above have no obvious written signals in the Greek text to alert us to
the fact that Paul is referring to the Corinthian voice. Scholars have
come to the conclusion that the voice is not Paul's because that is what
makes best sense of the flow of argument in each of those examples.
Again, this gives us cause to at least consider the same possibility in
1 Corinthians 11. Furthermore, Peppiatt argues that there *are* two
other instances in 1 Corinthians where a longer rhetorical argument
may be seen. She makes reference to Paul's teaching on speaking in
tongues in 1 Corinthians 14:20–25 and his teaching on women being
silent in 1 Corinthians 14:33b–36. Both of these texts follow a similar
format to 1 Corinthians 11:2–16 with 'obvious "breaks" in the text
where we know that there is a shift in thinking, or where Paul appears
to be contradicting himself … In each example we will note Paul's
use of the rhetorical question occurring in 11:13, 14:23, and 14:36.'[23]
If Peppiatt is right in her position, then there are other examples of
longer rhetorical arguments in use in 1 Corinthians, which obviously
strengthens the suggestion to read 1 Corinthians 11:2–16 in this way.

3. The Significance of 'Nevertheless' and 'in the Lord'

Nevertheless, in the Lord woman is not independent of man nor man of woman; for as woman was

made from man, so man is now born of woman.
And all things are from God. (1 Cor. 11:11–12)

Verse 11 sees a sudden transition in the argument. Where it seemed that Paul had been carefully building an argument for hierarchy between men and women, there is now an abrupt change as he turns to the interdependence of men and women. His finishing thought in verse 12, 'all things are from God,' interrupts the idea that men are from God, but women are from men. This conspicuous change in the direction of argument is introduced by the words, 'Nevertheless, in the Lord' in verse 11. These are significant words and warrant attention.

'It has been noted by many scholars that the word πλὴν (nevertheless) first is adversative and second is used "to break off a discussion and to emphasize what is important." Importantly, it is for this reason that Murphy-O'Connor and others make an exegetical decision to *prioritize* Paul's reciprocal picture of man and woman articulated in verses 11–16 over his patriarchal argument in verses 2–10.'[24]

Shoemaker makes a similar point: 'Although generally translated "only" or "nevertheless," I believe this particle takes on a special rhetorical function for Paul. Although used only four times in his letters (Philippians 1:18; 3:16; 4:14; and here), it appears to serve as a pointer in each case to an important statement. It is a term that introduces Paul's central theme in each context. Thus, I have chosen to render it "The point is."'[25]

Paul's words 'in the Lord' are equally significant. They are words that signify a complete transformation and 'radical new existence'.[26] We see this phrase 'in the Lord' again in Philemon 16, where Paul uses it as the basis of his argument for Philemon to see Onesimus no longer through the lens of the master/slave hierarchy but to see him as his equal: a brother in the Lord.

Hence, Paul's words at the beginning of verse 11 are provoking to the reader. There is a complete break with the line of argument that has come before, where hierarchy and shame are main players. Instead, Paul changes direction completely, communicating his 'central theme' as what is now a reality 'in the Lord': the interdependent relationship of man and woman. Even if we are not convinced that the words of 1 Corinthians 11:11 are a compelling reason for reading a rhetorical argument in this text, they still give us ample reason—as Murphy-O'Connor recognises—to give priority to Paul's thoughts in verse 11 over the earlier verses in the text.

4. No Such Custom

> Judge for yourselves: is it proper for a wife to pray to God with her head uncovered? Does not nature itself teach you that if a man wears long hair it is a disgrace for him, but if a woman has long hair, it is her glory? For her hair is given to her for a covering. If anyone is inclined to be contentious, we have no such practice, nor do the churches of God. (1 Cor. 11:13–16)

Verses 13–15 see Paul throwing the ball back into the Corinthian court with a rhetorical question. It is thought that his appeal to 'nature itself' signifies a stoic argument rather than a theological one.

In verse 15, he plays on the idea of glory again, but in a rather different way, for woman is not reliant on another for glory. She has been given her own.

However, it is verse 16 that is of the most interest to us in this section, particularly the words 'we have no such practice.' Some translations have given an alternative, opposite translation of 'no *other* practice' but 'it is generally acknowledged that "no other practice" (NIV) is a bad translation.'[27] Fee states that 'The Greek adjective *toiautēn* means "of such a kind, such as this" (BDAG); to stretch it, as most English translations tend to do, to equal *allos*, "other," is to make it conform to what one thinks Paul ought to have said.'[28] The point Fee is making is clear. If we read 1 Corinthians 11:2–16 as purely Pauline, we are left considerably perplexed as to why he would finish off his whole teaching claiming *not* to have the very custom he's been arguing for. It is because of the considerable problem this verse raises that the majority of translators have opted to stretch and twist the meaning in order to make it fit. Others who have maintained the original meaning have tried to argue that 'no such custom' must then be in reference to being contentious. But it is difficult to see how contention is equal to a custom.

This last phrase of the section gives us another strong reason to understand 1 Corinthians 11:2–16 as a mix of Corinthian and Pauline thought. In that case, Paul stating that there is 'no such custom' in any of the other communities of God makes perfect sense. A group in Corinth was trying to insist upon head coverings only for women to cement a hierarchy in the church community. Paul is clear that there is 'no such custom' that either the apostles or the churches of God recognise.

5. Resolution of Interpretive Problem

If we understand the first verses to represent the thoughts of a group within the Corinthian community, then some significant interpretive challenges are resolved. The text is no longer double minded with perplexing errors and inconsistencies but now makes sense as a consistent and provoking flow of thought. We no longer have to resolve in our minds why a brilliant, intentional theologian like Paul would present such a convoluted, inconsistent, and contradictory argument. In addition, regardless of whether we believe Paul taught complementarian or egalitarian theology, I hope we would all agree that he was not misogynistic in his behaviour towards women. Unfortunately, this 1 Corinthians 11 text, with its singling out of women by demanding such a shame-filled consequence for any who disobeyed the proposed customs with no corresponding consequences for disobedient men, is difficult to stomach. But, again, a reading that acknowledges Corinthian thought to be interlaced in this text allows us to see that Paul was in no way seeking to 'put women in their place' to the point of utter humiliation but was rather wanting to alert this Corinthian group of how far they'd veered off track with what they were trying to enforce.

Conclusion

A rhetorical argument viewpoint clearly changes the narrative that we have read into the text from one where the women are the problem to one where it is a leading faction of men that are the problem. Is this so difficult to imagine? We have bought into a narrative of unruly women for so long, but is it not just as easy to imagine overbearing men reasserting their patriarchal views over women, even after they have come into new life in Christ? Neither narrative can be proven. But the point is that it is at least as likely that men were falling back into patterns of behaviour that were deeply ingrained in them from childhood as it is to believe that women were misusing the freedom that they were experiencing for the first time in their lives. Both options are plausible.

The difficulty is that a rhetorical argument is impossible to prove. Paul did not put obvious markers (that we are aware of) to signify which parts of the passage are his own thought and which parts are his quotations of Corinthian thought. This reality, however, does not stop us from reading other texts to include Corinthian quotes if it allows the text to truly make sense. Perhaps it's time for us to apply the same logic here. Furthermore, as mentioned previously, Peppiatt has done some work to show that although we do not have obvious textual markers for quotations, there are recognisable patterns (break in the argument and use of rhetorical question) in 1 Corinthians 11 and twice in 1 Corinthians 14 which point to a change in thought. We will look at the implications of this for the 1 Corinthians 14 text in the next chapter.

In truth, this 1 Corinthians 11 text still holds some mysteries that the rhetorical interpretation doesn't conclusively answer. Significantly, we still cannot be sure what is meant by the sign of authority spoken of in verse 10, nor the question of angels. But what it does do is plausibly deal with most of the questions posed. Paul is not double minded but is wisely employing a device that was common in Greek thought and he himself is acknowledged to use elsewhere.

Ultimately, regardless of whether we are convinced by a rhetorical argument interpretation or not, what we have discussed from 1 Corinthians 11 gives us solid reason not to read this text as a supporting argument for hierarchy between men and women. Our discussion on the meaning of 'head' allows us to reject the idea of authority as being the point of the teaching in verse 3, and the discussion on the transition words in verse 11 suggests we should prioritise the theology of verses 11 and 12 over those that go before them. Adding to that, the significant inconsistencies that remain should we reject a rhetorical argument interpretation leaves any who wish to build a hierarchical argument from these verses on extremely difficult ground.

1 CORINTHIANS 14: WOMEN, BE SILENT

Now we arrive at the second of the tricky sections on gender roles in 1 Corinthians. As with 1 Corinthians 11:2–16, this text, 1 Corinthians 14:33–36, is found in Paul's extended teaching on matters relating to worship in the community. Let's look at the verses before spending some time discussing what Paul might mean in them:

> For God is not a God of confusion but of peace.
>
> As in all the churches of the saints, the women should keep silent in the churches. For they are not permitted to speak, but should be in submission, as the Law also says. If there is anything they desire to learn, let them ask their husbands at home. For it is shameful for a woman to speak in church.
>
> Or was it from you that the word of God came? Or are you the only ones it has reached? (1 Cor. 14:33–36)

It is interesting to note that, according to ancient Mediterranean cultures, 1 Corinthians 14:33–36 would not have felt at all out of place. Instructions for women to be silent in public would be a perfect fit with the social norms of the day. Payne quotes various ancient authors affirming that women should be silent (e.g., Sophocles (*Ajax* 293), 'Silence adorns a woman'; Democritus (*Saying* 110) 'Let a woman not practise speech; for that is terrible'[1]). In direct contrast to us, therefore, first-century readers would have found 1 Corinthians 14:33–36 to be completely in step with Corinthian culture, but the assumptions of 1 Corinthians 11 and 12—that women should have their voices heard in public—quite challenging.

It is the obvious contradiction between 1 Corinthians 11:2–16 and 1 Corinthians 14:33–36 that makes this latter section difficult to interpret. Had there been no verses in Paul's writings assuming that Corinthian women would speak in public, we might have been able to argue that Paul did want the women (at least in Corinth) to stay completely silent in the church. The trouble, of course, is that we do have verses that assume that women will be speaking in the community—not only in 1 Corinthians 11 but also in 1 Corinthians 14 itself where all speak in tongues (v. 5) and prophesy (v. 24). What then are we to make of 1 Corinthians 14:33–36? Unless we are willing to concede that Paul contradicted himself intentionally (perhaps he was in two minds whether women should speak or not?), then we are faced with the need to interpret 1 Corinthians 14 in such a way as to adequately explain why there is the command for women to remain silent in a letter that assumes that they should speak.

Some have tried to hold 1 Corinthians 14 as Paul's superior judgement on women speaking (see, for example, Origen: 'Even if she speaks marvelous and holy things [i.e., prophecy], "it is shameful for a woman to speak in church" simply because it comes from the mouth of a woman.')[2] Thankfully, this view is not a well-respected one and there is virtually unanimous consensus amongst scholars today on the one thing that 1 Corinthians 14:33–36 cannot mean: that women are actually to remain silent in the church.[3]

In order to make sense of these verses then, we will look at three approaches (in no particular order) that have been suggested to interpreting the passage. First, some scholars argue that Paul intended qualifications to what sort of speech is being restricted. Second, some suggest that these verses are not Paul's own view but are, in fact, Paul quoting a Corinthian slogan. Third, some scholars argue that verses 34 and 35 are not authentically Pauline and are a later insertion into the text. We will take some time to look at each of the arguments in due course.

Before weighing up the different interpretations, let us pause briefly to look at two phrases in the text that are often the subject of discussion.

Firstly, let's look at verse 33b: 'As in all the churches of the saints.' This is a phrase that has sparked debate because it is possible to make it either the end of the sentence from verse 33, or the beginning of the sentence going into verse 34. The first possibility means that Paul is advocating that the Corinthian church recognise that God is One of peace—as in all the churches of the saints. The second possibility means that Paul is wanting for women to keep silent in the Corinthian church—as in all the churches of the saints. That there is disagreement on which option is correct is evidenced by the different translations we have access to. The ESV, as seen above, attaches verse 33b to the subsequent sentence in verse 34, strengthening the idea that Paul's teaching on silence is applicable universally for all churches. The NIV, KJV, and NASB, in contrast, attach verse 33b to the preceding sentence in verse 33a. In reality, both readings are stylistically awkward—how does 'as in all the churches' add any meaning to the rest of verse 33?[4] But it is equally awkward to attach the phrase to verse 34, given the fact that that would mean Paul unnecessarily repeats 'in the churches' twice in the one sentence. Beyond these stylistic issues, Johnson raises a number of more academic points that may help us decide which way to read the verse:

> First, in other instances in the epistle an appeal to the churches' practice comes after Paul's discussion of a particular issue, not before (4:17; 7:17; 11:16). Second, when verses 34–35 are displaced to follow verse 40 in some manuscripts and versions, the last part of verse 33 does not go with the section on women/wives. Third, there does not seem to be a clear instance in biblical Greek literature (New Testament and LXX) of *hōs* ('as') beginning a sentence with a verbless dependent clause, which would be the case if the last part of verse 33 were attached to 34.[5]

Johnson's case for reading verse 33b as concluding the sentence found in verse 33 is convincing, particularly in the absence of any robust arguments to the contrary. Hence, from this point in this chapter, we will assume that verse 33b closes the preceding section and does not introduce the teaching on women in 1 Corinthians 14.

The second phrase to look at is found in verse 34: '[Women] should be in submission, as the Law also says.' This is a difficult and unusual statement which is often downplayed with unwarranted confidence. It is difficult because who or what women are to be submitted to is left for us to guess (despite what some may claim). It is unusual because of the lack of clarity of 'the Law' that he is referring to. To appeal to a law which is not cited (and for which no obvious citation has been agreed on by subsequent scholars) as the basis for a specific requirement for Christian behaviour in the community is unusual for Paul. Payne comments, 'Nowhere else … does Paul appeal to the law without a corresponding OT reference.'[6] It is therefore a cause for concern when comments are made on this text without caveats of uncertainty. See, for example, 'The *law* requires the acknowledgement of the distinctive roles of men and women (34), a reference to Gen. 2:20–24 or 3:16. Paul has already cited the former in 11:8–9.'[7] Despite the clarity communicated in this interpretation, there is nothing in 1 Corinthians 14:34 that speaks of the distinct roles for men and women, nor any link in the text of 'the Law' to the Genesis narrative. Neither does 1 Corinthians 11:8–9 suggest that it is referencing (or prescribing) a law when creation order is described. We should approach any claims that the meaning here is clear, particularly any assertions that are used to prop up a wider argument, very cautiously. On this, Belleville notes,

> The problem is that traditionalists have difficulty admitting ignorance or even ambiguity. They tend to treat these matters as plain and factual. All too often it is simply assumed Paul is commanding

women to submit to their husbands in keeping
with the so-called 'law' of Genesis 3:16 … Yet this
is a most improbable (if not impossible) interpretation. For one thing, neither Genesis 3:16 nor any
other OT text commands women to submit to
their husbands. Would Paul take an OT text (Gen.
3:16) that is descriptive of a post-fall, dysfunctional
marital relationship and cite it as prescriptive for
the husband-wife Christian relationship?[8]

My aim in highlighting the phrase from verse 34 is not to
bring a conclusive answer (I have none) but rather to underline the
importance of approaching the text cautiously. There is too much left
unsaid in the text for us to approach in any other manner.

Having established some preliminaries, let us turn our attention
to the different arguments offered. Right from the outset let us recognise that once again we find ourselves grappling with 1 Corinthians
in a not entirely satisfactory way. Debate on this section abounds
despite the fact that what we are dealing with is only three verses.
It has been noted that in assessing this text 'it is much easier to cite
views and dismiss them for various reasons than to offer a completely
satisfying alternative.'[9] We will therefore approach the text carefully
and with a good dose of humility!

Interpretation 1: Introducing Qualifications

Many scholars have suggested that the text hints at qualifications for
the instructions, allowing us to understand Paul's teaching within

the confines of specific boundary lines. In this way, 1 Corinthians 14:34–36 no longer stands in contradiction to other texts assuming that women will speak but rather provides the context of when speaking is appropriate, and when it is not.

There are different qualifications that have been suggested. This list is by no means exhaustive, but we will look at some of the more popular arguments that have been put forward. Some have argued that what Paul is instructing against is disruptive chatter from women in the community. Others suggest that the church meeting being described in 1 Corinthians 14 is a more public one than what 1 Corinthians 11 or 12 describe. Women are allowed to speak in more private meetings but not in public gatherings. Others have argued that the instruction is against women interrupting with questions in the middle of church meetings—they can (and should) do that at home. Still others argue that the qualification for silence is the context of weighing prophecy. In this argument, weighing prophecy requires superior authority to bringing prophecy and Paul's concern is that women do not overstep their authority by assuming the function of weighing words in the community. We will look at each of these briefly.

a. Chatter

The word translated as 'to speak' in 14:34–35 is the Greek word *lalein*. This word is used in classical Greek to mean 'chatter'.[10] Does this then mean that what Paul was referring to is not absolute silence but rather instructing women to stop disrupting the meetings with their chatter? Unfortunately, Paul's usage of *lalein* elsewhere in this passage does not allow for this argument. 'Each of the twenty-two other occurrences of λαλεῖν [*lalein*] in this passage describe inspired speech. Elsewhere in this chapter, any specific sense of "to speak" (e.g., "in tongues") is always specified.'[11]

b. Specific Church Meeting Context

Does 1 Corinthians 14 refer to a different, more public gathering than 1 Corinthians 11? It is difficult to see how it is possible to differentiate between the context of the two texts. It would be a neat way of explaining the contradictions between the two, but there are no indicators in the passages that the context of the instructions are any different, with the flow of teaching from chapter 11 to chapter 14 being quite clearly rooted in church gatherings (see 11:17, 18, 22; 12:7; 14:4). The fact that 1 Corinthians 11 assumes a public gathering is further evidenced by the instructions on head coverings built on the principles of shame and honour. That argument would only be relevant in public contexts. Carson notes, 'This interpretation does not seem very likely, for: (a) Paul thinks of prophecy primarily as revelation from God delivered through believers *in the context of the church*, where the prophecy may be evaluated (14:23–29). (b) Distinctions between "smaller house groups" and "church" may not have been all that intelligible to the first Christians, who commonly met in private homes.'[12]

c. Questions

Some scholars argue that verse 35 is the key to understanding Paul's instructions in verses 34–36. Verse 35 indicates that there was an issue where women who were wanting to learn were asking questions. It is then surmised that those questions voiced in public were causing some disruption. Hence, it is argued, when Paul brings instruction for the women to be silent, he is not commanding complete silence. Rather, he is telling the women not to ask questions that will disrupt the public gathering. Payne notes that this is 'probably the most widely held view'[13] in interpreting this text. The fact that women were at an educational disadvantage strengthens this argument.[14] It would be natural for women to want to ask questions in the meetings in order to learn more fully. This view does not suggest that Paul didn't want women to learn but simply that there was an appropriate place for them to do that learning and the public gathering was not that place. Although this interpretation fits well with verse 35, there are some difficulties. The fact that Paul does not state that women should not ask questions but that they should be 'silent' and 'are not permitted to speak' (v. 34) and that 'it is shameful for a woman to speak' (v. 35) is an issue here. None of these words reference questions as the issue but seem to be addressing the much broader issue of women speaking. A reduction of the meaning of these words to mean disruptive questions 'ignores the obvious meaning of "be silent."'[15]

d. Weighing Prophecy and the Issue of Authority

Another option presented is that the issue in these verses is one of authority. The argument is based on the fact that Paul's teaching on spiritual gifts and, in particular, prophecy directly precedes and follows the conversation on women (vv. 29–33 and vv. 37–40). If the text on women being silent is surrounded by instructions on the use of spiritual gifts, presumably the instructions themselves are based in that same topic? The strength of this argument is the immediate context of these verses. We know that Paul assumed women would prophesy (1 Cor. 11:5) but what about the practice of weighing prophecy that is mentioned in 1 Corinthians 14:29b? Is it possible that the silence Paul speaks of is not absolute, but is in reference to the weighing of prophecy? However, once again, we find some significant challenges to holding this view. Firstly, if Paul is talking about the weighing of prophecy, why does he not just say that? It seems an obtuse way to state something simple. Secondly, if weighing prophecy is the issue, why did Paul not bring the instructions of verses 34–36 straight after verse 29b? Why bring other instructions on prophecy for a few verses and then return to the idea of weighing without giving it mention and hope that your readers will be able to make the mental leap? Thirdly, some ancient manuscripts do not have the instruction on women at verses 34–36 but rather after verse 40. In this case, the idea that Paul was trying to link his words to the weighing of prophecy becomes even more unlikely to fathom. Fourthly, the comment on weighing prophecy in verse 29 makes it clear that whilst two or three prophets prophesy, it is the responsibility of 'the others' to weigh the words. Does 'the others' refer to the community of prophets or the whole community? It is difficult to be sure but, in either case, women would be present. It is strange for Paul to use this inclusive word in verse 29 and then hope his readers will catch his meaning negating it in verse 34.

Ultimately, this argument has gained traction because of two major assumptions:

> 1. That women have less authority than men for some church-recognised roles.
>
> 2. That weighing prophecy is a function of superior authority than prophesying because 'the careful weighing of prophecies falls under that magisterial function [of teaching].'[16]

The difficulty is that neither of these assumptions are found anywhere in the 1 Corinthians 14 text. Furthermore, if we want to pursue the idea that teaching exercises superior authority to prophesying, we will be hard pressed to find a scriptural foundation for that argument. To the contrary, when Paul states a 'hierarchy' of gifts in 1 Corinthians 12:28, he places prophet before teacher. Thus the argument that a weighing/teaching role must be held back from women because it is superior in authority to a prophetic role is rather undermined. There is no scriptural evidence whatsoever that weighing prophecy is seen as exercising superior authority to delivering prophecy.

Besides the specific difficulties encountered by each argument, all four of the above suggestions stumble at two significant obstacles:

Firstly, when the same teaching to remain silent is given to those who speak in tongues and prophesy, the qualifying context is clearly stated in each instruction, 'But if there is no one to interpret, let each of them keep silent' (v. 28) and, 'If a revelation is made to another sitting there, let the first be silent' (v. 30). If there was a clear qualifying context (such as one of those stated above), why would Paul omit it when he teaches about women, unlike his other references to silence? Many years ago I wrote an essay for a church leadership course. In that essay I argued that the fact that Paul tells three groups in this chapter to be silent softens the tone as Paul is not singling out women but dealing with disruptions in worship. The problem with my argument, however, was that it ignored Paul's qualifying statements to the first two groups and the absence of such to the third. Both those who speak in tongues and those who prophesy are given very clear contexts when they are to remain silent. The command for silence in women is entirely different. Women are not told to be silent because they are disruptive but because it is simply shameful for a woman to speak in public. The prohibition is not rooted in disruptive behaviour but in gender. Far from softening the tone, the presence of the first two instructions for silence serves to highlight the hard-hitting scope of the instruction in verses 34–35, given the notable absence of a qualification.

The second significant obstacle to reading qualifications into the text is found in the repetitious nature of the instructions in verses 34–35. The same idea is repeated three times in slightly different ways:

1. 'The women must keep silent' (v. 34). This word 'silent' is from the Greek word *sigaō* which means absolute silence, including any speech.
2. 'They are not permitted to speak' (v. 34).
3. 'For it is shameful for a woman to speak' (v. 35).

The instruction for women not to speak is insistent. Payne, citing Delling, shows how significant this would be to first-century readers: 'In the Greek and Hellenistic Roman world, "threefold utterance of a word, expression, or sentence gives it full validity and power ... three is characterised by fullness and solidity.'"[17] He goes on to say, 'Modern attempts to limit 14:34–35's threefold prohibition are so anachronistic they would strike first-century readers as obvious distortions of the writer's clear intent.'[18] Clearly, there is a problem here. The way the text is written leaves us little wiggle room. As much as we would like to insert qualifiers to the instructions, we cannot, not only because of the difficulties mentioned for each view, but even more so because of the manner in which the prohibition is communicated. It would seem that we need to move on to find another interpretation to help resolve this text's contradiction with Paul's teaching elsewhere.

The next two interpretations of this text are different from the one discussed above because they do not follow the narrative that women were the problem at Corinth. Rather, they suggest that the view of 1 Corinthians 14:34–35 is reflective of those who would prefer to adhere to the patriarchal norms of the day than to adopt the radical transition that the gospel signifies for how men and women are to relate. The argument from both of the next interpretations is that 1 Corinthians 14:34–35 is not Paul's viewpoint at all.

Interpretation 2: A Corinthian Slogan

Is it possible that Paul is quoting a slogan from a Corinthian 'prophet' (or group of 'prophets') in 1 Corinthians 14:34–35 and not communicating his own views? There are many scholars who give their voice to this interpretation, sometimes on quite different grounds (e.g., Snyder, Odell-Scott, Bilezikian, Flanagan, Peppiatt).

Let us look now at some of the arguments that accompany this interpretation (some of which have been noted earlier):

1. There is an inconsistency between 1 Corinthians 14:34–36 and Paul's views in 1 Corinthians 11–12 which needs resolution.

2. Paul uses Corinthian quotes elsewhere in his letter, and therefore, it is not implausible that he should be doing so in 1 Corinthians 14:34–35.[19]

3. The repetitious and absolute nature of the prohibition in 1 Corinthians 14:34–35 makes it difficult to justify an attempt to soften the text by inserting qualifications that are not present.[20] We are faced with a very strong restriction and have little option but to conclude that either Paul did intend for women to be in silence in the community (despite the inconsistency), or that the views communicated are not his own.

4. The problems with the flow of the passage are resolved if Paul is quoting a false prophet(s) in the community. The verses immediately preceding the text reference how all should have room to prophesy, learn, and be encouraged (v. 31), how prophets should exercise self-control (v. 32), and how God brings peace not confusion. If there was a controlling 'prophet' in the community who was masquerading patriarchal customs as the words of God to the detriment of all that Paul communicated in verses 31–33, then it would make perfect sense for Paul to quote that false prophet here. Verses 34–35 are in direct opposition to verse 31 (and to v. 39). They actively shut down the ability of the women to prophesy and learn within community gatherings. It would make sense for Paul to quote the prohibition that was being communicated, along with his disdain at such a teaching (vv. 36–38) and a reaffirmation of the freedom of all to exercise the gifts (v. 39).[21]

5. Immediately following verses 34–35, there is the Greek participle *ē* which some have suggested signals disapproval with those verses.[22]

6. There is an observable rhetorical pattern between 1 Corinthians 11:2–16, 1 Corinthians 14:20–25, and 1 Corinthians 14:34–36. Each text carries a contradictory teaching and has a rhetorical question attached. Is it possible that these are all longer examples of Paul's use of Corinthian thought?[23]

7. The reference to 'the law' without a citation is not normal usage in Paul's vocabulary and hence makes us question whether it is actually Paul who is making this the basis of his argument. This is further highlighted by the fact that there is no law in the Old Testament that would require the silent submission of women. Some try to stretch this 'law' reference to creation order because that order has already been mentioned in 1 Corinthians 11. But this is not convincing. For one thing, 1 Corinthians 11 does not acknowledge that its reference to creation order is either referencing or prescribing a law. Furthermore, if somehow creation order is the law that is being referenced, how does it justify the silencing of women so absolutely? It is interesting to note that whilst the prohibition in verses 34–35 appeals to the law, in the verses that follow it, Paul appeals to the command of the Lord (v. 37), which would certainly be a way of appealing to a higher authority if verses 36–38 are intended by Paul to refute verses 34–35.[24]

The argument is compelling, but once again, there are a few challenges to consider. The difficulty is that there is no introduction of this text as a Corinthian slogan. Although scholars acknowledge Paul quoting Corinthian slogans in other instances where there is no obvious marking in the text,[25] the lack of an explicit quotation here makes this interpretation a difficult one to prove conclusively. Furthermore, none of the other recognised Corinthian slogans used in the letter are as long as this text in 1 Corinthians 14.[26] This is not an insurmountable problem, however. The fact that Paul does use slogans certainly makes it possible that he might have on occasion chosen to use longer quotes. Additionally, if Peppiatt's argument is correct, then we do have other instances where Paul did use longer excerpts of Corinthian thought.

Some scholars have raised objections to the use of the Greek participle *ē* to justify this position. The egalitarian scholar Linda Belleville notes, 'The simple fact is that, while *ē* can denote an exclamation expressing disapproval, the standard Greek-English lexicon of Hellenistic Greek lists only two instances, and in both cases there is a double *ē ē* … and not the single *ē* we have in 1 Corinthians 14:36.'[27] It would seem then that we are on safer ground to read the participle *ē* at the beginning of verse 36 as a simple 'Or' rather than anything more akin to 'What?!' This does not necessarily mean that verses 34–35 are not a Corinthian slogan but does mean that the presence of the *ē* is an insufficient argument to prove that point.

One of the more compelling arguments against this view is the lack of obvious modifying teaching following verses 34–35.[28] In the other examples of Paul quoting Corinthian slogans, Paul refutes the incorrect view with his own viewpoint. But there is nothing explicit in verses 36–38 that specifically addresses the women to restore them to vocal freedom. Having said that, what we do see in verses 36–38 may be Paul refuting the authority of the 'prophet(s)' in question by his appeal to the command of the Lord given through him, as well as his reiteration that all should desire to prophesy and that no one should be forbidden from speaking in tongues (v. 39) which stands in direct contradiction to the command for half the congregation to be silent in verses 34–35.

In the end, although there are compelling elements to this argument, the difficulty is that there is not enough in the text to prove it. Let us move on to one more possible interpretation.

Interpretation 3: An Interpolation (a Later Insertion)

Some argue that verses 34–35 are an interpolation into the text and are not part of Paul's original instructions.[29] This assertion is not made simply because of the contradictions that the passage highlights in Paul's teachings but because of inconsistencies in the text found in ancient manuscripts that are not explained by other interpretations. The reality is, whilst the vast majority of Bible texts are undisputed for authenticity, most Bible scholars agree that some texts we have are most likely late insertions (e.g., John 7:53–8:11).[30] This argument then is not without precedent elsewhere in Scripture.

The difficulty for proponents of this view is that all ancient manuscripts we have access to do have the verses of 1 Corinthians 14:34–35 somewhere in the text. If these verses are an insertion after the original, the insertion would have had to come very early on in the copying process for us not to have a single manuscript with the verses omitted. Is this plausible? Are there any clues in the text that this might be so?

There is a significant manuscript inconsistency when we look at 1 Corinthians 14. Ancient manuscripts place verses 34–35 in two different positions. Western manuscripts place the verses after verse 40 whilst non-Western manuscripts place the verses after verse 33. Scribes were meticulous in copying texts carefully so as not to change the scriptures. How then is it possible that there are two different placements of these verses? Either some scribes, having access to a manuscript with one placement, intentionally decided to change the position of the verses in the text to the other placement, or an early manuscript (for reasons that we will go on to assess) gave rise to both of these two different placements.

It is extremely unlikely that the inconsistent placement of verses 34–35 came about as an intentional decision from scribes.

> It is virtually inconceivable that a scribe would take verses 34–35 out of an original position after verse 33 and place them after verse 40 [and vice versa] … Scribes copied texts word for word, line for line. They might make what they believed to be spelling or style corrections, but they did not transpose such large blocks of text to other places to improve the logic of a passage without obvious reason. Unless this is the only occurrence, no scribe of any extant manuscript of the Pauline letters ever moved this large a block of text this far to improve its logic for no clear reason.[31]

If the inconsistent placement is not likely to be due to intentional changes from scribes, what then could give rise to the two versions in manuscripts? Proponents of an interpolation view argue that if someone had inserted verses 34–35 into the margins of the text (which is recognised to have happened elsewhere in Scripture), then any subsequent scribes, having no idea that these words were not part of the original, would have to make a decision concerning the placement of these words. An insertion into a margin would span several verses in the text, and so any copying scribes would be faced with having to decide the position of the words from the margin. This could explain the occurrence of two different placements. At least two different copies must have been made from the interpolated text—one scribe choosing after verse 33 and another choosing after verse 40 for its placement. All subsequent copies would reflect the placement in the manuscript being used to copy from.[32]

To justify this interpretation, scholars point to a number of clues from early manuscripts:

1. One of the earliest manuscripts of 1 Corinthians 14 that we have, Codex Vaticanus, contains symbols (distigme) by the end of 1 Corinthians 14:33.[33] These symbols are recognised as a signal that there were variations of the text occurring at this position in the manuscripts available. It is pointed out that Codex Vaticanus does not have these same symbols after verse 40. Because the distigme are missing after verse 40, it would seem implausible that the variation Codex Vaticanus is making reference to is the two possible placements of verses 34–35. If that was the case, the same symbolic distigme would be present after verse 40. There must be another variation that Codex Vaticanus is pointing out with these symbols. The only other variant noted by scholars of the *NA27* (a foundational Greek New Testament) at this position is 'the conjecture that originally 14:34–35 was not in the text.'[34]

2. Codex Fuldensis—a copy written between AD 541 and AD 544—contains a rewritten correction of 1 Corinthians 14:34–40 in it, omitting verses 34–35.[35]

3. Verses 34–35 have an unusually high rate of textual variations across manuscripts, 'about twice as many word reversals and other small variants as other verses in the context.'[36] Textual variations are acknowledged to be a typical marker of interpolations.

Beyond these clues from early manuscripts, scholars point to the notable absence of 1 Corinthians 14:34–35 in comments from early church fathers, despite the enormous implications of the verses. 'Even though 1 Corinthians was the most quoted epistle by Christian writers in the second century, none of the Apostolic Fathers cite 1 Cor. 14:34–35 … The earliest extant citation of 1 Cor. 14:34–35 appears to be by Tertullian, writing about AD 200.'[37]

Furthermore, there are issues of vocabulary in 1 Corinthians 14:34–35 that could support an interpolation interpretation. As noted before in this chapter, it is unusual for Paul to appeal to the law in the way that verse 34 does. Additionally, there are striking similarities between the vocabulary of 1 Corinthians 14:34–35 and 1 Timothy 12:11–15. 'Many scholars view this extensive verbal correspondence as evidence that 1 Tim. 2:12 affected the wording of this interpolation.'[38]

Clearly, there are some plausible reasons to see 1 Corinthians 14:34–35 as a later insertion. The difficulty is, as with the Corinthian slogan interpretation, an interpolation is difficult to prove. The arguments are persuasive, but not conclusive.

It seems that we are left to settle on one of the interpretations presented, despite the misgivings for each one, or come up with an entirely new interpretation in order to make sense of the argument from Paul.

Conclusion

Within Paul's teaching on orderly worship lie three verses that have caused considerable consternation. If the words are Paul's own, they carry a significant contradiction to his thoughts elsewhere. Attempts have been made to reconcile the inconsistencies by inserting qualifications to his instructions, but as we have seen, placing qualifications where Paul did not is neither an easy nor a convincing task.

Others have suggested that the words are not likely to be Paul's own. They do not reflect his instructions elsewhere and contain words that are unusual for Pauline arguments. Far from bringing a radical blueprint of God's kingdom, these words fit as a direct transference of thoughts from the culture of the day—is it not plausible then that they are exactly that?

In the end, it is extremely difficult to settle on one of the interpretations with complete certainty. Having said that, unless we are willing to suggest Paul was double minded, we can conclude that Paul had no intention for women to be silent in the community and, in light of the evidence, and in the absence of alternatives, we have good reason to lean towards one of the two interpretations suggesting that the view of verses 34–35 was alien to Paul's own thinking.

5

1 TIMOTHY 2: TEACHING AND AUTHORITY

Now, onto the verses that have caused the most debate, and where the most significant battle lines are drawn. These are the verses that often lead to stalemate. I sometimes wonder if we didn't have the book of 1 Timothy, whether there would be any debate on the authority of women at all. But we do have the book and there are discussions to be had.

In reading any part of Scripture, there are some basic hermeneutical (interpretive) principles that we need to apply in order to get the right understanding. In the book of 1 Timothy, we have a letter that is separated from us today by time, culture, language, and occasion for its writing. As twenty-first-century readers, we have to do some work in order to bring into focus what would have been common knowledge between the author and original readers so that we don't end up making incorrect conclusions about the text.

All too often when I have had conversations around some pivotal verses in 1 Timothy, I have been met with the argument that 'the plain reading' of the letter is what we should follow rather than dig too deep, as if those who dig deep are seeking to twist the words of the letter but those who follow the 'plain reading' are allowing the letter to speak for itself. The trouble is that 'plain reading' is a fallacy. With the differences in our day from when the letter was written, it is inadequate. In embracing a 'plain reading', we may have pure intentions to preserve the words of the letter, but it is a dangerous approach to reading the Bible as we will miss the background and context needed for us to interpret the words correctly. We may end up preserving words at the cost of the meaning—which is sadly what I believe many have done. It is precisely that sort of argument that upheld slavery within Christian thought for a shamefully long time—the 'plain reading' of a handful of verses, distorting the heart of Scripture throughout. We have no choice but to dig deeper than surface level. This is true for all of Scripture but is especially pertinent where there is so much controversy.

It is important to recognise that, as with any historical writing and particularly so with letters, when Paul was raising specific issues within a community, he was raising those issues on a backdrop that both he and those he wrote to understood—one that is helpful for us to understand. If we do not, we will reach skewed conclusions. The backdrop of common knowledge would not be something he would necessarily explicitly point out, but that does not make it any less essential for us to identify if we are to accurately understand his meaning.

There are a number of ways we can flesh out our understanding of a book's historical context. Firstly, we can look to other passages in the Bible that overlap with the historical setting of the book we are studying in order to further inform us of what the people, city, and community were facing. Beyond that, we can look at extra-biblical resources that pertain to the people or city in question to give us a greater understanding of the setting.

But perhaps most importantly, looking at the writing itself, the issues raised will be signposts of what was going on in the community. In his pastoral letters, Paul was not just throwing out random theological thoughts but rather addressing specific concerns. For example, in reference to Paul's teaching on women to learn in quietness, Douglas Moo notes, 'But the encouragement does not come in a vacuum—almost certainly it is necessary because at least *some* women were *not* learning "in quietness."'[1] It's a little piece of common knowledge that we can fill in from the topics covered. Problems arise when we make the issues raised mean something beyond their intention.

Let me flesh this out by using an analogy from my everyday experience. I am mum to two boisterous toddlers, and I'm quickly learning that in parenting you have to choose your battles carefully if you want to be heard and if you don't want to go crazy in the process! If I wanted to, I could spend all day parenting my precious two on everything from the need to wear clothes in public to the wisdom of not hitting, kicking, or biting other people. But I am coming to realise that I need to hone in on the things that are most important in the moment—and they will be different for each child. My son is extremely good at sharing but not so good at not hitting his sister. My daughter is currently a breeze when it comes to gentle behaviour but extremely challenging on staying away from electric sockets. So in parenting my son, I'm focussing on him not being violent and for my daughter, on her not trying to electrocute herself.

You may be wondering where I'm going with this, so let me try to link my parenting story with 1 Timothy. Paul knew what it was to 'parent' churches. He'd been doing it very well for some time and with good success, and I'm sure he would have figured out then what I know with my children. You focus on the most relevant and important problem for the individuals you're addressing. That does not mean that your principles are not important for anyone else (I wouldn't want my son to attempt electrocuting himself either), but in that moment, you focus on the matter at hand for whomever you are speaking to.

Here's my point. When Paul is teaching that women should learn in submission, it's not necessarily an implication that men don't need to also learn in submission but rather highlighting for us what would have been common knowledge in that community: that it was the women who were having trouble learning in submission. When Paul teaches the men to use their hands in peace, that's not meant to tell us that it's okay for women to be violent but rather that, in that community, that was an issue for the men, not for the women. When Paul withholds permission for women to teach and to exercise authority, he's not just throwing out a random theological principle but addressing something that almost certainly had reason to be addressed within that community.

To make these problems permanently gender-specific ones is a mistake (just as it would be ridiculous for someone to hear a transcript of me parenting my children and assume that only girls need to be restrained from going to electric sockets and only boys need to be restrained from violence). Paul was addressing issues based on what was at work in that community.

With this in mind, we will take a step back from the verses that most interest us for a moment so that we can set the stage with the historical-cultural context of the book. My intention in this process will be to further flag pieces of common knowledge between author and original reader so that we can enter into their conversation having caught up on all that *didn't* need to be said between them. At that point we'll be on somewhat safer ground to view what *was* said.

Uncovering Common Knowledge: Historical Cultural Setting
Author and Recipient

There is some scholarly debate on whether or not 1 Timothy really was written by Paul. I am not going to enter into that here and will assume that Paul indeed was the author. If Paul wasn't the author, then, at least initially, the views of the book on women's roles fall second to more pressing questions of authorship and inspiration. If Paul was the author, we can go ahead and address the teaching found in the letter, so I will focus my attention there.

From the letter's opening words, we read that it was written by Paul to his spiritual son Timothy (1: 1–2). This is important. Most of Paul's letters were intended to be read to the whole community—as evidenced by their opening remarks. But 1 Timothy was not a letter addressing an entire community. It was a letter from a spiritual father to a spiritual son who needed wise counsel in leading a precarious community.

Paul mentions that the reason he asked Timothy to stay in Ephesus was so that he could challenge those who were bringing false teaching into the church (1:3). This letter has the stance of defending truth from those who would propagate falsehood (see 1 Tim. 1:18–19; 4:6–7; 6:12–14, 20–21). 'Paul's posture throughout is corrective rather than didactic'[2]—his desire to combat false teaching colours the entire letter. First Timothy is not Paul's general teaching on doctrine but is designed to mentor Timothy on how to address those leading a community into error, how to correct false ideas that have been propagated, and how to instate protective— even restrictive—practices that will safeguard this community from further error and restore it to health.

Ephesus

It's easy to understand why the church there would be facing some challenges—first-century Ephesus was complicated. Acts 18–20 provide us with some insight. The city itself was a significant cultural melting pot. It was home to one of the seven wonders of the ancient world: the temple of Artemis. This not only meant deep impact on the city by the Artemis cult (you only need to look at the unfolding riot in Acts 19:21–41 to see how significant a stronghold it was), but it also meant a steady stream of outsiders flocking to the city to see this ancient marvel.

We know that there were Jews and Gentiles living alongside one another in the city (Acts 18). And so, Ephesus housed a clash of religions and ideologies. There were those who were committed to the practices of Orthodox Judaism, and those who worshipped at the cult of Artemis, and a good measure of sorcery and witchcraft to boot (Acts 19:18–19). Into this context, you had the planting and growing of a Christian community, which we know from Acts 19 caused great upheaval in the city. Clearly, these strong religious forces would butt heads on many issues, but the one we are most interested in is their different views on gender roles.

The cult of Artemis, 'in which the female was exalted and considered superior to the male,'[3] would be quite a clash with the traditional patriarchal beliefs of those who came into the church from Orthodox Judaism. In addition to these, there is evidence of a movement amongst women in the Roman Empire in the first century termed by classical scholars as the 'New Roman Woman'. In essence, this was a trend that saw some women achieving unprecedented financial independence and social freedoms and throwing off sexual restraint and modesty. With regards to this, Steve Robbins cites first-century authors (including Sallust (c. 86–c. 35 BC) and Seneca (4 BC–AD 65)) who spoke of this trend in women dressing lavishly and provocatively as a sign of their sexual promiscuity and freedom, ending marriages, retaining property, challenging men in education, and pursuing cases in public courts.[4]

Without attempting to over-zealously reconstruct the historical context, it is important nevertheless to acknowledge that those who were coming into the church from these different worldviews would have completely different lenses that would need adjusting as they learnt what it meant to be the people of God. It is little wonder that there were serious quarrels, divisions, and false teachings at work in this church community. Furthermore, we know that the problems were not solely coming from a handful of difficult members on the periphery but rather from central leading characters in the community, even within the eldership (Acts 20:30). No wonder Paul asked

Timothy to stay in Ephesus to steady this church and felt the need to write this letter to him to bring further instruction. This was a community which was leading itself into error and needed some drastic measures to bring it back into health.

I am aware of those who have tried to downplay the significance of external cultural factors on the church in Ephesus. Whilst I would agree that it is not possible to quantify exactly to what extent the outside factors would have impacted the early Ephesian church, it seems strange that we would try to disregard them entirely. No church community exists in total isolation from its culture so we would be wise to pay external influences some attention. The downplaying of outside forces is a theoretical argument that loses substance very quickly in church practice. I am writing this book from my church office in South Africa. Anyone who would claim that my church community is not being impacted and fighting battles within, based on the racial tensions outside, is either wilfully ignorant or naive when it comes to church in practice. At the very least, let us acknowledge that outside cultural forces make up some of the common knowledge between writer and reader in 1 Timothy, and we need to be aware of them.

Uncovering Common Knowledge: Signposts in the Letter

When we read Paul's instructions to different areas of the community, we are introduced to some of the issues they were facing. This list is not exhaustive, but focuses in on the problem areas that are relevant for our area of study:

- False teaching throughout the church community—
  including instructions on the law and ancestry (1:4,
  7–11), commands to abstain from marriage and
  certain foods (4:2–3), and a focus on myths and
  'knowledge' (1:4; 4:7; 6:3, 20).
- Anger and quarrelling amongst the men (2:8).
- Immodest or ostentatious dress amongst the
  women (2:9).
- Women professing spirituality whilst living otherwise (2:9–10).
- Non-submissive or argumentative learning amongst
  the women (2:11).
- Unrest because of women teaching (2:11–13).
- Unrest because of how women are exercising
  authority over men (2:12).
- Women being deceived (2:14, see further in
  2 Tim. 3:6–7).
- Confusion around 'traditional' roles of moth-
  ering and childbearing amongst the women
  (1 Tim. 2:15; 4:1–4).
- Widows in the community bringing unnecessary
  financial strain on the community (5:4, 16) and
  propagating error (5:13).
- Friction, envy, slander, and suspicion amongst the
  community (6:4–5).

This was not a healthy church. The reality is, if the list above was
true of our local church community, we would not want anything

to do with it. Who wants to be part of a community where some of the elders are heretics and where there's a problem with rebellious, overbearing, deceived, and ignorant women? Who wants to sign up to go to a church where there's so much strife that prayer meetings result in a brawl? No matter what we think about the details, it is clear that the church in Ephesus was in trouble.

1 Timothy 2: Getting to the Nitty-Gritty

Now that we've clarified the backdrop of the letter, let's focus in on chapter 2 which contains some of the most potentially problematic verses for women in the church.

Chapter 2 starts with 'First of all, then ...' (note the use of the conjunction *oun* in the Greek, clearly linking this thought with the one before it). Chapter 2 is not taking a neutral theological stance but is written in direct relation to the concerns laid out in chapter 1. Paul has just charged Timothy with 'fighting the good warfare' in the context of coming against false teaching. Therefore, despite arguments to the contrary,[5] the opening of chapter 2 identifies the teaching of the chapter as a correction to error rather than simple instructions for everyday healthy Christian living. 'There is no question that the context of 1 Timothy is the presence of false teaching in Ephesus, against which Paul urges Timothy to stand fast ... Egalitarians correctly stress that Paul's restrictions on women in 2:11–12 must be interpreted in light of the dangers of heresy afoot in the church.'[6] On this, Douglas Moo concedes, 'It is likely that the false teaching does give rise to Paul's instruction in 2:9–15; but the crucial question is, how does it affect his instructions?'[7]

I fully agree. It is up to us to weigh up whether Paul's practical instructions in direct response to false teaching would be any different if they were in response to a community in health. It is important to note here that Paul is not giving Timothy the corrective *theological teaching* to bring against the false teaching. Instead, he is advising corrections in *practice* to curb the influence of the false teachers and their teaching. This reality must cause us to ask the question—if the false teachings were removed, would the practices enforced to curb and rectify falsehood need to be changed in any way?

Does the fact that this section is corrective rather than didactic make it any less relevant for the church today? Absolutely not! All Scripture is God-breathed and useful (2 Tim. 3:16). But what it does mean is that the *context* of the application of these verses needs to be carefully assessed. Let's bring a practical example. In a time of extreme unrest in a nation, martial law might be declared and the military may be deployed to bring the nation back into peace. The aim in that moment is a restoration of peace. It is a valid and necessary action within a specific context if peace is desired. However, in the context of peace already present in a nation, if martial law was applied and the military deployed, what would result would not be a maintenance of peace (even if that was the stated aim) but oppression of the people. When I am pointing out that Paul's teaching in 1 Timothy 2 is corrective, I am in no way suggesting that it is any less useful for edification. However, I am stating that, unless we are aware of what its aim is and what the context of its deployment is, we will use it to oppress rather than to ensure peace in a community. Context is key.

Paul's aim as he brings his instructions is seen in his repeated theme through chapter 2 of living in 'quietness and peace' (see

1 Tim. 2:2, 8, 11–12). 'This peace is a peace in contrast to the con-
tentiousness of the false teachers (e.g., 1:4).'[8] The essence here is not
living at a low level of noise, but rather being peaceable. This theme
is important to note because as we will go on to see, it forms a central
principle for the teaching on women's roles.

Initially, Paul's instructions for 'fighting the good warfare' against
the false teaching in the church look at the community as a whole,
that they should pray and thank God particularly for those in authority (1 Tim. 2:1–3). Then he moves on to teach specifically about the
men—that they should pray without quarrelling (v. 8). And then he
introduces his instructions specifically about the women, using the
word 'likewise' (v. 9), again linking the flow of thought in this entire
section together.

Adornment of Good Works

> Likewise also that women should adorn them-
> selves in respectable apparel, with modesty and
> self-control, not with braided hair and gold or
> pearls or costly attire, but with what is proper for
> women who profess godliness—with good works.
> (1 Tim. 2:9–10)

Paul's comments on women begin with some teaching on
what women who 'profess godliness' should adorn themselves
with—teaching against a focus on outward appearance but rather
encouraging modesty and the most appropriate adornment for those
who claim to be spiritual— 'good works' (v. 10). Paul was not so

much interested in women's fashion as he was in the outworking of godliness in the community. There was something about how the women were dressing that was causing problems. The reference to 'costly attire' makes it plausible that there were women making a show of their costly clothes to give them a level of status and superiority because of their obvious wealth. There were others who were causing problems because of their immodesty—something that would perhaps be natural for someone coming from the background of the Artemis cult. Regardless of motivation, there was something about their dress code that was causing unrest, so Paul emphasises the fact that true spirituality is marked by 'good works'.

Quiet Learning, Teaching, and Authority

> Let a woman learn quietly with all submissiveness.
> I do not permit a woman to teach or to exercise authority over a man; rather, she is to remain quiet.
> (1 Tim. 2:11–12)

Most English translations separate verses 11 and 12, whereas in the Greek text they form one sentence. Additionally, because of the differences between Greek and English grammar, English translations reorder the words from the Greek text in order to make the flow of words make sense to us. Of course, this is a necessary part of taking a foreign text and making it readable in a meaningful way in one's own culture. Unfortunately, however, for 1 Timothy 2:11–12, this restructuring means that we often miss a literary device that Paul used which is important to our understanding of the text. This is further compounded by the fact that the Greek word used twice in the sentence to create the literary device is often translated as two different words in English translations.

A literal translation of the Greek text shows that in the original writing, Paul started and finished his instructions in this one sentence with the adjective *hēsychia*: 'quietness'. This word encapsulates the whole sentence (vv. 11–12), framing Paul's instructions on learning, teaching, and authority.[9] With regards to his teaching in verses 11 and 12, 'quietness' is his opening and closing thought. It is an important word in the reading of this text, given Paul's choice to use it to bookend his teaching. It is not a secondary term in relating to the instructions but a defining term for them. We will therefore spend some time grappling with the meaning of the word *hēsychia*.

What did Paul mean in using this adjective? The translations vary from 'quietly' (ESV) and 'in quietness' (NIV) to 'in silence' (NRSV, KJV). What is unfortunate about these word choices is that they imply a meaning relating to noise and speaking, when that is not the likely nuance given the context. When we look at Paul's use of the related noun *hēsychios* in 1 Timothy 2:2, the meaning conveyed there is clearly not about noise level or about speaking but about being peaceable. Equally, when Paul uses *hēsychia* in verse 11, he uses it in the context of calling for learners to be submissive. Submission is not a word for silence, but for agreement. Given Paul's consistent assessment of this community in Ephesus using words associated with division, quarrelling, etc., there is further reason to understand Paul's three-time use of the adjective *hēsychia* and its related noun *hēsychios*, not as countering noisiness in the church community (which we have no mention of), but rather combatting a divisive quarrelling culture in the church (that we have ample mention of). '*Hēsychia* does not mean "silence" (cf. its only other NT uses outside this passage in Acts 22:2 and 2 Thess. 3:12). The cognate adjective *hēsychios* has appeared as recently as in 2:2 to refer to the kind of lives all believers are to live—"peaceful and *quiet,*" cooperative and caring, *not* never speaking!'[10] This same understanding is echoed in Hübner's work as he references influential complementarian scholars, including Schreiner and Hurley, concluding, 'Complementarians readily acknowledge this (Moo 1981:199, is an exception).'[11] Put simply, *hēsychia* is not anti-speaking but anti-divisiveness.[12]

Hence, we can confidently read *hēsychia* with peace rather than volume in mind, which allows us to see that Paul's instruction for women to learn, not to teach, and not to exercise authority are all permeated by his desire for the community to be peaceable. We will take some time in due course to assess whether women teaching and exercising authority are always mutually exclusive ideas with peace-ability, but for now, we will leave the discussion on *hēsychia* here, having highlighted its important place in Paul's teaching in these verses.

Learning

Let's now turn our attention to focus on the first part of the sentence: 'Let a woman learn quietly with all submissiveness' (v. 11).

The instruction for women to learn is the only imperative in this whole section. It should be noted that the very fact that Paul was giving instruction for women to learn was groundbreaking—particularly for those from a background of Orthodox Judaism. As has been noted by scholars, 'Such a practice was not generally encouraged by the Jews'[13] and 'This command for women to learn contrasts with the absence of women from any list of students in Ephesian schools of that time.'[14] So, though it may not carry the same weight in twenty-first-century culture, Paul is being remarkably pro-women here. As we have seen, Paul is not merely interested that women should learn but interested in the *manner* of their learning. He instructs for the learning to be 'in quietness'—in peaceability. Paul is asking women to learn but to do so peaceably rather than argumentatively.

Much has been made of the fact that Paul instructs that the women should learn in submission as evidence of him putting further restrictions on them. However, I struggle to follow this line of argument. Surely *any* learning must be done in submission if it is to be effective? Whether Paul meant submission to the teachers, or to the Scriptures, or to God we do not know, nor does it alter the general meaning of the moment—the point is that true learning requires being submitted to authority so that you can effectively receive what is taught. Some have spent a lot of time focussing on what or whom women are to submit to as if the conclusion of that argument will hold sway for women's roles. I cannot see how this would be the case. Regardless of whom or what he was meaning for the women to be submitted to, the reality is that if women were to learn effectively, they would need to do so in a posture of submission to those bringing instruction. Realistically, those teaching the women would most likely be men because the cultural reality of the day would be that, barring perhaps some rare exceptions, the men would have had the educational privilege to qualify them to teach, whereas the women would have been a step behind in that arena.

Regardless, submission to authority—be it Scripture, God, or people—is a principle that is vital for both male and female students. It's impossible to really learn if you are setting yourself up above your teacher. 'The general point seems clear enough: it is hard to learn if you're the one doing all the talking.'[15] Believing you are above your teacher will mean that you will not learn properly and so will believe that you know more than you actually do (a problem that Paul picks up in his reference to the false teachers in chapter 1: 'They want to be teachers of the law, but they do not know what they are talking about or what they so confidently affirm' [v. 7 NIV]). This is obviously dangerous ground in the context of a multiplying church. You need those who are learning to learn properly so that they will teach the next generation accurately!

Why didn't Paul then tell the men to learn in submission? A couple of obvious reasons:

1. There was already a culture of education for men, so it would make such basic instruction less necessary. They'd have been well versed in how to be students from childhood.

2. As pointed out before, Paul is addressing the issues here that directly relate to bringing solutions to the difficult context in Ephesus. Clearly, it was women in the community who were being argumentative students in a way the men were not. We can see from 1 Timothy 1:19–20 that the male ringleaders of false teaching had already been excommunicated, and so in 1 Timothy 2:11 we see Paul focussing his attention to address the learning of a group that we know were significantly infected by those false teachers: women. As I've previously noted, this by no means makes remarks on submission while learning a gender issue but highlights that, for the

community Paul was teaching, it was the women who were having problems in this regard.

Teaching and Authority

> I do not permit a woman to teach or to exercise authority over a man; rather, she is to remain quiet. (1 Tim. 2:12)

We could spend the better part of this chapter analysing the words 'teach' and 'authority' and get stuck in the question of whether *oude* links them into one thought (teaching with authority) or whether they are separate ideas where women should neither teach nor exercise authority over men. Because I don't believe that the answers to these questions hold the key to settling the debate on women's roles today, and because there are many excellent resources which look at these words in great depth, I am only going to do a brief review of the meaning of teaching and authority before we look further at where I believe the interpretive keys lie.

To teach (*didaskō*) is a relatively straightforward word to understand as it is used frequently in the New Testament and has a clear meaning of teaching or bringing instruction.

> Paul uses this verb not only of teaching others (Rom 2:21; Gal 1:12; Col 1:28) but of teaching oneself (Rom 2:21). He uses it of the gift of teaching (Rom 12:7) and of his own teaching in the churches (1 Cor 4:17), but he also encourages all believers to

'teach and admonish one another' (Col 3:16). Paul
refers to teaching by word of mouth or by letter (2
Thess 2:15). Paul even uses this same word to say
that nature 'teaches' that long hair disgraces a man
but is the glory of a woman (1 Cor 11:14–15).[16]

I have become very familiar with attempts to bring restriction
to the *context* of this word purely to what would be akin to our
modern-day Sunday church services and/or restriction of its *content*
to sermons containing 'authoritative doctrinal instruction'[17] but it
is difficult to see on what basis this definition is to be conclusively
reached given Paul's usage of the word. I have been invited to speak
at Saturday conferences in churches that would not have me preaching on a Sunday morning on the basis of their interpretation of
1 Timothy 2:12, or have been told that I can preach on a Sunday
as long as I am not bringing a word that includes any doctrine or
anything theologically weighty (what then is left for me to preach
on, I wonder?). As much as I admire the desire of these churches
to create alternative contexts for women to preach, I do not think
they have much theological footing for these boundary lines they
are creating. Whether I am speaking on a Saturday or Sunday or
even at a midweek community gathering is frankly irrelevant. Paul
was not differentiating between our Sunday congregations and our
special conference congregations! Neither did he have in mind for
our congregations to have to endure teaching that conveys nothing
important just so that our women will be allowed on platforms.
The problem with restricting content of 'teaching' to the scope of
doctrine or theology is that drawing the line becomes increasingly

arbitrary and subjective and leads to us carving around things that, in essence, have more to do with what we are comfortable with than they have basis in Scripture. Surely talking about anything that is about God, Scripture, or the church has an element of doctrine or theology to it? Paul certainly puts no obvious boundary lines in place here and clearly wouldn't be advocating that it *was* fine for women to bring whatever teaching they wished as long as doctrine wasn't included—the letter's stance against false teachings and myths and meaningless debates would beg to differ there!

So too, context becomes difficult to define as we think about Paul's community where house churches were a reality, and we acknowledge that, given the singular form of the words, the verse itself is prohibiting a woman from teaching or exercising authority over even just one man. How then do we decide if it's really okay for a woman to teach in our home groups today or even to lead small Bible studies? How and where do we draw the line? It seems that if we want to take a universal approach to 1 Timothy 2:12, then we have little choice but to apply the ban on a woman bringing teaching in all of our contexts or risk a schizophrenic application of the verse structured more around our preferences and sensibilities than Paul's words. The trouble, of course, is that a universal ban becomes difficult to advocate when reviewing wider New Testament teaching, but we will explore that in greater depth in a moment.

To 'exercise authority', as it is translated in the ESV, is unfortunately not quite such a straightforward word to understand. Paul opts for the word *authentein* which does not appear anywhere else in the New Testament. It's a strange word choice as he had at his disposal the word *exousia* which was the common Greek word for authority—one which he used throughout his letters. Why then opt for this word in this context? The fact Paul chose not to use the normal word for authority here is strongly suggestive that generic authority is not what he had in mind. The rendering "exercise authority" or "have authority over" seems less likely because of its generality. It would be quite odd if Paul chose an extremely rare word to only say the ordinary.'[18] Many scholars point to extensive analysis from Baldwin on which to base their conclusions on the meaning of *authentein*. Because it is such a significant study, Payne's reflections on how it is represented are all the more concerning: 'Baldwin's study of αὐθεντέω [*authenteō*] "narrows down the range of meaning that might be appropriate in 1 Tim. 2:12" to four possible meanings: to dominate, to compel, to assume authority over, and to flout the authority of. Baldwin says Schreiner will identify which best fits 1 Tim. 2:12. Schreiner, however, adopts none of these, but rather "exercise authority over".'[19] It is not within the scope of this book to do a full analysis on the meaning of *authentein* (*authenteō*), but bias towards a generic meaning of exercising authority, despite results from a study stating otherwise, is a worrying allegation.

Having said that, as debate on the meaning of *authentein* continues, and because I don't believe even the most conservative rendering of the word ultimately changes conclusions for us on gender roles, I will opt to use the conservative meaning of 'exercising authority' from this point on in this chapter. However, as Hübner aptly points out, 'It is one thing to say "we don't know exactly what the term meant in the first century or in 1 Timothy 2:12." It is quite another to say "we don't know exactly what the term meant in the first century or in 1 Timothy 2:12, so we're going to assume that there's no particular reason why Paul chose it, that it has no nuance of any kind and thus means the generic exercising of authority"—and then ban half the global church from being pastors. This is not sound reasoning.'[20]

A further complexity is added to verse 12 by the use of the conjunction *oude* (with possible meanings: and not, nor, but not, not even). It is possible (given the right sentence structure) for conjunctions to connect two ideas to convey one meaning. Therefore, the question in interpretation here becomes does *oude* mean that Paul is only making one prohibition (that a woman should not bring authoritative teaching over a man—made all the more significant if we read authority with negative nuance), or is it maintaining a dual prohibition (that a woman should neither teach nor exercise authority over a man)? There are well-respected scholars on both sides of the argument here. Köstenberger argues quite convincingly that the use of *oude* here does not create a single prohibition and that teaching and exercising authority should be kept as two separate elements. However, as he points out, 'It should be noted, this particular reading of 1 Tim. 2:12 does not by itself settle the issue.'[21] Therefore, I will move on from here to focus on what I do believe will lead us to more definitive answers on this text.

Interpretive Key 1: Paul's Guiding Principle

We have already shown that our English translations don't adequately convey the intricate framing that is seen in the Greek text. Paul uses *hēsychia* as a framing idea of his instructions in verses 11 and 12. The Greek reads *hēsychia* as the first and last idea in these verses.

This word is one that we've spent some time on already in our introduction to verses 11 and 12. It is a word which has been shown to be not about speaking and noise level but about being peaceable rather than divisive. Given that Paul encapsulates the instructions in verses 11 and 12 in this idea of peaceability, it certainly seems to be the aim which is at the forefront of his mind. This is further bolstered by Paul's use of the idea of peaceability in 1 Timothy 2:2. Peace and unity are what Paul wants upheld. And he wants measures in place to stop what is divisive in this community.

What this means for our reading of verse 12 is that we can see that Paul put a ban on women teaching or exercising authority over men (his application) with the explicit aim to uphold peace in the community (his principle). There was something in the manner of women in this community with regards to learning and teaching and exercising authority that was not promoting peace. Peaceability is a clear element of the text, one that I am surprised is paid very little attention to in a lot of commentaries.

If this principle of being peaceable is Paul's aim, it then raises the question for us today as we approach 1 Timothy 2:12: 'Which is it more important to uphold—his application or his principle?' We have to admit that whatever it may have meant in the Ephesian church of Paul's day (clearly some division!), women teaching or having authority over men are not actions that are mutually exclusive with being peaceable in today's culture. What do we do when a biblical principle and its application do not work as harmoniously together in our day as they did in the context of their authorship? This is where we have to do the honest and challenging work of hermeneutics. What is it that makes us stay true to Scripture? Is it us following words even when doing that might twist their original aim entirely? Or do we follow the originally intended principle, even if to do so requires the original application to be somewhat modified, in order to uphold Paul's intention in a way that will translate meaningfully in today's culture?

If we refer back to the analogy of martial law from earlier in the chapter, it would seem to me that what we are doing in many streams of Christianity today is seeing and upholding Paul's application of martial law here in verse 12—whilst ignoring the context that makes it necessary (gross division, ignorance, deception, and false teaching). The reality is that martial law applied in any context other than overwhelming unrest is not going to uphold peace but is going to instigate oppression—and tragically that is what many in the church are doing today, even with the very best of intentions.

Interpretive Key 2: Temporal vs. Universal

In reading 1 Timothy 2:12, we need to ask ourselves the question, 'Was this a prohibition that Paul intended for all places and all times (a universal prohibition), or was this a prohibition that was based on certain conditions (a temporal prohibition)?'

In order to answer this, we will look at Paul's choice of language in verse 12 and also look further afield to see how he related to women who taught and exercised authority.

Firstly, on the issue of Paul's language and phrasing. If we accept the premise that 1 Timothy 2:12 indeed was a universal prohibition, we are then forced to ask why Paul communicated the prohibition with no acknowledgement that Timothy already knew about it. Why was Paul communicating it to Timothy in this mentoring letter as something that would be instructive to Timothy if this was something that Timothy would be fully accustomed to already (which he surely would have been had it been Paul's usual practice)?

> What is most significant about the wording of the passage, however, is that Paul does not assume that Timothy already knows this rule. Had this rule been established and universal, is it possible that Timothy, who had worked many years with Paul, would not have known it already? Paul often reminds readers of traditions they should know by saying, 'You know,' or 'Do you not know?' or 'According to the traditions which I delivered to you.' In his letters to Timothy Paul appeals to 'we know' (e.g., 1 Tim. 1:8), 'faithful sayings' (e.g., 1 Tim. 1:15), and cites Timothy's knowledge of Paul's own life (2 Tim. 3:10–11).[22]

In this prohibition in verse 12, however, none of those phrases indicating prior knowledge are present.

Furthermore, Philip Payne does some helpful work on the use of *epitrepō*, which is often translated as 'I do not permit/allow'. He shows how a more accurate translation given the grammatical form of the verb is 'I am not permitting'. This perhaps seems like a small change but has very significant implications. 'I do not permit' has the weight of a universal command. 'I am not permitting' is a *presently* ongoing prohibition. 'Paul often chose the first person

singular ("I") present active indicative ("am not permitting") to
indicate his own personal advice or position for a situation that is
not universal'[23] (as seen in 1 Cor. 7:7, 26, 32, and 40). For universal
instructions it is more common for Paul to use imperatives rather
than what we see here. Even Moo states, 'As far as the present tense
of the verb goes, this allows us to conclude only that Paul was *at
the time of writing* insisting on these prohibitions.'[24] But he quali-
fies this by saying that it is the context that would help us decide
whether Paul intended for this to be a universal ban or not, which,
of course, I am in full agreement with. Issues of context aside for a
moment, on the basis of grammar alone we must therefore concede
that Paul was not *necessarily* intending to put in a ban for all places
and all times.

Further still, if we look at Paul's interactions with women who
taught or had authority, we see broader confirmation that 1 Timothy
2:12 was not a universal ban he wanted upheld. His approval and affirmation of Priscilla (also referred to as Prisca in the New Testament)
is telling—a woman who taught with enough authority to shape the
theology of an apostle, Apollos. We cannot somehow factor her out
of that teaching context. Luke even puts her name first in his account
in Acts 18:26, making it implausible to suggest she was simply a
bystander as her husband taught Apollos correct theology. Equally,
it is insufficient for us to adhere to a universal understanding of
1 Timothy 2 but to explain away Priscilla's involvement of teaching
by suggesting that her teaching was validated by the fact that she did
it 'under the covering' of her husband. Paul never gives that as an
option in his prohibition in 1 Timothy 2:12. Likewise, we cannot
minimise the Acts scenario by suggesting that her teaching was not

what Paul had in mind because she was only teaching one man. As stated earlier, 1 Timothy 2:12 is a sentence of singulars not plurals. Equally, we cannot argue that because the word used in Acts 18:26 to describe Priscilla's action is *exethento* (explained) and not *edidaxe* (taught), this wasn't true teaching. Luke uses the word *exethento* again in Acts 28:23 of Paul teaching in Rome[25] and we would be hard pressed to say that what that word is describing is not real teaching. And lastly, for any who want to suggest that Priscilla's teaching didn't involve doctrine, what else would it mean to draw someone aside to explain to him 'the way of God more accurately' (Acts 18:26)? Having heard Apollos' theology as he preached, Priscilla and Aquila needed to draw him aside to teach him further. We have to admit that what we see in descriptive form in Acts is very much what Paul seems to prohibit in 1 Timothy 2:12, and so I find little option, from even just this one example (we will look at others later in the book), but to come either to the conclusion that Paul was inconsistent or to weigh up contextual application more carefully.

However, before we get too carried away with the reasoning for reading Paul's words as a temporal prohibition, it is common for complementarians to use the reference to Genesis found in verses 13 and 14 as evidence that Paul's teaching here *must* be universal. Let us turn our attention to that section for a moment.

Foundations in Genesis?

For Adam was formed first, then Eve; and Adam was not deceived, but the woman was deceived and became a transgressor. (1 Tim. 2:13–14)

It is argued that because Paul chose to use an illustration from Genesis for his instructions in verses 11 and 12 rather than an appeal to the context in Ephesus, his teaching in those verses must have universal reach rather than simply be temporal to the context of the day. It is a good argument and warrants attention.

As has been pointed out previously, the Greek text does not separate out verses 11 and 12 as we are apt to do, and so when we read verses 13 and 14, we must understand them to be concluding the whole thought introduced by both verse 11 *and* 12 rather than just be attached merely to a curbing of teaching and authority.

Paul's reference to Genesis focuses on two things:

1. The fact that Adam was made before Eve.
2. The fact that Eve was deceived (not Adam), leading to transgression.

When we start unpacking what Paul actually wrote in reference to Genesis, it becomes increasingly likely that Paul's Genesis reference was more an apt illustration of why women should learn well (and the dangers of them not learning) than an illustration for why women shouldn't teach or have authority. I say this for a number of reasons:

Paul points to Eve's deception rather than her leading of Adam into sin. If Paul had wanted to bolster his instruction on women not teaching or exercising authority by using the Genesis account, it would have made much more sense for him to highlight that it was Eve who led Adam astray by giving him the fruit. It would be perfectly logical to build his point by saying women shouldn't teach because when Eve spoke, she misled Adam, or women shouldn't exercise authority because look what happened when she exercised authority in leading Adam to sin. But that is not what Paul is getting at at all. Eve is not being used as a demonstration of a woman illegitimately speaking or exercising authority, or even leading another into deception, but of a woman herself being deceived.[26] You are only at risk of deception if your understanding of truth is lacking. Again, Paul's problem is not Eve's *propagating* of disobedience (which would be the obvious link with teaching and an illegitimate use of authority) but her *vulnerability* to being led astray herself (which is the obvious link to learning). Contrary to what some have tried to assert about the reference to Genesis being an illustration of God's design of male authority (which we will look at more closely in a moment), the reference to Genesis, therefore, makes much more sense as an illustration of why women need to learn accurately.

Paul uses creation order and Eve's deception as linked ideas in his argument—with her deception being the punchline. If creation order is being synonymously used here with a God-ordained authoritative hierarchy between male and female (which is commonly argued), we must then ask how that authoritative hierarchy concludes logically in Eve's deception? Having less authority does not in itself leave you more vulnerable to deception. The latter is not an obvious conclusion of the former. Moo asserts that the reference to creation order is clearly 'indicative of the headship that man is to have over woman',[27] but if that is what Paul is getting at, how is Eve's deception a relevant punchline? Genesis doesn't give any indication that Eve's deception was linked to her undermining the man's rightful authority but places the woman's deception in the context of 'the serpent's distortion of

God's word.'[28] The link between authoritative hierarchy and deception is unclear.

But there *is* another explanation that would draw all the thoughts
of this section together quite coherently and would certainly fit into
the wider brushstrokes of Scripture more easily. If creation order and
the act of being deceived are linked ideas, then we must consider on
what basis being created second would make Eve more vulnerable
to deception. Would it not be on the basis of her understanding
of what God had told Adam? Adam had received instruction from
God before Eve was even created (Gen. 2:16–17). And Eve, being
created second, was, therefore, reliant on learning those instructions
from Adam to walk in truth. Though his equal, she was in a place
of needing to learn from Adam because he had been made first.
This illustration makes perfect sense for the context being faced in
Ephesus. Women in Ephesus were reliant on their male counterparts
who would have had access to education, including of Scripture,
that the women, in general, would not have had because of cultural
realities. This didn't mean that women would never be in a position of equality but that, in the baby church in Ephesus, women
would need to submit to learning what the men around them had
had a head start in if they were ever to come to a place of equality of understanding. If not, they would be at risk of desiring to be
teachers 'without understanding either what they are saying or the
things about which they make confident assertions' (1 Tim. 1:7). In
the context of Ephesus, Paul's choice to refer to how 'the woman
was deceived' makes perfect sense as it is clear that, in this community, women *were* the ones being deceived (further underlined in
2 Timothy 3:6). Hence, in his instructions and the illustration from

Genesis, Paul is bringing a safeguard to the group who were most significantly being swept away by false teachers—the women—and telling them that they needed to get grounded in the truth properly so that they would no longer be convinced and deceived by the errors being brought into the community.

A final point on this topic: Even if Paul's Genesis reference *was* explicitly related to teaching and exercising authority, there is still an interpretive challenge for complementarians who wish to use it as proof of the universal nature of Paul's instructions. Douglas Moo highlights this challenge when he states, 'New Testament authors will sometimes appeal to creation, or to the Old Testament generally, to establish a principle on which a specific form of behaviour is demanded. In these cases, while the principle always remains in effect, the specific form of behaviour will not. This seems to be the situation, for instance in 1 Corinthians 11:2–16.'[29] The point Moo is making is that, if there is a clear principle in the text, it is important that we work to uphold that principle, making the application culturally meaningful in today's terms—hence the reference to the teaching around head coverings in 1 Corinthians. Head coverings simply don't mean the same thing today as they meant in Paul's day, and so upholding their use would somewhat ironically twist the principle that was intended to be upheld in the first place. I wholeheartedly agree with Moo and would venture to say that what he states here points us to one of the keys of settling the argument over 1 Timothy 2. I am somewhat puzzled, however, because Moo then goes on to say, 'But the difference between this [1 Corinthians 11] and 1 Timothy 2:12–13 is simply this: in 1 Timothy 2:12–18 the principle cannot be separated from the form of behaviour.'[30] I find Moo's stance here perplexing because I would argue that there is a clear principle displayed in this section. It is one that we have explored already, the principle of 'quietness'. Paul gives it prime position in the text in his framing device. It is a principle that is not so difficult to find but has often been rather neglected.

What the presence of *hēsychia* does for us is that, in offering a plausible principle, it brings a solid rebuttal to any argument that wishes to use the Genesis reference as a universal binder for Paul's application in verse 12. We do not do that elsewhere in Scripture and have no good justification to do that here.

Concluding Thoughts

Into a community where the women were bringing division and unrest through how they were learning and speaking, Paul advised Timothy to apply very careful and restrictive boundaries. His aim? To restore health and uphold peace and unity. Whether these women were part of an original group of false teachers, we don't know for sure. But what we do know is that they certainly were a group significantly impacted by the false teaching at work and were propagating it further still (see 1 Timothy 5:13—a verse not about gossiping but about spreading false ideas and nonsense. The word *phlyaroi* used there was 'commonly used to identify teachings or philosophies that are opposed to the truth'[31]). Despite the putting out of significant false teachers from the community (see 1 Tim. 1:20), their influence was still poisoning the church and Paul was coaching Timothy to stop this flow.

This view, far from making 1 Timothy irrelevant to us today, makes it one of the most relevant pastoral mentoring books for those leading communities that are falling into unhealthy practice. First Timothy gives us guidelines of how to restore health to a community on the edge—apply rigorous boundaries, especially target those groups that are the biggest concern—both in propagating and in receiving the error—and raise the standards of who is allowed to pass on biblical truth and lead. Those boundaries need not be in place forever as they will restrict life in the community when it is functioning healthily, but they are needed for a time as a safeguard until the community is brought into life again. To use an illustration from the world of medicine, a plaster cast is only needed to restrict a bone that is broken. Once the bone is healed, the cast must be taken off again in order to allow the body to function to fullness.

Ultimately, we have a choice as we approach verses 11–14 in 1 Timothy 2. Either we can defend a universal application of these verses (despite good reason to do otherwise from the verses themselves) and thereby need to bring awkward interpretations to a large number of verses elsewhere in the New Testament to justify our stance, or we can acknowledge a clear principle throughout the text and allow that to shine comfortably alongside the rest of the New Testament.

I am concerned that a universal approach to 1 Timothy 2:11–14 not only leads to a violation of the principle Paul intended in those verses themselves (bringing oppression, not peace) but also leads to a violation of a much larger number of verses throughout the New Testament. A universal approach to 1 Timothy 2:11–14 is mutually exclusive with Paul's teaching in Romans 12:4–8, Colossians 3:16, Ephesians 4:11–13, to mention a few, unless we take it upon ourselves (something that Paul certainly didn't do) to insert into these verses invisible gender disclaimers and disqualifiers. A universal approach to 1 Timothy 2:11–14 means that we have no choice but to belittle what we read in Acts 18:24–26 and Romans 16:1–16, refusing to acknowledge that it is unlikely that women were famous in the house churches across provinces for anything other than significant public ministries. A universal approach to 1 Timothy 2:11–14 leads us to read Genesis 1–3 with a lens of hierarchy where there is no such suggestion in the text itself. And ultimately, a universal reading of 1 Timothy 2:11–14 impacts greatly on what it means to be men and women, equal co-heirs in Christ.

1 TIMOTHY 3: A QUESTION OF ELDERSHIP

I used to feel stumped by 1 Timothy 3. I was fairly confident that Paul's words in 1 Timothy 2 couldn't possibly mean what they appear to mean on a surface level, because in that case they would be at odds with multiple other scriptures. But I must admit that the question of eldership[1] left me much more perplexed. Every time I felt like I'd reasonably grappled with chapter 2, I would run right into chapter 3 and feel uncertain all over again. The language is explicitly male in 1 Timothy 3—surely that speaks for itself?

I know I am not alone in thinking this. I have had many conversations with church leaders who will say to me that they have no problem with women teaching and having authority—they have been convinced from Scripture that God does not hold these areas back from women. But they draw the line at ordaining women elders because 1 Timothy 3 is very clear that this is a male-only role. At least that's what they believe. At least, that's what I believed.

And then I started researching more deeply for this book and could not have been more surprised by what I read. I had looked at chapter 3 as perhaps the hardest to grapple with until I started reading more literature from both the complementarian as well as the egalitarian camp, which signalled otherwise.

A clue that 1 Timothy 3 is not the 'jewel in the crown' for the male-only eldership argument is that there is actually far less airtime given to 1 Timothy 3 than to 1 Timothy 2. Far from being centre stage in the argument for male-only eldership, 1 Timothy 3 only gets a cursory glance in the literature on gender roles—despite being the only text out of the two that actually mentions eldership. The lack of focus on 1 Timothy 3 highlights the fact that this passage is a far cry from being an obvious silencer to any argument for female elders and is not a favoured text to build a convincing argument for gender roles.

Therefore, despite the inclusion of 1 Timothy 3 in the CBMW (The Council on Biblical Manhood and Womanhood) website as one of five New Testament passages 'which speak of restrictions on women's roles in the church',[2] both complementarian and egalitarian scholars (including Linda Belleville,[3] Craig Blomberg, and Susan Foh) have noted that this is not the case. Blomberg states, 'Matthew 10:1–42; 1 Timothy 3:1–7; and Titus 1:5–9 are not terribly relevant …'[4] and Susan Foh (like Blomberg, an influential complementarian scholar) asserts, 'There is only one valid argument against women's ordination to the ministry: scriptural prohibition. This prohibition is found in 1 Tim. 2:12.'[5] Now, whilst I do not agree with Foh on her reading of 1 Timothy 2:12, I find her assertion helpful and enlightening. Making the assumption that 1 Timothy 3 is convincing proof of male-only eldership is clearly a mistake—not even significant scholars in the complementarian camp believe that. As it turns out, 1 Timothy 3 ends up being nothing like the 'silver bullet' of the male-only eldership argument that I had imagined it to be.

And so, if you are one of the people I described at the beginning of this chapter—perhaps convinced that women should teach and exercise authority but unable to see a way to assess 1 Timothy 3 as anything other than an instruction for male eldership—keep reading. I trust that this chapter will be a help to you, as the research of it was a help to me.

The Nature of Greek

When we read the New Testament, we must bear in mind that the ancient Greek language it is written in is primarily androcentric (male orientated). Terms written in male language do not prove that only males are present or that the author is wanting to permanently exclude women. The barring of women needs to be explicitly stated to be convincing as a required exclusion.

We see this with multiple examples throughout the New Testament. In Acts 1:12–16 we have a clear example of both men and women gathered together in the upper room in prayer and fellowship. Yet, when Peter gets up to speak to the group, he addresses the brothers (*adelphos*)—even though he could easily have also added the word for sisters (*adelphē*), which would have certainly been in his vocabulary. In using the explicitly masculine word, are we to surmise that Peter was only speaking to the men in the room? Clearly not. We understand that Greek is an androcentric language, which means that when addressing both men and women, it would be natural to use masculine terms, and we therefore read through that lens. In fact, where we see 'brothers' throughout the New Testament—unless women are explicitly stated to be excluded—we understand it to mean 'brothers and sisters' despite the literal translation from the Greek text being 'brothers'. We never use the argument that, because Peter *could* have used the feminine 'sisters' as well, it shows that he meant brothers only (an argument sometimes applied to 1 Timothy 3). That is simply not how Greek works.

In 1 Timothy 4, Paul follows his teaching and instructions with the statement, 'If you put these things before the brothers [*adelphois*]' (v. 6). His masculine focus is not understood by scholars today as exclusivity against women—that issues of doctrine or church practice should be exclusively presented to men—but simply of the nature of the ancient Greek language.

Another example is seen in the gift list of Ephesians 4:11. All of the words listed are in masculine form but, to my knowledge, the masculine form of the words is not credibly used as proof that women are excluded from these roles. If someone wants to assert that women are excluded from any of these gifts, they would have to base their argument elsewhere, for Ephesians 4 does not explicitly state that these are male-only gifts and gives no justification to claim it is so. Rather, 'The leadership list in Ephesians 4:11 (NIV) is a good example of the gender inclusivity of the Greek masculine.'[6]

D.A. Carson (a complementarian scholar) argues this same point of androcentricity when he refers to the absurdity of reading a masculine word only in reference to men in 1 Corinthians 14:36: 'That the word for "only" is masculine is irrelevant: people considered generically are regularly found in the masculine gender in the

Greek. It is more natural to read verse 36 as addressed to the church, not just to the men in the church.'[7]

The examples could go on and on, but I hope the point here is clear—Greek is an androcentric language, and we have to remember that when reading male language in any text. Unless there is an explicit exclusion of women, the language itself does not give us cause to assume that exclusion.

And so, when we read 1 Timothy 3 and realise that the word used for overseer/bishop is masculine (*episkopos*), the gender of the word itself is an inadequate argument for male-only eldership. To use the gender of the word as the basis of our argument shows an insensitivity to how androcentric Greek texts are as a norm. Just because a text uses masculine language, that is not in itself evidence that the author was making a point that women are to be permanently excluded.

Interestingly, though the word *episkopos* used in chapter 3 from verse 2 onwards is a masculine one, the word 'overseer' (often translated 'office of overseer') in chapter 3 verse 1, is in the feminine form: *episkopé*. Paul introduces the whole chapter with the gender-inclusive 'anyone' rather than 'any man' and states if anyone desires the 'office of overseer' (feminine form), he or she (the Greek text has no pronoun) desires a noble task.

Just to be clear, I believe it is inadequate to use the femininity of *episkopé* as proof for women elders. That is not what male and female words necessarily mean in the Greek. However, the difficulty of making much of the masculinity of the word *episkopos* whilst playing down the femininity of the word *episkopé* should be obvious. Either the gender of the words are crucial to our understanding, in which case we are forced to give weight to the feminine form in verse

1 as we do to the masculine form from verse 2, or the gender of the words are not proof of gender inclusions/exclusions, in which case we must go on to further study. What we cannot do is have it both ways by ignoring the gender of the word in verse 1 and then basing our argument on the gender of the word from verse 2.

As well as, and arguably more important than, the androcentric nature of the ancient Greek *language*, we need to bear in mind too the androcentric nature of ancient *culture*. The world of the Bible was a patriarchal world. Life was built around the privilege and opportunity of men over women simply as a norm, and masculine terminology when addressing both genders is just one expression of the reality of a male-centric culture. Given this male-orientated culture, it is very likely that many elders (and doubtless, all, in some communities) were men. But just because something *is* so, we should not assume that it was *intended* to be so. As we read Scripture, it is important for us to assess which layers are part of the perfect intentions of God and which layers are the reality of godly principles being applied to a specific context. Bearing this in mind, even if we were to assume that the masculine language in 1 Timothy 3 *was* because only men were being referenced at the time, that in itself is still not viable proof of an intentional future exclusion of women. There is no statement of exclusion in the text. It is precisely because of this that many complementarians do not use 1 Timothy 3 as a basis of argument. Picking up on this point and highlighting both androcentricity of language as well as culture, Tom Wright writes, 'Paul refers to the bishop throughout as a man. My reading of the rest of the New Testament inclines me to think that this is more because that's how Greek grammar normally refers to both genders together, and because in the very early days of the church the leaders of most communities were probably men. I don't see it as debarring women from this particular ministry and vocation.'[8]

And so, we can see that the masculine nature of words are not a conclusive argument for male-only eldership. Masculine words are easily understood either as part of an androcentric language or as a reality of an androcentric culture. To turn them into explicit and universal instructions on gender is to stretch the text beyond what many scholars (including complementarian ones) are comfortable with.

Having discussed this issue of androcentricity, let's now turn our attention to some other arguments that are posed on this topic of eldership.

Male-Only Phrases

Those who do assert male-only eldership from 1 Timothy 3 argue that two phrases within the list of eldership characteristics are examples of Paul making explicit the exclusion of women. We will look at each in turn.

a. One-Woman Man

The phrase most commonly pointed to is found in verse 2, 'one-woman man', often translated as 'husband of one wife' (1 Tim. 3:2). Clearly, women cannot fulfil the role of being a husband, and therefore, it is argued that the phrase proves that Paul was assuming elders would and should be male-only. However, to raise this argument is extremely problematic—so much so that influential complementarian scholars (e.g., Moo,[9] Schreiner[10]) conclude that the phrase is insufficient to exclude women.

Firstly, 'one-woman man' is acknowledged to be a set phrase. 'The phrase *one-woman man* (or *one-man woman*) is an idiom inscribed on numerous ancient gravestones celebrating the virtue of a husband (or wife) who had not remarried. By noting that he (or she) was married only once, it suggests the virtue of extraordinary fidelity.'[11] The difficulty with idiomatic terms is that if we try to apply them too literally, we can end up twisting their meaning altogether. This particularly is the case when we focus on separate parts of the phrase rather than to allow it to convey a meaning as a whole.

Furthermore, by focussing on 'man' as a *requirement* in the set phrase 'one-woman man', we are met with an additional challenge as this phrase is largely agreed to function as an *exclusion* in the passage. In other words, 'one-woman man' is not intended as a requirement that all elders must be married but rather is a phrase used to exclude anyone in the community who was married but was not faithful to their spouse, or was in a polygamous relationship. We cannot make part of the phrase ('man') a universal requirement if we are not reading the whole phrase as such.

Payne picks up on this danger, stating, 'Since "one woman man" is a set phrase that functions as an exclusion, any claim that a single word of it ("man") also functions separately as a requirement must posit a double meaning. This is not warranted by the context. It is bad hermeneutics to isolate a single word ("man") from a set phrase ("one woman man") that functions as an exclusion (of polygamists and probably adulterous husbands) and to elevate that single word to the status of an independent requirement (that all overseers be men).'[12]

Thus, it is difficult to justify using 'one-woman man' as an argument for male-only eldership. To insist on a requirement within a phrase of exclusion is problematic. By that logic, what is to stop us from doing the same a little further on in chapter 3 where Paul states that the overseer 'must manage his own household well' and highlighting 'own household' to add an additional requirement that all overseers must be homeowners?[13] Clearly, we are on dangerous ground when we start dissecting set phrases in this way.

Now, in response, some may want to defend the phrase as a requirement as a whole. But, frankly, an argument to that end quickly loses steam. Paul himself was single, and he advised his hearers to remain single in order to be better able to give themselves to the work of ministry (1 Cor. 7:26–40). Making marriage a requirement (for both eldership and deaconship) is hardly a viable option if Paul was saying neither he (nor Jesus for that matter!) nor those who followed his advice to devote themselves to ministry in singleness would be qualified to function as either elders or deacons.

And so, the more we study, the more obvious it becomes that 'one-woman man' is not a good platform from which to argue a requirement for male elders, and those who choose to do so are walking in difficult hermeneutical territory.

b. Managing One's Own Household

Another phrase pointed to as proof of masculine exclusivity is the instruction to 'manage his own household well' (1 Tim. 3:4). Payne quotes Wayne Grudem's view that women cannot be overseers since 'the NT never uses *proistēmi* to speak of women "managing" or governing a household, but only of men.'[14] Despite Grudem's assertion, however, the verb *proistēmi* is used in Romans 12:6–8 where there is nothing specifically directed to men in the text (please ignore any masculine pronouns that some English translations insert—they do not exist in the Greek). Equally, the one noun form of the verb *proistēmi* that we have in the New Testament is used to describe a woman—Phoebe—in Romans 16. And lastly, whilst Paul doesn't use the verb *proistēmi* explicitly in singling out women, he *does* use an even stronger word for 'ruling' households—*oikodespotein*—of women in 1 Timothy 5:14, showing that this is not an action reserved for men alone.[15]

What about Titus?

For those of us who might be tempted to explain away the list in 1 Timothy 3 as only context-specific, there is a nearly identical list found in the book of Titus for us to read, and so that option is not open to us. It is clear that Paul's eldership requirements were applied to different regions in the ancient world.

The list in Titus 1:6–9 has virtually the same requirements as 1 Timothy 3 and starts in the same way with the gender-inclusive word 'anyone' rather than 'any man'. Whilst these do not prove female eldership, they do lead us towards a significant thought. Given that the letter to Titus did not have any prohibitions on the ministry of women (in contrast to 1 Tim. 2:12), there is no convincing reason to believe that Titus or the community he was serving would have taken the eldership requirements as instructions barring women from eldership. It would have been natural for them to see masculine terms as gender inclusive, even if men were the only elders at the time of writing. If Paul wanted to explicitly exclude women, he would need to state that plainly.

In view of this, Paul was certainly risking a considerable amount of misunderstanding and error by omitting a statement of female exclusion, which is strange given his intention to bring order to the community and in view of how meticulous his stated requirements are.

It would seem then, that the presence of the list in Titus becomes a bit of a liability for those who would want to argue for male-only eldership from 1 Timothy 3. From the scriptures we have, there is no reason to think that Titus' readers would reach that conclusion.

A Matter of Statistics

Many scholars have pointed out that in the book of 1 Timothy, there are remarkable similarities between Paul's listed requirements for elders and the instructions he gives to women in the community. Almost half of the requirements are seen virtually word-for-word in instructions to women, and the other half are seen in conceptual equivalents (e.g., elders to be 'not addicted to too much wine' (3:3) and women to be 'sober' (3:11)).

Philip Payne has done some statistical analysis on this. In analysing the word-for-word pairings only (in order to take a conservative approach), we see that the probability of the phrases on elders also occurring in the 1 Timothy texts on women are 6 in 1 million when using the pastoral epistles alone and 5 in 1 trillion when taking all the Pauline texts into account. Clearly these are significant results.

Furthermore, if conceptual parallels are included in the analysis, then the statistics become even more significant.[16]

'The use of so much identical terminology in the verses explicitly about women in 1 Timothy is statistically so improbable that it makes sense that Paul deliberately described women with these words.'[17] However, before we run ahead and put too much emphasis on these results, let us be careful. The statistics show us that a correlation exists. They do not, however, show us *why* that correlation exists.

I have included the statistical argument here because the results are too significant simply to ignore. The numbers warrant for us to at least pause enough to ask the question, 'What did Paul want to achieve when he chose to use the same terminology in his teaching to these two groups?' Certainly one possible reason is that he wanted to demonstrate that he believed women in the community should and could fulfil the requirements of elders. I cannot think of another likely motivation to intentionally draw such a line between elders and women, but, perhaps, one might exist and it is hence difficult to become dogmatic in arguing from these statistics alone. The results are worthy of some thought from us and certainly give increased momentum to an argument for the inclusion of women in eldership, but as they are not conclusive as to Paul's motivation, we will move on to further arguments.

Aren't Old Testament Priests and New Testament Elders Equivalent Roles?

Some have tried to argue that priests and elders are equivalent roles of leading the people of God in two different covenants. Since it is clear that in the old covenant the priesthood was exclusively male, it is argued that in the new covenant, eldership should be exclusively male.

The argument requires that priesthood and eldership are equivalent roles and also that old covenant logic applies in the same way in new covenant contexts. However, the premise of the argument is one that I am not convinced is a biblical one in either case.

Is it actually true that Old Testament priests and New Testament elders are equivalent functions? To take a simple approach here, let me focus on two firm challenges to this view. Firstly, Scripture itself never draws a parallel between the Old Testament priesthood and New Testament eldership. If that parallel is not obvious for New Testament writers, it shouldn't be one that we adopt. Secondly, Scripture *does* show us a new covenant expression of the old covenant priesthood, and it is not eldership, but rather Jesus as the ultimate High Priest (Hebrews 5–8) and every believer now included in the priesthood (1 Pet. 2:5). 'The New Testament portrayal of the church as a priesthood of believers implies that the parallel to the Levitical priesthood is not the ordained office (or leadership function) but the church as a whole.'[18] To ignore the parallel that Scripture does give us and insert a parallel that it does not is neither helpful nor accurate and belittles the wonderful truth that every believer now has rights to enter into the presence of God without a human mediator.

Under the old covenant, priests were there to minister on behalf of a people who had no right of access to God. Jesus ended the need for the old covenant priesthood, He Himself now being the One who brings us into the presence of God, and so we all gain access rights to God. 'There is no continuity between the office of priest, which ceased when Christ sacrificed himself once for all

(Heb. 7:11–10:25), and the office of elder or pastor-teacher. The duties of the two are very different.'[19]

To apply old covenant logic to new covenant reality grossly ignores the seismic changes that occur between the two and puts eldership into a box that New Testament writers neither acknowledge nor enforce. If anything, the New Testament inclusion of *every* believer into the priesthood (note—not only every *male* believer) clarifies for us how this male-only system under the old covenant has now been superseded and just how much of a restoration of male and female *alongside* one another has been achieved in the redemptive work of Christ. 'Because Christ has qualified all believers to stand in God's presence, regardless of race, social status or gender, we are all ministers within the fellowship. As priests of God—and only because we are priests—we are called by the Spirit to ministries among Christ's people, and some of these ministries include positions of leadership.'[20]

The Lack of Examples of Female Elders

The fact that we do not have any explicitly named female elders is sometimes used to bolster a complementarian male-only eldership argument. If female elders existed, presumably we would have a few named in Scripture.

The problem, however, is that the New Testament gives us *no* named examples of elders—whether male or female. We cannot argue that the lack of a named example makes it unlikely that they existed because we know from Scripture that elders existed and yet, there are none whom we can name.

Furthermore, let us again acknowledge the cultural realities at the time of the writing of the New Testament so as not to demand examples that are unrealistic. Otherwise, we risk falling not only into a sexism that is not God-intended but into a racism that is contrary to His heart.

> In addition to androcentrism, we must also be reminded that the world of the first-century is inarguably patriarchal. It [is] common for critics of women elders to say such things as, 'the New Testament commends the activities of women in various sorts of ministries except those that would violate the male leadership principle' (Knight 2006: 358). But if this 'male leadership principle'—little more than an alternative label for male control—is to some degree actually patriarchy, androcentrism, and sexism generated by the fall, the reader of the New Testament ought to be particularly careful not to attribute such historical phenomena to an absolute, universal moral norm … To make the point differently, the Bible gives far more attention to Jewish people than to other ethnicities, but no Christian would demand an equal treatment of all ethnicities in Scripture to have a 'biblical argument' for racial equality. That men dominate the scene of Christian leadership in the early church is expected; the question is how much significance should be given to it. Is it prescriptive, or descriptive? It is,

therefore, superficial to demand an account of women in ministry directly comparable to men in ministry from the Scriptures. Not only are the purposes of Scripture limited and its historical contexts fixed, but its own internal principles (e.g., the institution of the New Covenant and its elevation of women) have not reached full realization even today.[21]

The Obligation for Consistency: The Trouble with Picking and Choosing through Restrictions

I have been in many churches where women are categorically excluded from eldership, but there is nowhere near the same level of militancy in excluding men who do not fulfil all of the requirements Paul sets out. I wonder why this is?

I struggle to see the logic or the integrity of being so dogmatic in our exclusion of women but more 'understanding' (is this the motivation?) when it comes to the full list of requirements. Even if Paul was excluding women from his requirements (which is quite a difficult stretch), we cannot with integrity insist on the enforcement of that exclusion in our communities today unless we are willing to insist on all of the criteria set out with the same immovability.

This, of course, is not an argument for or against female eldership in itself, rather an argument for greater integrity in how we follow our own interpretation of Scripture.

If you want to be dogmatic in your exclusion of women, then please be equally dogmatic in all your exclusions. I wonder why we often find it more important to be dogmatic on a stipulation not present in the text, rather than dogmatic on the stipulations present for all to see?

If you are a church leader who believes that women should be excluded from eldership, please ensure that neither yourself nor anyone on your eldership team falls into any of these categories:

- Men who are not married.
- Men who have been widowed and have remarried. (For we cannot literally use 'one-woman man' as an argument for the exclusion of women if we will not then follow its further literal translation to exclude those who have been with more than one woman—whatever the reason.)
- Men who have divorced and have remarried.
- Men who are married but don't have children.
- Men who are married but only have one child. (Note, all the verses in relation to children are plural.)
- Men who have children who are rebellious. (Which parent of a toddler or teenager would be exempt from this, I wonder?)
- Men who have children who are not saved. (Which would presumably mean men with very young children are excluded because how are they to prove that their children are saved?)

- Men who are not hospitable. (This might not be
  fashionable in our current-day understanding of
  introverts, but any elders who are not opening
  their homes to people in the community stand in
  direct contradiction to this.)
- Men who are quarrelsome or violent.
- Men who drink too much alcohol. (Who is to set
  the bar on this, I wonder? I know a number of
  church leaders who drink more alcohol than the
  medically recommended limit.)
- Men who are recent converts.
- Men who are not self-controlled.

Please note, consistency in application of all of these will not
necessarily mean that our stance on women is correct, but will mean
that at least we are standing in integrity as we dogmatically assert
what we see to be scriptural exclusions.

Conclusion

It seems to me that many Christians stumble at 1 Timothy 3, believing it to be a convincing hurdle to female eldership, where many
scholars see 1 Timothy 3 in a very different light. At one time, I
thought of 1 Timothy 3 as a text which effectively blocked any ideas
of women in leadership. I am now thoroughly convinced that it cannot feasibly be used for this.

When we take into account the androcentric Greek language
and culture as well as the lack of any prohibition of female elders

in an otherwise meticulous list of requirements and exclusions, any argument for male-only eldership from this text begins to lose momentum. Adding to that the evidence for Paul's intentionality in using identical terminology in his teaching on elders and on women, as well as the lack of named elders (whether male or female) in the New Testament, we end up with a strong argument for seeing 1 Timothy 3 as gender *inclusive,* not exclusive. Furthermore, we have seen that the presence of the very similar list in Titus, but with the absence of limitations on women's roles, strengthens a gender-inclusive argument in interpreting these requirements for eldership.

Finally, we have looked at the difficulty of using this text dogmatically to exclude women—particularly when we are hesitant to use it as dogmatically to exclude certain men. This brings to light the challenge we face as we grapple with gender roles in the body—not simply to answer the question, or even to answer it correctly, but to act in consistency and integrity whichever side of the argument we land on.

EPHESIANS 5: MARRIAGE

Some years ago, my husband, Julian, and I were part of a church team grappling with the idea of hierarchy in leadership. The conversation was animated as the team discussed potential pros and cons to how we were approaching leadership in the church. In that discussion, my husband mentioned how, in our family, we approach marriage without a fixed authoritative hierarchy, where Julian is not the permanent leader but both Julian and I lead in different moments depending on our gifts and strengths. That moment is etched into my mind as one of the most uncomfortable moments I've experienced in all my years in church ministry. It was as if someone flipped a very big, angry switch. Julian may as well have thrown a hand grenade into the group. Suddenly tensions flared and conviction was overtaken by hostility as people began to raise their voices to defend that husbands *must* take the lead in marriage. The strength of emotion induced from all sides at Julian's words was both fascinating and extremely sad. Without commenting on the merit of his (or the group's) opinion, it occurred to me then, as it does now as I write this, that the subject of headship in marriage is one of the most emotionally charged aspects of the gender roles debate.

With this in mind, I ask that you keep an open mind in this chapter. How we view marriage has profound, far-reaching implications.

Ephesians 5: Context

Paul wrote the letter of Ephesians to the church in Ephesus (and in all likelihood intended it as a circular letter to other cities in Asia) whilst under arrest. The letter is 'apocalyptic' in nature[1]—superimposing the reality of another world onto our everyday experience. The first three chapters focus on the new reality of every believer—reconciled and seated in Christ with a completely different vantage point and experience from when we were alienated from God. Chapters 4 through 6:1–9 then go on to flesh out what that new reality looks like in practice with the repeated word 'walk' throughout the verses. Now that you know where you're seated, learn how to walk it out. The last part of the book, in chapter 6:10–20, focuses in on what warfare looks like for the believer: standing. You who are in Christ, stand your ground. The cross and resurrection have placed you on victorious ground. Do not give way to enemy schemes. And so, we can trace out the other-worldly teachings of the letter through the simple summary of three words, 'sit, walk, stand'.[2] But don't be fooled by the simplicity of the summary. The letter is a theological treasure trove, breathtaking and magnificent in its scope.

In the section detailing how to walk out the new reality of every believer, Paul brings some instructions about Spirit-filled living in the community and goes on to address three groups of people: husbands and wives, fathers and children, and masters and slaves. In modern culture, the focus of Paul's teaching can be confusing. The fact that he instructs slaves rather than denounces slavery raises some questions. So too does his focus on fathers, rather than instructing both parents. And, of course, there are well-known questions raised by his instructions to husbands and wives. Why are wives singled out to submit? Why are husbands singled out to lay their lives down?

Before looking at some of these questions in greater depth, let us note, as a matter of initial importance, that Paul did not pick these three groups arbitrarily but highlighted them because they were already the focus of the moral-ethical discussions of ancient household codes in the Greco-Roman world.[3] In Ephesians 5, Paul is giving believers a masterclass in being relevant to culture in order to transform it. Too often as Christians, we enter conversations that no one is having and wonder why we are not seeing the change that we are believing for. What Paul did in his writing of Ephesians 5 was profound. He joined the conversation his world was engaged in, in order to bring meaningful transformation from the inside. Answering questions no one is asking is a waste of time and energy. Answering questions that everyone is asking with game-changing kingdom wisdom is part of the mandate on every believer. Join the conversation, and then provoke it to wholeness. Notice, Paul's method of engagement was not to blow up the conversation entirely (e.g., by denouncing slavery), but rather he accepted the peripheral boundaries of the conversation and then meticulously dismantled the premise internally. We do not do ourselves (or the world) any favours if we denounce conversations without journeying with unbelievers in them.

When we see that Paul did not arbitrarily pick the three groups but that instead he focussed his discussion on what was relevant for his cultural context, then we are able to read his singling out of these three groups not as proof of an implicit approval of hierarchical structures but as something quite different and radical. It is how Paul deals with each group, particularly in contrast to how his world dealt with each, that points to what he himself believed.

In the Greco-Roman world, husbands, fathers, and masters held absolute, unquestioned authority and, therefore, 'Secular "household tables" focus on the patriarch controlling his wife, children and slaves.'[4] Furthermore, ancient household codes had a completely one-sided approach with their discussions, taking interest only in those who were in authority: 'The secular forms do not include direct address to the "inferior" parties.'[5] Wives, children, and slaves were not seen as important enough to warrant reciprocal teaching. But clearly, in Paul's eyes, each group was a valued part of the community of God. He took a one-sided conversation and opened it up to allow room for all parties. This may seem simple and small to us. It would not have been simple or small in his day. Not only did he include all parties in his instructions, but in each context, he *required* something from husbands, fathers, and masters in how they related to their counterparts. This would have been challenging and offensive for many readers. To instruct husbands that they needed to love to the point of self-sacrifice, and fathers not to exasperate their children, and masters that ultimately they served the same master as their slaves and so stood on equal ground was countercultural. In his teachings on the three groups, Paul was disrupting the status quo of his day. Quietly, prudently, but nevertheless quite radically.

The book of Ephesians sets up careful foundations for the instructions to households. The thrust of the first few chapters of the letter makes it clear that all are invited now to participate in Christ. God, and all the riches that flow from Him, are not reserved for the chosen, superior few. Everyone and anyone is invited in to be in Him, even enthroned with Him (2:6). The 'inferior' Gentiles invited in every bit as much as the chosen Jews (2:18). What was once acknowledged as superior is now drawn into equality. Chapters 4 and 5 present what is appropriate for those who walk in Christ— community pursuing unity (4:3), kindness (4:32), humility and gentleness (4:2), bearing with one another (4:2), loving as Christ loves us (5:2). Lording it over one another is not a behaviour appropriate for those who are now in Christ.

This teaching of unity in the Spirit, sacrificial love, and the preferring of one another over ourselves is underlined in Ephesians 5:18–21, which is the immediate foundation on which Paul's household instructions are given. These verses are very much a *part* of the instructions, particularly on marriage, as Paul 'embeds his call to wives in a single long sentence that includes everything in Eph 5:18–24.'[6] This is further highlighted by the fact that in the Greek text, in contrast to English translations, verse 22 does not contain the word 'submit'—it is understood from verse 21. In view of this, let us take a closer look at the verses that form the first part of the sentence where Paul begins his instructions on marriage.

Ephesians 5:18–21

> And do not get drunk with wine, for that is debauchery, but be filled with the Spirit, addressing one another in psalms and hymns and spiritual

> songs, singing and making melody to the Lord with
> your heart, giving thanks always and for everything
> to God the Father in the name of our Lord Jesus
> Christ, submitting to one another out of reverence
> for Christ.

Verse 18 instructs believers to be filled with the Spirit (the tense of the verb indicates an ongoing action to keep on being filled) and the overflow of that filling is seen in the series of participles: believers addressing one another with songs, singing to the Lord, giving thanks always, and submitting to one another. It is important to recognise that Paul's instructions to the community here are off the springboard of the Holy Spirit's activity in us. We have no hope of understanding Paul's teaching here in the absence of being filled with God's Spirit, for Paul's instructions require something that is different to the natural workings of the world.

The final participle—submitting to one another—acts as a hinge which connects actions illustrating life in the Spirit in the entire community to more specific instructions to certain household groups. A literal translation from the Greek text reads, 'submitting to one another out of reverence for Christ [v.21], wives to your own husbands as to the Lord [v.22] ...'[7] Verse 22, therefore, is rooted in the premise that the community (which presumably includes married couples) is to submit to one another in a reciprocal manner. This is a problem for those who would argue that submission is a role that is exclusively from wives to husbands but not the other way around.

In view of this, some have tried to reduce the reciprocal nature of 'submit to one another' to actually mean 'some of you always submit to others of you'. In this way, an argument for fixed hierarchical leadership in marriage can be maintained, where the husband is always in authority and the wife must always submit to him. Wayne Grudem is a proponent of this view and presents two arguments to justify his position:

> a. The verb 'submit' (*hypotassō*) 'always implies a relationship of submission to an authority.'[8]
> b. 'One to another' (*allēlous*) can be seen in 'many cases where it rather means "some to others".'[9]

Hence, according to Grudem, there is good reason to translate the verse as 'some being subject to some others' rather than the reciprocal 'one to another'.

On his first point, Grudem cites many verses that do show submission as an action to a superior authority (including Rom. 13:1, 1 Cor. 15:27, and Titus 3:1 to name a few). There is no doubt that the word 'submit' can be used in this way. However, Grudem is mistaken in his claim that this is *always* how the verb is used. There are clear examples where the same word 'submit' is used in a context of equals or even to a subordinate, including:[10]

- 1 Corinthians 14:32, 'The spirits of prophets are subject to prophets.'
- 1 Corinthians 16:15–16, 'Now I urge you, brothers ... be subject to such as these [the household of Stephanas], and to every fellow worker and labourer.'

- Luke 2:51, 'And he [Jesus] went down with them [Joseph and Mary] and came to Nazareth and was submissive to them.' (Grudem cites this verse in favour of the word submission always being used to signify the submission of an inferior to one of greater authority. However, I wonder if Grudem might be missing the point of Luke 2 somewhat. Luke writes this sentence directly after Jesus has claimed God as His Father in verse 49. The point, then, of Jesus submitting to His parents is not that He submitted to those of greater authority than Him, but an illustration of how Jesus humbled Himself in submission to earthly parents despite being the Son of God!)

Beyond the fact that these examples show that the word 'submit' *can* be used in relation towards equals or even subordinates, there is further reason to understand submission in Ephesians 5:21 as more than an action from an inferior to a superior. The idea of submission even to subordinates is a biblical one. Hence, Grudem's argument seems doubly improbable given the encouragement in Scripture to 'count others more significant than yourselves' (Phil. 2:3) and to lower ourselves to servanthood even as a sign of our superior authority and greatness (Luke 22:26–27).

On his second point, Grudem again cites several verses to back up his claim (Luke 2:15; Luke 12:1; Luke 24:32; 1 Cor. 11:33; Gal. 6:2; Rev. 6:4). However, contrary to Grudem's assertion, in each verse that he cites, there *is* a reciprocal action. Perhaps Grudem has been

sidetracked by his belief that 'interpreters *assume* that the Greek pronoun *allēlous* ("one another") must be completely reciprocal (that it
must mean "everyone to everyone").'[11] But Grudem is misled here,
'The straw man idea he proposes of "everyone to everyone" is not commonly, if ever assumed.'[12] Clearly, for submission to be meaningfully
carried out, some individuals submit to others in different moments.
The question, however, is whether Paul wanted one individual (or
groups of individuals) to be *permanently* the ones submitting to another
individual (or groups of individuals) without any reciprocation. The
word *allēlous* does not give us any reason to believe that. Even in the
examples Grudem cites, within the specified group in each verse, the
behaviour is very much reciprocal. A rendition of 'submit one always
to the other' is to ignore how *allēlous* is used in Scripture.

Given the arguments above, it is reassuring to note that the
highly respected Greek-English dictionary BDAG identifies every
occurrence of *allēlous* as '"the reciprocal pronoun" with English
equivalents "each other, one another, mutually"'[13] and, furthermore, defines *hypotassō* in verse 21 as 'submission in the sense of
voluntary yielding in love …'[14] It is little wonder then that many
scholars, including complementarians such as Knight and Hurley,
do not share Grudem's views. Knight is quite clear that verse 21 is
indeed reciprocal and inclusive of the whole community and that
this mutual submission is the foundation for the instructions that
follow: 'Thus verse 21, explicitly insisting that believers submit to
one another, sets the tone for the entire section.'[15]

Having thus established the foundation of mutual submission in
the community (which assumes the inclusion of both wives and husbands), let us move on to look at Paul's specific instructions on marriage.

Submission and Love

Wives, submit to your own husbands, as to the Lord.
For the husband is the head of the wife even as Christ
is the head of the church, his body, and is himself its
Saviour. Now as the church submits to Christ, so also
wives should submit in everything to their husbands.

Husbands, love your wives, as Christ loved the
church and gave himself up for her, that he might
sanctify her, having cleansed her by the washing of
water with the word, so that he might present the
church to himself in splendour, without spot or
wrinkle or any such thing, that she might be holy and
without blemish. In the same way husbands should
love their wives as their own bodies. He who loves
his wife loves himself. For no one ever hated his own
flesh, but nourishes and cherishes it, just as Christ
does the church, because we are members of his body.
'Therefore a man shall leave his father and mother and
hold fast to his wife, and the two shall become one
flesh.' This mystery is profound, and I am saying that
it refers to Christ and the church. However, let each
one of you love his wife as himself, and let the wife see
that she respects her husband. (Eph. 5:22–33)

Traditionally, these verses have been read to mean that husbands are in a position of authority over the wife as the 'head' of the
home. Wives are to submit, recognising their husband's God-given

authority. Husbands are to lead in a loving, self-sacrificial way. Not lording it over their wives, but leading them with love and kindness. These roles are gender exclusive. Wives submit and husbands lead and never in reverse. This interpretation is largely based on:

> a. The fact that Paul talks to the wives about submitting, but does not do the same to the husbands. This leads to the assertion that Paul expected wives, but not husbands, to submit.
>
> b. The use of the word 'head' which, it is argued, is a clear position of authority strengthened by the analogy of Christ being the head of the church.

Quite aside that this rendition ignores a foundation of mutual submission, there are a number of other very good reasons *not* to read the verses in the way that the traditionalists would. We will look at these reasons in some detail together.

Reason 1: The Analogy of Headship

We have seen in the earlier chapter on 1 Corinthians 11 that the Greek word 'head' can mean many different things, including source, leader, authority, anatomical head, preeminent, etc. What was it that Paul meant in Ephesians 5? It is the context that will help us determine that. Paul places two parallel thoughts together in using the word 'head' that gives us the key to his meaning. 'For the husband is the head of the wife even as Christ is the head of the church, his body, and is himself its Saviour.' Notice that 'saviour' is an apposition to 'head' thus meaning that 'saviour' is the word which explains 'head'.[16] The headship of husbands to wives is likened to the headship of Christ *as Saviour* to the church. Paul does not use the picture of Christ's *Lordship* to demonstrate what he means by head, which is a point ignored by a number of complementarian scholars (e.g., Schreiner, 'The primary role of leadership ... for the husband is clearly taught here, just as the church is to submit to the lordship of Christ'[17]). Christ as Lord would signify leadership and authority. Christ as Saviour signifies something quite different: self-sacrifice for the benefit of others. In view of this, Gordon Fee asserts, 'Just as the church is totally dependent on Christ for life and growth, so the wife in the first-century household was totally dependent on her husband as her "savior," in the sense of being dependent on him for her life in the world.'[18]

Furthermore, the way Paul uses the picture of Christ as head of the church elsewhere in his epistles is not primarily a picture of authority exerted over the church but rather a picture of the unity that the church has with Christ and the empowerment to the church brought by that union. Ephesians 1:22–23 shows Christ given as head to the church, His body, so that His fullness might be in them, and so they too stand in authority over all things that are under Jesus' feet. Ephesians 4:15–16 shows that Christ empowers and gives life to the whole body in order that it may grow and be built up in every way into Him. If Paul had wanted to use a picture of Christ relating to the church authoritatively to underline an authoritative hierarchy in marriage, there are other pictures that may have signified that. But the picture of Christ as head and the church as His body is not an obvious choice.

As Christ as Saviour is the focus in the Ephesians 5 text, and the headship of Christ in relation to the church is not used with the emphasis of Christ's authority exerted over the church elsewhere in the New Testament, it is extremely doubtful that Paul is instructing wives to submit because the husband is her authoritative leader. If that is not the picture that Paul is pointing to in Christ, then it cannot be the picture that he is intending when it comes to husbands. An interpretation of authority is not reflected in the text. Wayne Grudem has gone to extensive lengths with word studies on *kephalē* (head) to argue that headship should be read as authority in this context, but as Marshall states, 'Grudem deals mainly with the external evidence, but as Fee, Belleville and others insist, Paul's usage must be understood by considering how he uses the word in its various contexts.'[19]

Reason 2: The Missing Language of Authority

Isn't it strange that in the entire text Paul never uses the words 'lead' or 'have authority' and yet that is exactly what many have interpreted the text to mean? It is significant that Paul does not use the opposite of submit when he talks to husbands (lead, exercise authority, etc.), but *love*. What he is instructing is not two opposite roles—because he does not reference opposite actions. 'Were Paul intending to establish the traditional, hierarchical theology [of] marriage, he probably would have followed all of his commands for wives to submit to their husbands with a command for their husbands to exercise authority over their wives. But he never does … This is important because it is often missed that "love" is not the opposite activity of "submit." Scripture never teaches "wives, submit to your husbands … husbands, exercise authority over your wives."'[20]

Furthermore, not only is the language of authority missing in the context of headship in Ephesians 5, but the language of headship is missing in the context of people in roles of authority elsewhere in the New Testament. 'The New Testament contains scores of references to leaders from all walks of life: religious leaders, community leaders, military leaders, governmental leaders, patriarchal leaders, and church leaders. Never is any of them designated as "head" or as "head over". A profusion of other titles is used for them throughout the New Testament, but "head" is conspicuously absent from the list. The obvious explanation for this singularity is that *head* did not mean "leader" in the language of the New Testament.'[21] To further drive this point home, as mentioned earlier in this book, Greek translators did not believe 'head' (*kephalē*) to be the best word to convey the idea of leader (despite this being a natural metaphorical link in Hebrew) and hence overwhelmingly chose to translate the Old Testament Hebrew metaphors of 'head' to something other than *kephalē*.[22]

Reason 3: The Non-Exclusivity of the Terms

Complementarians argue that submission must be uniquely a wifely role given the fact that Paul does not explicitly instruct husbands to submit. The problem with this argument is that it is not feasibly applied elsewhere. Does the fact that Paul doesn't instruct wives to love means that he was not expecting wives to love their husbands? Of course not! There is repeated teaching in the New Testament for believers to love (e.g., Eph. 5:2; John 15:12–14) and, therefore, wives, being believers, are included in that teaching, even in relation to their husbands despite Ephesians 5 only giving that instruction to the men.

In the same way, believers in the New Testament are taught to submit to one another (Eph. 5:21), count others as more significant than themselves (Phil. 2:3), and humble themselves for the benefit of others (Eph. 4:2; John 13:13–14). Husbands, being believers, are not exempt from these instructions simply because 'the other' that is before them is their wife. We cannot argue one thing for the exclusivity of the instruction for women to submit when we would not dream of doing that for the exclusivity of the instruction for husbands to love.[23] There is a dishonesty at work when we use different scales for different genders. There are many instructions given in Scripture to certain groups that we understand to be a comment not of exclusivity but of relevance in the moment to that group. For example, 1 Timothy 2:9 states that women should dress modestly. We do not see the exclusion of men from that instruction as indicative of that being a gender-exclusive instruction, but rather indicating that in that community it was the women who needed help with modesty.

Reason 4: Role Reversals in Scripture

Despite the assertion of complementarians that husbands leading and wives submitting are permanent, God-ordained roles, there are examples in Scripture of the reversal of these roles which are either commanded or commended by God. See how God tells Abraham to submit to Sarah's plan (Gen. 21:12) and how Abigail, who is distinctly unsubmissive to Nabal, is portrayed as a woman of great wisdom in 1 Samuel 25. On this, Hübner quotes Walter Kaiser Jr., '[God was not] displeased with an Abigail (1 Sam. 25), who showed more discernment and wisdom than her foolish husband Nabal, who almost led that whole household into mortal danger had not Abigail intervened. Not only did King David praise her for preventing him from acting foolishly, but Scripture attests to the rightness of her actions over against those of her husband Nabal by saying that, ten days later, the Lord struck Nabal down and he died" (2005:6–10).'[24]

Reason 5: The Equality of 1 Corinthians 7

> But because of the temptation to sexual immorality, each man should have his own wife and each woman her own husband. The husband should give to his wife her conjugal rights, and likewise the wife to her husband. For the wife does not have authority over her own body, but the husband does. Likewise the husband does not have authority over his own body, but the wife does. Do not deprive one another, except perhaps by agreement for a limited time, that you may devote yourselves to prayer; but then come together again, so that Satan may not tempt you because of your lack of self-control. (1 Cor. 7:2–5)

First Corinthians 7:2–5 is a profound text on the mutuality of marriage. This is the only text in Scripture that *does* use the word 'authority' in the context of marriage, but the picture it gives is one of complete equality and no hierarchy. Paul's statements here are utterly radical. Husbands have authority over the wife's body, but before a hierarchy is assumed (which would be natural in his day), Paul states that wives likewise have authority over their husbands' bodies. Paul goes further to show how decisions on sex in marriage should be reached: 'by agreement'. There is no sign of a gender-exclusive command for wives to always submit to their husbands but, rather, an equality of mutual submission. Some try to soften the impact of 1 Corinthians 7 by stating the text is talking about 'just sex' (which would still stand as a direct contradiction to a hierarchical reading of Ephesians 5:24's 'submit *in everything*'). I find this mildly amusing because I don't think I've ever seen the word 'just' followed by the word 'sex' in any other Christian context. No pastor ever advised those in adultery that it was okay because what's taking place is 'just sex'. When we are thinking honestly, Christians recognise that sex is much more than just a physical act but is a deeply spiritual act that goes far beyond the body and is the culmination of two lives being joined together. The argument that 'body' here is *merely* (!) used in relation to sex is further confounded by the use of the word 'body' in 1 Corinthians 6:13–20 where Paul is giving instructions on sexual purity on the basis that our bodies are joined to Christ. Clearly, the word 'body' isn't isolated to the physical act of sex.[25] No matter how uncomfortable it may make some feel, there is no way to get around it. Paul explicitly argues for an equality of authority in marriage in 1 Corinthians 7.

Reason 6: The Equality of Genesis 1–2

To argue that God ordains different roles for men and women where wives are to submit and husbands are to lead is to ignore (or rewrite) the creation narrative. Genesis gives no hint whatsoever that leadership was a role reserved for men. Rather, in direct contradiction to such a claim, it is clear that both male and female were commanded to rule and subdue (Gen. 1:27–28). Complementarians often acknowledge this Genesis verse, whilst saying the 'ruling' of male and female looks different for each gender, by way of different roles with men taking leadership roles and women taking more serving roles. The problem is, if the role the church is insisting on is one of the permanent submission of wives to husbands, then no matter how much we try to pretend otherwise, that role is in direct contradiction to the command to rule in Genesis 1. You cannot actually be ruling if you are permanently to follow another person who intrinsically carries superior authority to you. In that case, the other person is ruling, you are simply following.

Reason 7: The Challenge of the Instructions on Slavery

I believe that Paul was bringing instructions within the structures of his day because he understood how to transform an ongoing conversation from within. I do not believe that we should read an approval of hierarchy from his teachings—that ignores the radical nuances he plants within each instruction. No doubt some will disagree with me. But there is a hermeneutical challenge for those who do so. If we maintain that Paul was pro-hierarchy in husbands and wives, we stand on uneven ground when we try to argue that Paul was *not* pro-slavery. We run into trouble if we simply take the words of Ephesians 5:22–33, assuming an affirmation of authoritative hierarchy, if we do not want to do that with Ephesians 6:5–9.[26] With regards to the biblical teaching on slavery, most scholars today (thankfully!) agree that whilst the Bible may not be completely explicit in denouncing slavery, it certainly sets the course for that trajectory as it plants seeds of equality within references to the reality of slavery in its day (see Paul's letter to Philemon as well as the equality of standing before God mentioned in Ephesians 6:9). For those who disagree that the Bible explicitly teaches equality between men and women, there is still the valid argument of biblical trajectory to overcome. Marshall asserts, 'That there is a general trajectory in Scripture toward a recognition of the equality of men and women in salvation is incontestable.' He goes on to reference the biblical trajectory on slavery and concludes, 'A similar development with regard to marriage is both appropriate and necessary.'[27]

If It's Not Authoritative Hierarchy, What Is It?

Not all the reasons listed above carry equal weight, but together they do form a formidable argument against a complementarian approach to Ephesians 5. We must then ask, if Paul was not stating that husbands are the permanent authoritative head of the house, what was he saying?

I believe Paul was (as he often was!) concerned with the *manner* of behaviour in the body (see the emphasis on manner in the teachings on fathers and children and masters and slaves too). No woman in ancient times needed instruction to submit to her husband—she would be fully aware that was what was expected of her. 'Social conventions of the time, both Greco-Roman and Jewish, expected subordination from the wife.'[28] Seeing as such a teaching would be utterly superfluous, we must look further than asserting that Paul's point was simply that wives should submit. Rather, having stated the need for mutual submission, Paul was teaching wives about the *manner* and *motivation* of their submission.[29] The submission of wives to husbands in godly community is not to be one of robotic (even resentful) obedience but is to be one that is full of honour and respect. Wives are encouraged to see husbands in their role as head—even as Christ is the head of the church—a sacrificial, nourishing, other-preferring, sustaining role. The focus here is not an authoritative head, but rather a life laid down for another. This is essentially the submission of one to another who is already submitted in servanthood.[30] Because of this, the manner of 'mutually submit one to another' from wives to their husbands should be motivated by honour and respect. There's nothing automatic or powerless about such a submission.

Equally, Paul is concerned about the manner that husbands would carry out his instruction of 'mutually submit one to another' in a marriage context. Such a countercultural statement was bound to be a challenge to men who had been told their whole lives that they were the authoritative head of households. But what Paul lays out in the instructions to husbands is something that does not allow for a begrudging or patronising carrying out of Ephesians 5:21. Instead, husbands are instructed to follow a model of such radical sacrificial love that is demonstrated by Christ Himself (vv. 25–27). They are to lay themselves down willingly, not begrudgingly. So too they are to understand that their love is not a patronising bestowing of favour on wives because, ultimately, anyone who loves his wife, actually loves himself (v. 28).

What does Paul's teaching of such a marriage relationship culminate with? Union. The head and body analogy means that man and woman coming together forms one flesh—two parts joining together to form one substance. But what is most profound about 'this mystery' (v. 32) is that the marriage union is not only about the oneness of the man and woman, but reflects the radical nature of what it means for the church to be in union with Christ. It reveals to us God's extravagant, almost scandalous, desire to bring the church into oneness with His Son.

Conclusion

On the basis of the radical instruction of mutual submission, Paul applies kingdom values to assumed structures in his day. In his teaching to wives and husbands, he does not use words about leading or having authority but, rather, presents the parallel ideas of submission and sacrifice and love and respect with great clarity. The idea of an authoritative hierarchy in marriage is a foreign concept to the text. It does not originate in the verses of Ephesians 5. We have often dealt with Ephesians 5 as two opposite actions in the two genders (submit and lead) rather than what the text presents, which is two parallel outworkings of the one action (mutual submission—v. 21). This is further evidenced by the equality of authority in marriage instructed in 1 Corinthians 7 and the equality of rulership in marriage seen in Genesis 1. Paul's teaching in Ephesians 5 culminates in the mystery of being one flesh. A hierarchy is no mystery at all—it was to be expected in the culture of Paul's day. But a union which leads to equality, *that* is a profound mystery.

WOMEN IN THE NEW TESTAMENT

Craig Keener writes, 'The biggest problem with interpreting 1 Timothy 2:11–15 as excluding women from teaching roles in the church is that Paul clearly commended women for such roles.'[1] Clearly, the examples of what Paul and the early church community lived out in practice are important for us in order to gauge whether we have understood Paul's teaching on gender roles correctly. Our conclusions should not only be accurate in theoretical isolation but should be consistent with the practice of the early church. To this end, we will spend this chapter looking a little wider at both New Testament teaching and New Testament examples in order to put flesh and blood onto what we have discussed in theory.

The Inauguration of the Church

Right at the beginning of the church community, we see a beautiful picture of Holy Spirit–activated unity. Acts 1 shows us the tiny seed-bed of the church: 120 people (men and women) gathered together waiting for the coming of the Spirit. These men and women would be revolutionised into fearless witnesses of the risen Christ, transforming the whole world and the rest of history with their testimony.

The narrative of the birthing of the church community provides some details that are pertinent to our discussion. 'The account of Pentecost places considerable emphasis on the unifying power of the Holy Spirit. Men and women "numbering about a hundred and twenty" persons (Acts 1:14–15) were all gathered "together together" (deliberate redundancy in the Greek text, Acts 2:1). The hurricane sound surrounded *all* of them, and *all* of them were singularly designated as recipients of the Holy Spirit with a living flame. They were *all* filled with the Spirit and started speaking in a dozen foreign languages.'[2] The coming of the Spirit signalled a new day for the people of God. No longer was the Spirit given temporarily to certain special individuals, but He was poured out on the entire community to dwell permanently in the temple of His people.

The group was so overcome by the presence and power of the Spirit that they spilled out onto the streets, causing quite a commotion. With the questions (and accusations) from onlookers as to what might be going on, Peter stood up to give what is essentially the church's inaugural address. We will look briefly at the beginning of his message:

> Men of Judea and all who dwell in Jerusalem, let
> this be known to you, and give ear to my words. For
> these people are not drunk, as you suppose, since it
> is only the third hour of the day. But this is what
> was uttered through the prophet Joel:

'And in the last days it shall be, God declares,

that I will pour out my Spirit on all flesh,

and your sons and your daughters shall prophesy,

and your young men shall see visions,

and your old men shall dream dreams;

even on my male servants and female servants

in those days I will pour out my Spirit,

and they shall prophesy ...'

(Acts 2:14–18)

In order to explain what is going on, Peter quotes verses from the prophet Joel about the last days. It is interesting to note that the birthing of the church marks the onset of 'the last days'. As we look through Joel's words, it is clear that the coming of the Spirit signals a levelling of the playing field for all people from all walks of life. The promise from the prophet starts with the Holy Spirit being poured out on *all* flesh (v. 17). There is a glaring absence of Jewish focus here. The Jews that heard Peter's speech would be scandalised by that. God being equally available to all flesh was not part of their understanding. But, nevertheless, in the inauguration of the church, we see that racism and nationalism have no part in kingdom activity. Racial diversity is to be celebrated, but it is not to be seen as a platform for advantage. Joel's prophecy then goes on to note a lack of sexism in engagement with the Spirit—both sons and daughters are to prophesy (v. 17). Whilst there are accounts of female prophets in the Old Testament, the reality is that they are greatly outnumbered by male prophets. But with the pouring out of the Spirit on the new covenant people of God, there is an equality at work for both genders. Life in the Spirit is not male-centric. The revelation of equality continues with the involvement of both young and old. In a society where the youth deferred to the mature, this would be quite remarkable.[3] The point is not who is seeing the visions or dreams. The point is that, no matter the age, all are included in the empowerment of the Spirit. There is neither a 'junior' Holy Spirit nor an 'elderly' One but the same Spirit poured out on all. There is no ageism in the new community that God is building. And lastly, male and female servants have access to that same Spirit. Whether slave or free, God is available to all. Classism has no part to play in the kingdom.

In the deeply embedded social structure of the day, this prophecy was radical. Being a Jew, male, mature in age, or freeman gave you significant advantage over your counterparts in relating to God. But in the age of the Spirit, all of that was to change. This community was to be built on grace, not on background or achievement. Every group, every background is a target of the favour, the power, the gifting, and the person of the Spirit. 'Whereas the Spirit came and went to empower select people for mighty deeds in OT times, now he would indwell and empower *all* believers, irrespective of gender, age, or status.'[4] As Peter used the words of Joel's prophecy to explain the birthing of the church community, he was announcing a completely new way of being the people of God and blowing apart the boxes of superiority that were a fixed marker of religion. 'With the inauguration of the church, God's plan for the ages has come to fruition … The pouring out of the Holy Spirit has an ennobling impact on each individual receiving it … As a result, the old distinctions of race, sex, rank, and class pale into insignificance. That which becomes important is the shared identity and the shared ministry of new covenant believers.'[5]

Whilst diversity is beautiful and undoubtedly part of God's plan, a sense of superiority or a 'head start' based on diversity is utterly foreign to the work of the Spirit. With the dawning of the church, we see that, whilst diversity remains, no one ethnicity, gender, age-group, or social class has greater access to the Spirit's person or power than another. 'In summary, Pentecost essentially "sets the tone" for "Spirit-directed ministry" in the "Spirit-indwelled community" (Bock 2012:374). This ministry is definitional to the church and consists of carrying God's message ... Acts 2 demonstrates that gender equality (of some kind associated with Christian ministry) is characteristic of the New Covenant community.'[6]

Gifts of the Spirit

The equality we see in the narrative of Acts 2 is very much reflected in the teaching about gifts of the Spirit from the apostle Paul. First Corinthians 12 and Romans 12:6–8 display different gifts of the Spirit given as a means of grace to members of the body. The gifts include prophecy, teaching (the same word as used in 1 Timothy 2:12), exhortation, and leading. Not a single one of these gifts is specified to be applicable to one gender (despite the strange choice by some translations to insert masculine pronouns that are absent in the Greek text only in reference to the gifts of teaching and exhortation in Romans 12:7–8). These texts do not give us reason to argue gender qualifications for whichever gift we feel uncomfortable with women operating in, and there is no indication that women may only use their gifts in women-only contexts. Rather, Paul states, 'To each is given the manifestation of the Spirit for the common good'

(1 Cor. 12:7) within the context of instructions about the entire gathered church community.

In addition to the gifts given by the Spirit as seen in 1 Corinthians 12 and Romans 12, Ephesians 4:11–16 talks of gifts given by Jesus to equip the body to grow in every way into the fullness of Christ. The gifts given by Jesus are slightly different to those given by the Spirit, for the gifts given by Jesus are *people* whereas the gifts given by the Spirit are *functions*. The Spirit blesses the church with 'doing' gifts (e.g., prophecy, discerning spirits, etc.). If you can prophesy, that is not who you are, but is something you can do. Each function is given as needed to individuals for the common good. In Ephesians 4, there's a slightly different nuance to the gifts given. Jesus blesses the church by placing in the community 'being' gifts of apostles, prophets, evangelists, pastors and teachers. The nature of the Ephesians 4 gifts is not simply a Spirit-empowered ability. The nature of the Ephesians 4 gifts is a person who embodies an office. If you are the gift of an apostle to the church, that is who you are; it's not just simply one of the abilities you have. Importantly, as with the gifts of the Spirit, the Ephesians 4 gifts are gender inclusive. Ephesians 4 gives no reason to think that women are not given by Christ to the church to be apostles, prophets, evangelists, pastors, or teachers.

By and large, complementarian scholars agree with the gender equality of spiritual gifts as seen in 1 Corinthians, Romans, and Ephesians. Schreiner notes, 'Women share every spiritual gift,'[7] and Blomberg asserts, 'Virtually every thoughtful Bible student today agrees that when these terms [he specifies these as apostles, prophets, teachers, administrators, leaders, evangelists, and pastor-teachers] are used of spiritual gifts, women may receive and exercise them just as powerfully as men may.'[8] However, Blomberg goes on to try to soften what this may look like in practice for women, arguing that we must 'distinguish spiritual gifts from church offices'[9] where women can function in gifts but that does not mean they should occupy the church office of those gifts. This argument is not convincing on two counts. Firstly, it is an arbitrary distinction of authority that Scripture does not give us. On what ground is it possible to argue that he who exercises the Spirit's gift of leadership has less authority than he who is given the title of a leader by the church board? More so, Blomberg's argument fails because it totally disregards the fact that the Ephesians 4 gifts are in and of themselves gifts of office. You cannot take the office out of the person in Ephesians 4 and, as Blomberg states, none of the Ephesians 4 gifts exclude women.

Given the gender inclusivity of the gifts of function and office, it seems that we are on safest ground simply to acknowledge that the gifts given by the Spirit and by Christ to the church are accompanied by no gender disqualifications but assume an equality between men and women. This obviously poses somewhat of a problem for those from a complementarian viewpoint. What does it mean for Christ to give a female apostle to the body to lead it into maturity? What does it mean for women to receive the gift of the 'utterance of wisdom' (1 Cor. 12:8) for the 'common good' of the gathered church? What does it mean for a woman to be given as a teacher to equip the body into fullness in Christ? For those who read 1 Timothy 2:12 as a universal prohibition, these questions are difficult ones to answer without bringing additional qualifiers into the texts. Qualifiers that the apostle Paul does not give.

Galatians 3:28

> There is neither Jew nor Greek, there is neither slave
> nor free, there is no male and female, for you are all
> one in Christ Jesus.

This famous declaration from the apostle Paul has been the basis for much debate within conversations on gender roles. It is a verse that has not always been treated completely fairly, with its ramifications either being somewhat over-exaggerated or unfairly belittled in order to provide support for the different beliefs around gender equality. Blomberg notes these different approaches: 'Most discussions of this passage either claim too little or too much from this one text.'[10] On one side of the spectrum, some complementarians deny that this passage is talking about anything other than salvation and hence relegate what Paul is saying only to the fact that we all are saved through faith in Christ on equal terms. On the other side, some egalitarians use this verse as a trump card as if this one verse automatically silences all others on the subject of race, gender, and status. I find it hard to align myself with either extreme.

It is true, as many complementarians point out, that the wider context of the verse is salvation by faith. Paul spends some time unpacking what living under the law entailed for the individual and the freedom that comes now that 'faith has come' (Gal. 3:25) making us sons of God in Christ Jesus. Hence, verse 28 is revealing that, no matter the ethnicity, gender, or status, we all come to salvation in Christ on equal ground. However, the context of verse 28 alludes to more than just the *moment* of salvation but to a *life* of salvation that has considerably wider impact. The preceding verse talks about baptism—an outward sign of an inner work. Baptism was a marker of being the people of God, and was a remarkably egalitarian one, as it replaced 'the Jewish initiation rite of circumcision that applied only to men.'[11] Tom Wright notes, 'This is not simply a spiritual state resulting from, or consisting in, a certain type of inner experience. For Paul, it is a matter of belonging to a particular community, the new royal family, the Messiah's people; and this family is entered through baptism ... Those who are baptized have thus "put on the Messiah". They are the Messiah's family. As a result, old distinctions cease to be relevant in terms of their status in the family, their standing before God or one another.'[12] Verse 29 follows on with Paul stating that we are not only offspring, but heirs. The context of verse 28, then, is not only isolated to the justification element of salvation but includes the reality of a life of adoption and, hence, seems to have a broader application than some complementarians would have us believe. As Bilezikian states, verse 28 'pertains to the nature of the community of oneness, not just to the point of entrance into it of individual believers.'[13]

Pioneering Women

Thankfully, the Bible does not only give us instructions on what the new community should look like but gives tangible examples of formidable men and women who spent themselves in the service of Christ in order to see His kingdom reach the ends of the earth. The New Testament is littered with the names of heroes of the faith, and, wonderfully, these heroes are not exclusively male. There are examples of women within the pages of the New Testament who operated in all kinds of spiritual gifts and exercised a variety of leadership roles. Blomberg notes, 'Women play a surprisingly prominent role in the early Christian movement',[14] and Hübner states, 'When one realizes the saturated level of androcentricity in the New Testament documents, the cases of women performing various ministerial and "manly" tasks (whether "manly" according to first-century culture or to our own culture today) become all the more significant.'[15] When we pay attention to the named examples in Scripture, we do not see women operating as assistants to men who 'did the stuff', but we see women themselves engaged in strategic and influential roles in the church community. We see women who were deacons (Rom. 16:1 NIV), apostles (Rom. 16:7), prophets (Acts 21:9; 1 Cor. 11:5), evangelists (Phil. 4:2–3), and teachers (Acts 18:26). These are not insignificant examples or roles and would have involved both teaching and the exercising of authority. The example of female prophets is particularly interesting as many scholars note that, 'To be a prophet, in the context of second temple Judaism, was to be a teacher of a kind. "For Paul prophecy apparently is a formal term embracing certain kinds of inspired teaching. The teaching of the prophet appears to overlap that of the teacher and can be distinguished from it only by the manner in which it is given or by the recognised status as 'prophet' of the one who is teaching."'[16] It seems that the only major ministry role that we don't have a named female example of is that of elder, but then we don't have a single male-named example in that role either. Hence, 'Virtually every leadership role that names a man also names a woman.'[17]

All we need to do is take a glance at Romans 16 to know that Paul affirmed, honoured, and trusted women who were known to be in roles of public ministry. It's interesting that 'while Paul greets more men than women here, he commends the ministries of women much more often than the ministries of men.'[18] Paul refers to the women in Romans 16 with the same *ministry* phrases that he refers to the men that he worked with. In verse 1, Phoebe is introduced as a deacon. Priscilla is commended as a 'fellow worker' (v. 3), which is the same ministry descriptor given to Timothy (Rom. 16:21). Mary, Tryphaena, Tryphosa, and Persis 'worked hard in the Lord' (v. 6, 12), a term which 'often describes his [Paul's] own ministry (1 Cor. 4:12; 15:10; Gal. 4:11; Phil. 2:16; Col. 1:29; 1 Tim. 4:10). In some texts, leaders are said to labor, or work hard (1 Cor. 16:16; 1 Thess. 5:12; 1 Tim. 5:17).'[19] Hence, we can see that Paul's level of honour for these women was not communicated in terms of their great *character*, but communicated in terms of their great *ministry*. Let us take some time to look more closely at some of these remarkable women.

Phoebe

Paul entrusts his letter to the Romans to the hands of Phoebe, a *diakonos* of the church at Cenchreae. Despite a number of translations rendering the word *diakonos* simply as 'servant', it is the identical word that is translated as 'deacon' in 1 Timothy 3:8–13. Although both terms are possible, a translation of 'deacon' is more plausible given Paul's addition of the local church context of Phoebe's service. 'In other contexts, a *diakonos* can be a more informal helper of many different sorts, but given that Paul calls Phoebe a *diakonos* "of the church in Cenchreae" (Rom. 16:1), it is likely she is one of its deacons.'[20] Schreiner agrees with this assessment, stating, 'It seems that Phoebe filled an office in Romans 16:1, for she is spoken of as a "deacon of the church at [TNIV, "in"] Cenchreae" (NRSV). The addition of the words "of the church at Cenchreae" after *diakonos* suggests an official position, for it appears she filled a particular role in a specific local church.'[21]

Despite this, some have resisted a translation that would acknowledge Phoebe in a leadership role, arguing that *diakonos* is a masculine term and, hence, 'deacon' must be a male-only role. Belleville aptly refutes this, stating, 'But this overlooks the fact that there was simply no feminine form in use at this time—*diakonissa* ("deaconess") is post apostolic. Nor was it needed, for the masculine singular in Greek often did double duty … This was certainly the way the church fathers understood it.'[22]

In view of the above, it is unsurprising that 'more and more scholars recognise that women served as deacons in the NT (Rom. 16:1; 1 Tim. 3:11), and such a view is confirmed by a reading of early church history.'[23] The uphill battle to see Phoebe acknowledged as a deacon in modern scholarship reveals something of the bias against allowing biblical examples of women to simply speak for themselves. 'Why is it that the translators, when interpreting it [*diakonos*] for men, used the word *ministers*, when for women, the word *servant*?'[24] This is a telling question. On the one hand, complementarians ask for evidence of biblical examples of women in authoritative roles in order to believe an egalitarian viewpoint, and on the other hand, they silence those very examples with translational choices. It is difficult to find an example if it has been all but scrubbed out.

Priscilla

In a number of Paul's letters, as well as in the book of Acts, we see Priscilla (or, more formally, Prisca), who served alongside the apostle Paul with her husband, Aquila. That she was significant in the early church is evidenced by her impact on the apostle Apollos through her teaching (Acts 18:26–28) as well as the number of times Paul refers to her in the context of ministry (Rom. 16:3; 1 Cor. 16:19; 2 Tim. 4:19). Interestingly, Priscilla is mentioned before her husband, Aquila, in four of the six times she is mentioned in the New Testament, including in the references to her teaching (Acts 18:26) and being Paul's co-worker (Rom. 16:3). The New Testament gives us no possibility of seeing Priscilla as Aquila's subordinate but firmly places her alongside him in ministry. Blomberg notes that 'presumably, she was the more prominent partner in some respect, perhaps in their ministry.'[25]

The significance of Priscilla's teaching has been discussed at some length earlier in this book in the chapter on 1 Timothy 2. Suffice it to say that those who want to negate the significance of her actions are forced to place distinctions between what sort of teaching is mentioned in 1 Timothy 2:12 and what sort of teaching is involved in Acts 18:26. Despite these claims, however, the description of Priscilla's role in Acts 18 is precisely the sort of action that is prohibited in 1 Timothy 2. First Timothy 2 is a sentence of singulars not plurals, and attempts to distinguish private vs. public or authoritative vs. non-authoritative biblical teaching fall flat because those distinctions are alien to these New Testament texts. Hence, Belleville states, 'Such distinctions, however, are decidedly modern ones. The NT knows no such distinctions.'[26] No matter how inconvenient she may be to our theological persuasion, Priscilla stands as a firm example of a woman who exercised her teaching gift over a man and had an undeniably significant role in public ministry warranting Paul to mention her in three of his letters which were sent across Asia. Blomberg notes that, in Priscilla, 'at the very least we have a positive example of a Christian woman helping to teach an adult Christian man in the area of religious doctrine.'[27]

Junia

Perhaps one of the most significant New Testament examples of a woman in leadership is a woman who is mentioned in one verse in Romans 16:7: Junia. The significance of this woman is demonstrated by the amount of debate that has surrounded both her gender as well as her ministry. If Junia is indeed a woman and was indeed counted among the apostles, then she poses a significant challenge to those of a complementarian persuasion. In his chapter in Grudem and Piper's *Recovering Biblical Manhood and Womanhood*, Schreiner states, 'Of course, if Junias was a woman apostle (Romans 16:7), then a tension is created between the apostleship of Junias (if Junias was a woman) and the other arguments adduced in this chapter [arguments to limit the role of women in ministry], for apostles were certainly the most authoritative messengers of God in the New Testament.'[28]

To assess the significance of Junia, let us first turn our attention to the question of gender. Is the name *Iounian* in Romans 16:7 to be translated as the feminine Junia or the masculine Junias as some have claimed? Linda Belleville, who has done considerable work on this subject, writes:

Yet there is no reason to read *Iounian* in any way but feminine. Both older versions and translations (Vulg., Syr., Copt., Wycliffe, Tyndale, Great, Geneva, Bishop, KJV, Rheims, Webster, Reina-Valera, Weymouth, BBE) and more recent revisions and translations (NRSV, REB, Revised NAB, NKJV, NCV, NLT, GWT, NET, ESV, CSB, TNIV) render *Iounian* as the feminine Junia. And rightly so. The masculine name Junias simply does not occur in any inscription, on any tombstone, in any letterhead or letter, or in any literary work contemporary with NT writings. In fact, 'Junias' does not exist in any extant Greek or Latin document of the Greco-Roman period. On the other hand, the feminine 'Junia' is quite common and well attested in both Greek and Latin inscriptions. Over 250 examples to date have been documented in Rome alone. Add to this the fact that none of the early versions of the Greek NT considered *Iounian* as anything but feminine … The fact is that no translation or commentary prior to the Middle Ages understood Iounian as other than feminine. Indeed, there is an unbroken tradition in the 'Who's Who' lists from Origen in the third century through Peter Lombard in the twelfth century that not only recognised a female apostle but lauded her as 'notable among the apostles.' John Chrysostom (fourth-century bishop of Constantinople) said: 'How great is the

devotion of this woman [Junia] that she should be
even counted worthy of the appellation of apostle'
(*Hom. Rom.* 31 [on Romans 16:7]).[29]

Despite this, some traditionalists have continued to argue that
Iounian should be translated as the masculine 'Junias', stating that
Iounian was a nickname of the masculine name *Iounianus* (Junianus).
However, this argument has been clearly refuted by a large number
of scholars. *Iounian* is a Latin name, and Latin names were not
typically shortened to form a nickname, but were lengthened to one,
e.g., Prisca to Priscilla. It is Greek names that were shortened to form
nicknames (e.g., Epaphroditos to Epaphras), but as stated, *Iounian* is
not a Greek name. Furthermore, if somehow there was an exception
where *Iounianus* was shortened, the resulting name would be *Iounan*
not *Iounian* because 'when there was a final *i* in the stem of the
shortened name, it was omitted in the transcribing. So the shortened
form of *Iounianos* (if it existed) would be *Iounas*, not *Iounias*.'[30]

In view of the considerable evidence that *Iounian* is a female
name, most scholars now concede the translation of Junia (feminine)
rather than Junias (masculine). Notably, despite detailing the queries
around the gender of *Iounian*, Schreiner states, 'Personally, I believe
a woman is in view. This was the majority view in the history of the
church until at least the thirteenth century. Moreover, a contraction
of Junianus is nowhere else found in Greek literature, and so I think
we can be confident Junia was a woman.'[31]

With regards to the significance of Junia, the second question
that is raised is whether we are to understand that she was part of
the group of apostles herself, or whether she was simply known to

the group of apostles. In other words, does the Greek text *episēmos en* mean 'outstanding among' or 'outstanding in the eyes of' the apostles? 'More recently, the NET and the ESV concede the feminine *Junia* but change the attribution from the long-standing "of note *among* the apostles" to "well known *to* the apostles." The justification for this change is the contention that all biblical and extra-biblical parallels to Romans 16:7 are *exclusive* ("esteemed *by* the apostles," "well known *to* the apostles") rather than *inclusive* ("honoured *as one of* the apostles," "notable *among* the apostles").'[32] However, as Belleville points out, the evidence shows the exact opposite to this assertion. The word *episēmos* literally means 'having a mark' or 'bearing the marks of'[33] and the grammar of the sentence points firmly to an *inclusive*, not *exclusive*, rendering. 'The preposition *en* plus the dative plural with rare exception is *inclusive* "in"/"among" and not *exclusive* "to".'[34] Belleville then goes on to list a number of examples from ancient texts that prove her point exactly. It is unsurprising, then, that Belleville's assertion is echoed by a number of complementarians, including Blomberg: 'Despite attempts of some complementarians to make this mean merely "well known to the apostles," the use of *en* followed by a plural object is far more naturally and commonly rendered "among".'[35] Thus, in view of the evidence, it appears that Junia was not only a woman, but she was also among the apostles.

But before egalitarians start celebrating at such a breakthrough, it seems that complementarians, having had to concede the first two questions, have raised a third objection: what does it actually mean for Junia to be an apostle? Schreiner states, 'It should be noted, however, that the word "apostles" here probably refers to "church planters" or "missionaries" and so does not place Junia and Andronicus at the same level as the Twelve or Paul.'[36] And Blomberg states, 'In contemporary Christian parlance, we would call these people "missionaries" or, if they don't travel too far from home, "church planters". This too is clearly an authoritative role of Christian leadership that includes teaching doctrine to adult men and women, but it was not designed to be an office of local, ongoing church administration and instruction. Properly functioning missionaries should, in fact, be appointing (or perhaps even ordaining) elders to perform this task, thus working themselves out of a job so that they can move on to a new location (Acts 14:23).'[37]

Let us first look at Schreiner's assertion. It is an interesting statement which introduces somewhat of a red herring into the whole discussion. I am not aware of anyone who is arguing that Junia was an apostle exactly like the Twelve or Paul. Surely there is virtually unanimous agreement that the twelve apostles and Paul are in a slightly different category of apostleship to all other apostles, having walked with Jesus and been commissioned by Him in person. But Schreiner's comment somewhat misses the point. The question isn't whether Junia is in the same category of apostleship as the Twelve and Paul, but rather whether Junia is in the same category of apostleship as Barnabas and Apollos and James. To this, there is no reason to answer anything other than in the affirmative, especially given that she is praised for being 'outstanding' in that group. Thus, Junia is in exactly the same category of apostleship as all apostles who have been gifted to the church subsequent to the Twelve and Paul. We may try to soften the meaning by claiming all apostles are just church planters or missionaries (as if those are not roles that exercise authority and involve considerable teaching), but the point remains the same:

in Junia we have an example of a woman operating in the highest authoritative gifting that the modern church experiences.

Blomberg's statement has a slightly different angle from which he tries to soften the significance of having a female apostle. If I am understanding Blomberg correctly, he is arguing that exercising authority in pioneering positions where perhaps your timeline of ministry is months or years before you establish an eldership team (just as would have been true of Paul the apostle's ministry, incidentally) is somehow less significant than the authority that is exercised in that community from that point on. But I find it difficult to follow this line of logic. First Timothy 2:12 neither distinguishes authority based on how long it is exercised nor allows for authority to be exercised as long as the aim is to work yourself out of a job. Keener's response to Blomberg's argument is apt: 'Craig's distinction among different kinds of apostles (to evade the implications of Junia) is arbitrary; apart from "apostles of churches" (in both cases clearly identified as such), Paul uses "apostles" without explanation for those who performed the same sort of missionary tasks as he as an apostle did, a circle larger than the Twelve (1 Cor. 15:5–7). Certainly they exercised more authority (charismatic, but continuous) than local elders.'[38]

Furthermore, it is interesting that both scholars use 'missionary' or 'church planter' here as if those terms are less significant than 'apostle'. It is not clear quite how one would reach that conclusion.

> How does Junia being a 'church planter' or 'missionary' subordinate her in relation to the Apostle Paul—who was precisely that? To define Junia's

apostleship as missionary work is to align it precisely with the work of the apostle Paul. Of course, one may point to the uniqueness of Paul's apostleship in an effort to drive a wedge between Paul and Junia, but this uniqueness (e.g., his conversion on Damascus road, his writing of the numerous NT epistles, his past life as a persecutor of Christians) sets Paul apart from *all* of the other apostles (including the Twelve), not just Junia. Additionally, part of Paul's intent is to align himself with Junia in the first place, calling her and Andronicus 'my kinsmen and my fellow prisoners'.[39]

Sadly, it seems that the obvious conclusions from the example of Junia in Romans 16:7 is what many, in one way or another, are trying to evade. Despite good reason, her significance is resisted and denied. But when we are willing to keep changing the goal posts of the argument in order to justify our original position, one wonders whether the truth is what we're really interested in, or the justification of our premise? Junia has been shown to be both a woman and an apostle. At what point will what is shown of her be enough? At the end of the day, if Junia was who Paul said she was, she stands in direct contradiction to a universal application of 1 Timothy 2:12. We can try to change the definition of apostle or assume time limits on that office to somehow try to hold both Junia's existence and a universal view of the 1 Timothy 2 prohibition together, but those attempts are not viable. I am perplexed as to why Schreiner has not paid heed to his own words as quoted in the beginning of this section: 'Of course, if Junias was a woman apostle (Romans 16:7), then a tension is created between the apostleship of Junias (if Junias was a woman) and the other arguments adduced in this chapter [arguments for placing limits on the role of women in ministry], for apostles were certainly the most authoritative messengers of God in the New Testament.'[40]

Conclusion

In this chapter, we have looked at the birth of the church and how intimacy with the person of the Spirit as well as access to His gifts and power have no gender bias. Furthermore, we have looked at Paul's teaching of equality in salvation life in Galatians 3 and his manner towards powerful women whom he commends and aligns himself with in Romans 16.

The three women we focussed our study on are noteworthy because each one is an example of a woman in an authoritative role in the community of God. These women do not fit the stereotype of what many assume female ministers must look like. They were not children's pastors, women's pastors, or church administrators (these are not insignificant roles in themselves, but the issue is that they should not be seen as limits for what any woman is allowed to do). Most significantly, the example we have in Junia provides us with solid evidence of a woman in the most foundational and authoritative role in the church—the role of apostle. This is no small thing. 'Although today we often think of ministry especially in terms of senior pastors, apostles and prophets were in some sense the highest-ranking ministers of the NT church; whenever Paul lists them among gifts or ministries he lists them first ... they were more prominent than local pastors, and, in at least some churches, "prophets and teachers" apparently *were* the pastors (Acts 13:1).'[41] Hence, the named examples of women in ministry give us serious reason to doubt the legitimacy of any teaching that claims that God intended for there to be a limit on the roles women can have. These examples don't justify such a claim.

Paul's teaching in practice in his day looked like female apostles, prophets, teachers, evangelists, deacons, and ministers of various descriptions (and we have no reason to believe elders were not included in this list) springing up and receiving public honour for their ministry. What does Paul's teaching in practice in our day look like? I wonder what is springing up in the wake of what we teach on gender roles? If the fruit of our teaching does not match the fruit that Paul saw, then perhaps it's time for us to go back to the drawing board, for we must not be portraying his words correctly.

GENDER EQUALITY AND THE TRINITY

By way of introduction to this chapter, let me ask you a few questions: Who do you think is in charge in the Trinity? Out of Father, Son, and Spirit, who gives the orders and carries the greatest authority? Is one of them the leader, or do they all lead in various ways? Orthodox Christianity adheres to the belief that the members of the Trinity are all equal and all God, but what does that actually look like in the practicality of how they make decisions and how they relate to one another? Although we may never have thought about these questions, what we believe about how God operates and whether there is a chain of command in the Trinity can significantly impact our beliefs about gender roles.

A few years ago, I was teaching a class on the book of Ephesians, and we got into some interesting territory as I started talking through marriage roles in chapter 5. Not being one to shy away from controversial topics, I led us into a discussion that became quite passionate as students asked questions and gave their views on the idea of headship. During the discussion my friend who leads the school (and whom I greatly respect) said something that just didn't sit right with me. In defending the idea of male headship, he pointed to how even Jesus had said the Father is greater than Himself. And so having men as 'greater' than women in headship must be a good and beautiful thing, just as it is in the Trinity. In the moment, I found myself ill-equipped to answer him but felt uneasy about the ramifications of his assertion. Of course, I don't disagree that Jesus made that statement—it's recorded right there in John 14:28. But I found my brain grappling with the question, 'Surely that doesn't mean that the Father is *actually* greater than Jesus ... How does an equal Trinity even exist if one member is greater than the other ...?'

Despite my unfamiliarity with the assertion at the time, the argument that my friend raised is not an uncommon one. Many see the Father in a role akin to being the CEO of the Trinity with Jesus and Holy Spirit submitted to His purposes. See, for example, Wayne Grudem's assertion that 'the Son and Holy Spirit are equal in deity to God the Father, but they are subordinate in their roles.'[1] In this model, the Trinity operates in a hierarchy with the Father at the top of the ladder. But the argument doesn't end there. In recent years, Trinitarian theology has been used by a number of scholars (e.g., Grudem, Ware) as a basis for views on gender. In these arguments, the role of men is linked to the role of the Father and the role of women is linked to the 'subordinate' role of Jesus. Grudem takes the correlation even further than most by arguing that, 'The husband's role is parallel to that of God the Father and the wife's role is parallel to that of God the Son ... And, although it is not explicitly mentioned in Scripture, the gift of children within marriage, coming from both the father and the mother, and subject to the authority of both father and mother, is analogous to the relationship of the Holy Spirit to the Father and Son in the Trinity.'[2] How Grudem arrives at that conclusion is somewhat of a mystery, and Kevin Giles' comment on this analogy is telling: 'This family picture of God has nothing to do with the revealed doctrine of the Trinity. It sounds more like Greek mythology.'[3]

Before we get into the full swing of discussion here, I want to clarify a few things in case I am misunderstood.

Firstly, it *is* possible to believe one thing about the ordering of the Trinity and something entirely different about ordering in gender roles. Being made in the image of God does not mean that we reflect absolutely everything about Him (anyone been omnipresent lately?), and therefore, just because something is true about God does not necessarily prove that the same is true of us. There are complementarians who believe that there is no hierarchy in the Trinity, and there are egalitarians who believe that there is. And there are egalitarians (such as myself) who believe in no hierarchy in the Trinity but do not believe that the latter view is necessarily justification for the former. Despite this, for many Christians, convictions around ordering in the Trinity *do* greatly impact their understanding of whether hierarchy is part of God's plan for how men and women are to relate. Hence, I believe this chapter is an important one to include in this book.

Secondly, I believe doctrine of the Trinity to be of priority over beliefs on gender roles. For this reason, if we believe there is a correlation between the Trinity and gender roles, let us be careful to use the former as our starting point, and not the latter. We are walking on dangerous ground when we superimpose what we believe about gender onto the Trinity rather than allowing beliefs about the Trinity to shape our understanding of gender roles. In modern scholarship, there has been some concern that over the last few decades the gender debate has wrongly influenced deeper truths about the Trinity in order to justify convictions on the roles of men and women. This concern is reflected in books such as Erickson's *Who's Tampering with the Trinity?* which discusses this problem in some depth.

Finally, the question of hierarchy in the Trinity is a complex one, and I am not assuming that this chapter is sufficient to address all the intricacies of the topic. My aim is to raise some salient points of discussion and hope that this might prompt some further thinking and study for those who find it of interest. With that being said, I offer this chapter as an introduction for those who wish to use the Trinity as a platform for discussions on gender roles.

Getting Our Bearings

Genesis 1:27 shows the creation of male and female being modelled after the Trinity—men and women together reflecting something of the Godhead. Because of this, some would argue that what we believe about relationships between the persons in the Trinity should have a decisive impact on what we believe about relationships between men and women.

If the perfect Trinity operates with a permanent chain of command where one member is the eternal 'Head' and the others work in submission to that Head, then it is not beyond the realm of possibility that human relationships were created to operate in this way, reflecting the One who made them. If we believe that Father, Son, and Spirit carry different levels of authority, we may be justified to believe men and women, though equal in value, were created with gender-based differences in authority in order to reflect this. Grudem argues in support of this: 'Because God in himself has both unity and diversity, it is not surprising that unity and diversity are also reflected in the human relationships he has established. We see this first in marriage ... Here, just as the Father has authority over the Son in the Trinity, so the husband has authority over the wife in marriage.'[4]

Conversely, if the members of the Trinity all carry equal authority and therefore do not operate with any authority-based hierarchy, arguing for a permanent authoritative hierarchy between men and women can be more difficult. If hierarchy is not a feature of the Trinity's relationship in perfection, should it be a feature of how men and women relate? If the persons of the Trinity all have equal authority to lead, command, and act depending on the moment, then perhaps male/female relationships that model themselves on the Trinity should reflect more of this fluidity where both men and women have the authority to step up to lead as the needs of the moment demand.

Historical Debate

Questions about authority and hierarchy in the Trinity are not new. Right at the beginning of the church's history, debates arose as to the nature of relationships within the Trinity. In the third and fourth centuries, heresies such as Arianism (which claimed that Jesus was a created being and hence inferior to God the Father) and Modalism (which claimed that the Trinity is just one person with three different expressions) arose. Around the same time, councils gathered to address these issues with particular focus on the relationship of Jesus to the Father. In the Council of Nicea (AD 325) Arianism was firmly rejected as heresy. Out of that council came the Nicene Creed declaring: 'We believe in ... one Lord Jesus Christ, the only-begotten Son of God, begotten of his Father [before all worlds]; (God of God), Light of Light, very God of very God, begotten, not made, being of one substance with the Father.'[5] The council was clear. Jesus was begotten not created. But, before being 'begotten' makes us assume He is somehow less, they followed up that assertion with a series of ways of saying one thing: in every way Jesus is exactly equal to the Father. Furthermore, the Nicene council declared to believe in 'One Lord, Jesus Christ'. This is significant. 'Lord/*Kurios* is the name of God in the Greek OT. In this confession, we are therefore saying we believe the "one Lord", identified as Jesus Christ, is God without any caveats, yet not a second God. In other words, we are confessing Jesus Christ to be Yahweh, omnipotent God.'[6]

It is interesting to note that, as with the Nicene Creed, other early church creeds (e.g., Niceno-Constantinopolitan Creed, Chalcedonian Creed, Athanasian Creed) affirm the equality of substance between the Father and the Son, but not a single one states an eternal subordination of the Son to the Father, nor defends any functional inequality in roles or a hierarchy of authority.[7] In other words, the creeds are univocal in their understanding of a Trinity who is equal in *every* way, rather than equal in essence alone like some claim. Because of this, Giles argues that 'the divide on the Trinity is not between evangelical egalitarians and complementarians but between creedal and confessional evangelicals and non-creedal and confessional evangelicals.'[8]

Modern Debate

Today, debate on the question of Trinitarian authority continues with two main camps of thought having emerged in evangelical circles. Though they have one central point of disagreement, they broadly agree on these points:

1. All persons in the Trinity are fully God and are equal in essence, value, and worth. Both those who argue for a hierarchy in the Trinity and those who argue against strongly support the view that in substance all members of the Trinity are equal.[9] This emphasis is a vital one to distance modern scholars who believe in Trinitarian hierarchy from the early church heresy of Arianism.

2. During the incarnation, an authoritative hierarchy was present in the Trinity where Jesus was functionally subordinate to the Father.[10] Whilst on earth, Jesus submitted Himself to the authority of the Father. Both groups agree that this subordination of Jesus during this time was only functional (based on what He did) not ontological (based on who He is). Pertinently for me, given my friend's assertion that led me to this study in the first place, this belief makes sense of Jesus' statement, 'The Father is greater than I', as well as the many other moments we see Him holding the Father in a position of authority over Himself.

The crux of the debate, then, rests on one issue. Is the hierarchy that we see during the incarnation a *permanent* reality of how the Trinity operates, where the Father carries the greatest authority and Jesus and Holy Spirit carry incrementally less, or was the hierarchy present during the incarnation a *temporary* reality necessary only for Jesus to fulfil His role in incarnation and redemption? In other words, is Jesus eternally subordinate to the Father because He intrinsically carries less authority, or was He only temporarily subordinate in order to fulfil His role in redemption? The first view sees hierarchy as an essential component of the nature of the Trinity, while the second sees hierarchy as a component of the role of incarnation and redemption—but no further.

In order to work towards a conclusion, we will take some time to look through Scripture together. The difficulty, of course, is that it is possible to find scriptures to support both viewpoints quite adequately. The truth is that finding a verse and being able to quote it doesn't alone justify a strongly held view. We have to tread more carefully than that. Yes, we've got to see what individual verses say, but then we've also got to look further at what fits most consistently with the breadth of Scripture. We need Holy Spirit wisdom to navigate this complicated topic. You will note that, for the most part, our study will focus on the relationship between the Father and Jesus. This is because that is where the majority of scholars base their arguments, but clearly, the logic of authoritative structure is to be extrapolated to Holy Spirit as well.

As we look at Scripture, we will ask ourselves three broad questions:

1. Do the names of the persons of the Trinity communicate something about their individual authority?

2. Do the roles carried out by persons of the Trinity communicate something about their individual authority?

3. Do our glimpses of the Trinity's eternal positioning communicate something about their individual authority?

The Names of the Trinity: What's in a Name?

Are the names Father, Son, and Spirit significant in and of themselves in communicating the authority of each person? From a human perspective, the name Father seems to carry more authority than either the names Son or Spirit. Is that what we are to understand in the revelation of these names?

Grudem argues exactly that, proposing that the very names Father and Son reveal a difference in authority and, therefore, necessitate a difference in role. He states,

> The Father and the Son relate to one another as a father and son relate to one another in a human family: The father directs and has authority over the son, and the son obeys and is responsive to the directions of the father. The Holy Spirit is obedient to the directives of both the Father and the Son ... the role of commanding, directing, and sending is appropriate to the position of the Father, after whom all human fatherhood is patterned (Eph. 3:14–15). And the role of obeying, going as the Father sends, and revealing God to us is appropriate to the role of the Son ...[11]

Since the names Father, Son, and Spirit are used outside of the incarnation, there is reason to believe that, for all eternity, the Father has roles of authority that are appropriate to one who bears that name, and the Son and Spirit have roles of lesser authority that are appropriate to their names.

But there is a significant problem with this kind of thinking. Giles notes that the gospel of John uses a word that is later echoed in the Nicene Creed of Jesus' Sonship. This is the word *monogenēs* which means 'only' in the sense of being entirely unique.

> John uses the word *monogenēs* of Jesus Christ five times (Jn 1:14, 18, 3:16, 18, 1 Jn 4:9). This designation of the Son was deliberately included in the creed because it explicitly excludes the disastrous error made by all the Arians of various brands, namely that human sonship defines divine sonship. All the Arians argued that because Jesus Christ is called the Son of God he is like a human son, he is subordinate to and must obey his father. What this clause in the creed is saying is that Jesus' sonship is *not* like human sonship. There is something about his sonship that is absolutely different to creaturely sonship.[12]

There is a difficulty, then, with Grudem's argument because his approach is the wrong way round. What he knows about human sonship is what he argues for in Christ's Sonship. But given that Christ is a Son in an entirely unique way, that mode of argument is unlikely to lead to an accurate understanding of who Jesus is (and in turn, who the Father is).

Instead, when we look to Scripture to define what the name 'Son' signifies, we get a markedly different picture to what we might assume from human sonship. New Testament writers do not make a correlation of subordination to a greater authority as they reveal Jesus as Son to the Father but rather view Sonship to God as a revelation of *equality and likeness*. John 5:18 tells us, 'This was why the Jews were seeking all the more to kill him, because not only was he breaking the Sabbath, but he was even calling God his own Father, making himself equal with God.' For the Jewish audience of Jesus' day, claiming to be the Son of God did not equate to being less than the Father but put Jesus on equal footing with the Father. If the writers and hearers of Jesus' day did not associate subordination with the name 'Son', then perhaps it is wise for us not to either.

This equality of the Son with the Father is further supported in the messianic prophecy spoken of the Son, 'His name shall be called … Everlasting Father' (Isa. 9:6) and Jesus' statement in John 14:9, 'Whoever has seen me has seen the Father'.

In view of the above, it is difficult to see how the names Father, Son, and Spirit can be used to prove a permanent difference in authority in the persons of the Trinity. There is nothing explicit in Scripture to support that view, and John 5:18 and Isaiah 9:6 stand as somewhat contradictory verses to such an assertion, as does the description of Jesus as the *monogenēs* Son.

The Names of the Trinity: Order

Another idea that has been put forward in relation to the names of God is that there is a very particular ordering which indicates the order of their authority. Ware describes this order of names or taxis: 'There is an ordering in the Godhead, a "built-in" structure of authority and submission that marks a significant respect in which the Persons of the Godhead are distinguished from one another ... The order is not random or arbitrary; it is not Spirit first, Son second, and Father third, nor is it any way other than the one way that the early church, reflecting Scripture itself (Matt. 28:19), insisted on: Father, Son, and Holy Spirit.'[13] Ware's argument rests heavily on the ordering of the Godhead as seen in the Great Commission. He asserts that Matthew 28 is the definitive ordering supported by Scripture and the early church.

To further prove his point, Ware points to 1 Corinthians 11:3 to provide evidence for his argument of taxis being a signal to us of a permanent authoritative structure in the Trinity: 'I would argue that 1 Corinthians 11:3 offers a truth-claim about the relationship between the Father and Son that reflects an eternal verity. That God is the head of Christ is not presented here as an ad hoc relationship for Christ's mission during the incarnation. It is rather stated as an absolute fact regarding this relationship. God is the head of Christ. The Father has authority over the Son. There is a relationship of authority and submission in the very Godhead on which the other authority-submission relationships of Christ and man, and man and woman, depend.'[14]

But Ware's assertions are easily refuted. As we look through New Testament writings, it becomes apparent that the earliest church fathers did not use a permanent ordering for the Trinity at all. 'In the roughly 70 times where the New Testament writers associate together the three divine persons, sometimes the Father is mentioned first (Matt 28:19); sometimes the Son (2 Cor 13:13[14]) and sometimes the Spirit (1 Cor 12:4–6).'[15] If there is an ordering or taxis of the Trinity that is to prove an authoritative hierarchy, the New Testament writers are not aware of it. Additionally, Ware's argument on 1 Corinthians 11:3 rests entirely on the assumption that the word 'head' in each couplet means 'authority over' thus creating the authority-submission relationships that will support his point. However, as has been argued earlier in this book, there is solid opposition to a translation of 'head' to mean 'authority over' in 1 Corinthians 11:3. Giles notes, 'This is not a trinitarian text; the Spirit is not mentioned, and it would seem that the Greek word *kephale* (Eng. "head") almost certainly carries the metaphorical meaning of "source". Woman comes from man (Adam) (1 Cor 11:8, 12) and the Son comes "from" the Father.'[16]

The Roles of the Trinity: What You Do Is Who You Are

The next question we want to consider is whether we can see exclusive roles carried out by each person in the Trinity and, if so, whether these roles are evidence of an authoritative hierarchy at work. Is one member of the Trinity permanently carrying out roles that would be associated with being the leader, or are there some examples of role crossover?

If the Father is essentially 'in charge' and Jesus and Holy Spirit follow Him, then Scripture would show very clearly boundaried roles, both inside and outside the incarnation, where the Father is exercising His leadership according to His will and Jesus and Holy Spirit are seen to act in submission to the Father's initiative. Most importantly, if the roles are ordained based on the authority of each person, then that would make any role overlap impossible—because that would mean certain persons in the Trinity overstepping the boundaries of their authority.

A brief study of the New Testament certainly seems to suggest that the Father is the one who initiates His purposes within the Trinity. For example, a look at Ephesians 1 reveals the Father choosing us even before creation (v. 4), the Father predestining adoption through Christ according to His will (v. 5), and the Father making His purposes known in Christ (v. 9). Romans 8:29 follows this pattern of the Father working out His will and purposes—He foreknew, He predestined—all before the incarnation took place. Then we have the verses in John's gospel (Ware counts over thirty instances[17]) clearly showing that Jesus was sent in order for the incarnation to take place at the Father's bidding (e.g., John 3:16; John 10:36). These verses set a strong case for the Father being the one working out His will with Jesus (and Holy Spirit) acting in submission to His plan.

However, whilst these verses are significant and certainly show the Father taking the lead in these instances, more is needed to prove that these roles are decided on the basis of *authority*. To demonstrate this, we must show that there are no moments where Jesus or Holy Spirit are the ones initiating or leading in the Trinity. An authoritative hierarchy can only be proven if roles that would be associated with one who is 'in charge' are exclusively seen to be carried out by the Father.

The Roles of the Trinity: Exceptions

Digging a little deeper into this idea we encounter a few inconsistencies:

a. We have noted that the Father is seen as the One who chooses and elects. What then do we do with verses where Jesus is claiming to be making those choices (John 5:21; John 13:18; John 15:19)?

b. We have many examples of the Father being the One who leads and initiates. But Matthew 4:1, Mark 1:12, and Luke 4:1 give a rather different view with Holy Spirit (who, following the logic of an authoritative hierarchy, has the least authority in the Trinity) leading Jesus—or even stronger, driving Jesus—into the desert. Jesus submits to the Holy Spirit's leadership and follows His prompting. But if the full logic of hierarchy is to be applied, this is not a role that is appropriate for Holy Spirit if He is indeed inferior in authority to Jesus.

c. A glance at Scripture may lead us to believe that the Father takes the role of Judge in the Trinity (Job 36:31; Ps. 9:8; Ps. 50:6; Isa. 33:22; Rom. 3:6; Heb. 12:23), and this would certainly make sense if He is the one carrying the most authority in the Trinity. But what then do we do with Jesus the 'righteous Judge' in 2 Timothy 4:8 and Jesus' teaching on judgement in Matthew 25:31–46 where 'The Son of Man comes in his glory, and all the angels with him, then he will sit on his glorious throne. Before him will be gathered all the nations, and he will separate people one from another.' The Father isn't even mentioned here—it is the *Son* on *His* throne in *His* glory at the consummation of the world, and *He* is acting judge. Further questions arise from John 5:22–23. In verse 22, we see the Father gives over the role of judging to the Son, which may lend support for seeing the Father with superior authority. But then we're told the intention is for the Son to be recognised as on equal footing with the Father, which would suggest the opposite of subordination. And then John 8:16 raises further questions—for now the Father and Son are making the same judgements.

Beyond these areas of overlap, we also see the Father and Son both sending Holy Spirit into the world (John 14:26; 15:26; 16:7);

Father, Son, and Spirit all dwelling in those who are in Christ (John 14:23; 1 Cor. 3:16; 2 Cor. 13:5; Col. 1:27); Father, Son, and Spirit all giving gifts (Matt. 7:11; John 10:28–30; 1 Cor. 12:11; Eph. 4:7–11; James 1:17); the Son and Spirit both making intercession for us (Rom. 8:26–27; Heb. 7:25); the Son and Father both receiving prayer (Luke 23:46; Acts 7:59–60).[18] Thus, Erickson states, 'The various works attributed to the different persons of the Trinity are in fact works of the triune God.'[19]

Erickson's view is by no means a novel one. In reference to the Father's sending of the Son in the incarnation, which could be seen as the Father's superior authority at work, the early church father Augustine states: 'For perhaps our meaning will be more plainly unfolded, if we ask in what manner God sent His Son … certainly it was done by a word, and the Word of God is the Son of God Himself. Wherefore, since the Father sent Him by a word, His being sent was the work of both the Father and His Word; therefore the same Son was sent by the Father and the Son, because the Son Himself is the Word of the Father …'[20]

Augustine's interpretation, then, views the action of sending not isolated to the Father, but inevitably inclusive of the Son, who is the very Word which commands the sending.

The Roles of the Trinity: Obedience

Let us look at two more scriptures together to bring a final angle to this discussion on Trinitarian roles. It has been asserted that while the Father's role is one of Leader and Initiator, the Son's role (by virtue of His Sonship) is obedience to the Father's leading. Are there any examples from Scripture that would contradict this view? Some scholars point to Philippians 2:5–11 to argue that Jesus is not an example of a subordinate Son, eternally following commands, but a demonstration of a Son who is fully God, willingly laying Himself down for His creation. On this, Bilezikian states, "'He humbled himself" (Phil. 2:8). He was not forced to become a servant; he was not compelled to be obedient; he was not dragged to his death against his will. The Bible puts it tersely: "He humbled himself." Therefore it is much more appropriate, and theologically accurate, to speak of Christ's self-humiliation rather than of his subordination. Nobody subordinated him, and he was originally subordinated to no one. He humbled himself.'[21]

Echoing this idea, but perhaps stating it even more strongly, is the assertion of Hebrews 5:8, 'Although he [Jesus] was a son, he learned obedience through what he suffered.' There are two fascinating things about this verse. Firstly, it denies that obedience is something that was eternally true of Jesus. Rather, it claims that Jesus had to *learn* it. Secondly, it denies that obedience is an inherent outworking of Sonship. The writer of Hebrews uses the word *kaiper* ('although'), expressing that Jesus' learning obedience was *despite* His Sonship, not because of it. This verse then directly opposes the assertion that Jesus was eternally subordinate and in obedience to the Father by virtue of being a Son. If there was a point at which Jesus learnt obedience, then there was a point at which He was not familiar with it.[22]

As we draw the discussion on Trinitarian roles to a close, we must admit that Scripture *does* have more verses that reveal the Father's role as initiating and taking the lead. But the problem for those who claim that His leading is on the basis of His inherent authoritative superiority is that there are examples of exceptions to this which considerably weaken that argument. Additionally, both Philippians 2 and Hebrews 5 give us reason to believe that a viewpoint of an eternal chain of command in the Trinity is simply inaccurate, with the Son not knowing obedience prior to the incarnation. In addition to these scriptures, Augustine's insight into the involvement of Father and Son in the very sending of the Son endorses an alternative non-hierarchical lens through which to approach Trinitarian roles. In Augustine's understanding, the Trinity is working in collaboration, not hierarchy.

The Eternal Position of the Trinity: Reigning Supreme

The final question we want to look at is whether the glimpses of eternity we get in Scripture tell us something about the authority of the persons in the Trinity.

There are repeated references in Scripture that show us Jesus sitting at the right hand of the Father after His ascension (e.g., Matt. 26:64; Acts 7:55–56; Rom. 8:34). For some, this positioning of Jesus is indicative of His lesser authority, where the Father takes the central throne and invites Jesus to a place of privilege, but not equal authority. Grudem states, 'Nowhere is this pattern reversed. Nowhere is it said that the Father sits at the Son's right hand. Nowhere does the Son give the Father the authority to sit with Him on His throne. The supreme authority always belongs to the Father.'[23]

A difficulty to Grudem's claim is that, although the majority of references reveal Jesus sitting at the Father's right hand, there are verses that show us Jesus seated on the Father's throne itself (e.g., Rev. 3:21; Rev. 12:5). Furthermore, in Revelation 22:3 the throne of God and of the Lamb are one and the same. If Jesus' right-hand position is reflective of His inferiority of authority, wouldn't sitting on the Father's throne or having the same throne as the Father be an overstepping of His authority?

In this section, the most compelling scriptural support for a permanent hierarchy in the Trinity comes from 1 Corinthians 15:24–28:

> Then comes the end, when he delivers the kingdom to God the Father after destroying every rule and every authority and power. For he must reign until he has put all his enemies under his feet. The last enemy to be destroyed is death. For 'God has put all things in subjection under his feet.' But when it says, 'all things are put in subjection', it is plain that he is excepted who put all things in subjection under him. When all things are subjected to him, then the Son himself will also be subjected to him who put all things in subjection under him, that God may be all in all.

It is argued that the introductory words 'Then comes the end' signify that these verses are not simply talking about Jesus' ministry in incarnation but that they reveal an eternal reality: 'Unless there is strong evidence in Scripture showing a later change in that situation (which there is not), the passage leads us to think that that situation will continue for eternity.'[24]

However, again there are difficulties with holding this position. The challenge to using this text to support a hierarchical view stems from the context of this passage focussing on Jesus as the second Adam, and the verses themselves looking at the conclusion of Christ's redemptive work. Paul is taking great pains in this section to bring revelation of Jesus' humanity—highlighted further in his quoting Psalm 8 which is about everything being made subject to *mankind*. It seems that Paul is making a case for the fullness of Jesus' humanity being made subject to the fullness of the divinity of God. Jesus, as the second Adam, fulfils all that the first Adam failed in. Hence, on conclusion of His redemptive function, Jesus as the second Adam hands the kingdom to the Godhead in His humanity, fully submitted to Father, Son, and Spirit.

Calvin explains it as such:

> But Christ will then restore the kingdom which he has received, that we may cleave wholly to God. Nor will he in this way resign the kingdom, but will transfer it in a manner from his humanity to his glorious divinity because a way of approach will then be opened up, from which our infirmity now keeps us back. Thus then Christ will be subjected to the Father, because the veil being then removed, we shall openly behold God reigning in his majesty, and Christ's humanity will then no longer be interposed to keep us back from a closer view of God.[25]

Interestingly, significant scholars who have argued for Trinitarian hierarchy disagree that this passage should be used in support of it. For example, Charles Hodge states:

> The subjection here spoken of is not predicated of the eternal Logos, the second person of the Trinity, any more than the kingdom spoken of in v. 24 [1 Corinthians 15] is the dominion which belongs essentially to Christ as God ... the word Son here designate[s], not the Logos as such, but the Logos as incarnate ... It is not the subjection of the Son as Son, but of the Son as Theanthropos [God-man] of which the apostle here speaks ... the words αὐτὸς ὁ υἱὸς, the Son himself, here designate, as in so many other places, not the second person of the Trinity as such, but that person as clothed in our nature.[26]

Thus, the context of 1 Corinthians with its focus on the humanity of Christ gives us reason to approach this text not as a revelation of Trinitarian roles in eternity, but as a revelation of the consummation of the redemptive role of the God-man Jesus Christ.

Again, we may find Augustine helpful in providing insight here. Augustine states that, in approaching scriptures concerning the Son of God, we must distinguish between Jesus as God and Jesus as a servant:

According to the form of a servant He [Jesus] is less than the Father, because He Himself has said, 'My Father is greater than I;' and He is less than Himself, because it is said of Him, 'He emptied Himself;' and He is less than the Holy Spirit, because He Himself says, 'Whosoever speaketh a word against the Son of man, it shall be forgiven him; but whosoever speaketh against the Holy Ghost, it shall not be forgiven him.' … According to the form of God, all things were made by Him; according to the form of a servant, He was Himself made of a woman, made under the law. According to the form of God, He and the Father are one; according to the form of a servant, He came not to do His own will, but the will of Him that sent Him …[27]

Seeing Jesus through this bifold lens helps us answer the question of whether Jesus is fully equal to the Father: 'And not, therefore, without cause the Scripture says both the one and the other, both that the Son is equal to the Father, and that the Father is greater than the Son. For there is no confusion when the former is understood as on account of the form of God, and the latter as on account of the form of a servant.'[28]

Does It Make Sense?

I have one final thought on the topic of hierarchy which is not one based in Scripture, but one based in logic. In the end, we must ask whether it is really possible to believe that God in essence is the same if God in authority is intrinsically different. Despite the verses that are presented from those who argue for hierarchy, I remain unconvinced (along with many scholars) that the argument of 'equal in essence, different in authority' can logically hold its weight if the difference in authority is part of the permanent intrinsic make-up of the person. The difficulty of arguing for functional *inequality* whilst trying to maintain ontological *equality* becomes obvious in the writings of some who come suspiciously (if not explicitly) close to asserting an ontological subordination of the Son despite the deviation from orthodoxy that this assertion requires.

Take, for example, the writings from the early church father Novatian in the third century:

> In receiving, then, sanctification from the Father, He [Jesus] is inferior to the Father … Now, however, by declaring that He has received sanctification from the Father, by the very fact of proving Himself to be less than the Father, by receiving from Him sanctification, He has shown that He is the Son, and not the Father. Besides, He says that He is sent: so that by that obedience wherewith the Lord Christ came, being sent, He might be proved to be not the Father, but the Son, who assuredly would have sent had He been the Father; but being sent, He was not the Father, lest the Father should be proved, in being sent, to be subjected to another God.[29]

Novatian's argument for an eternal subordination of the Son to the Father appears to be on the basis of a lot more than function. Certainly his assessment that the Son is 'less than the Father' and his belief that being sent proves being 'subjected to another God' suggests an argument for something somewhat deeper than being equal in essence but different in function. In view of this, it is interesting that Ware, who cites Novatian to support his view of a purely *functional* eternal subordination, simply brushes past this: 'Clearly Novatian means only here that the Son follows the Father's command and submits to the Father's will.'[30] However, as Erickson rightly notes, 'It does not seem so clear that this is all that Novatian means.'[31]

Novatian is not alone in blurring the lines. Charles Hodge suggests a subordination beyond the carrying out of roles when he writes that the subordination of the Son and Spirit occurs in 'the mode of subsistence and operations of the persons.'[32] Robert Letham asserts that 'There is not only an order in the economy [function] of redemption but also in the eternal ontological relations [being] of the persons of the Trinity … The revelation of the economic Trinity truly indicates the ontological Trinity.'[33] These texts demonstrate that it is difficult, if not impossible, to press the point of an eternally subordinate Christ in function without losing something of His equality of essence in the meantime.

If it is by nature of being Father that the Father has authority over the Son, and by nature of being Son that the Son is subordinate, we get into territory where the nature of these two persons of the Trinity have necessary differences which go directly against orthodox Christianity's understanding that their natures are one. As Erickson aptly states:

The problem is this. If authority over the Son is an essential, not an accidental [moment specific], attribute of the Father, and subordination to the Father is an essential, not an accidental, attribute of the Son, then something significant follows. Authority is part of the Father's essence, and subordination is part of the Son's essence, and each attribute is not part of the essence of the other person. That means that the essence of the Son is different from the essence of the Father. The Father's essence includes omnipresence, omniscience, love, etc., and authority over the Son. The Son's essence includes omnipresence, omniscience, love, etc., and submission to the Father. But that is equivalent to saying that they are not *homoousious* [of the same substance] with one another. Here is surely a problem for the gradationists, for they want to affirm the *homoousious*, in order to reject Arianism. On face value, therefore, there seems to be an internal contradiction in this doctrine.[34]

Conclusion

We have looked at a number of passages of Scripture as well as the thoughts of some well-respected early church fathers and scholars throughout this discussion on Trinitarian hierarchy. As mentioned at the opening of this chapter, conclusions on the Trinity should not necessarily impact conversations on gender roles, however, given how some scholars have argued gender on the basis of the Trinity, this chapter has been an important inclusion in this book.

In our survey of Scripture, we have noted how Jesus, in acknowledging God as His Father, outraged the religious teachers of His day for assuming equality with God. Alongside this we have noted how the early church creeds took great care to teach the equality of the Son to the Father in *every* way and described the Son as *monogenēs* (only, unique) lest we should compare His Sonship with earthly sonship. We have seen how there are many verses that reveal the Father in a leading and initiating role but that there are examples of role exceptions which suggest that leading is not a role reserved for the Father on the basis of superior authority. We have explored how Augustine's suggested lens through which to see Christ helps us understand Him as subordinate in His redemptive role but equal in His divinity. And finally, we have seen how difficult it is to argue for an isolated functional subordination without encroaching into ontological territory.

Though this discussion has been brief in view of the weightiness of the subject, my hope is that I have demonstrated how there is compelling evidence to view the Trinity not as a hierarchy of authority and command, but as a profound and beautiful collaboration of three distinct persons of equal value, authority, and substance. Whilst this conclusion may not justify egalitarian gender roles, it does form a rebuttal to those who seek to rationalise arguments for a hierarchy between men and women on the basis of Trinitarian hierarchy. There is not enough evidence for such an approach.

EGALITARIANISM IN PRACTICE

A number of years ago, I had a dream which had a profound impact on me, even to the extent of defining how I live my life today and how I serve in ministry. In my dream I was back at work as a doctor in emergency medicine. As I was going about my duties, I looked down and noticed that my badge did not display my name, but displayed a man's name. I started panicking as I realised that for whatever reason I had decided to pretend to be a man while I did my job, rather than use my ordinary badge with my name on, and do my job as myself. The majority of the dream entailed me fighting anxiety as I tried to see to my patients, aware that at some point someone would realise that I was not the man the badge said I was. I kept beating myself up in the dream, thinking to myself, 'I have my own badge! I am a doctor under my own name! Why did I pretend to be a man to do my own job?' I woke from the dream with a start and with the images and feelings still vivid within me. In that moment, I heard God speak to me a warning: 'If you try to do what I have called you to do as a man rather than as a woman, what you do will become illegitimate. I have called you as a woman. Minister as a woman.'

So far in this book we've spent a considerable amount of time looking through biblical passages and themes in order to weigh up whether an egalitarian belief system is a viable option from Scripture. Underpinning all that we have discussed is a question of equality. An equality not only in *value* (which is where most complementarians would focus to define the word), but equality too of *authority* and an equality in opportunities to pursue our call. If we have come to the conclusion that complete equality *is* God's intention for humanity, what do we do in order to make that a practical reality? How do we work out equality in our church teams and marriages in a meaningful way?

But, crucially, as my dream pointed out, how do we work out equality in a way that does not deny or nullify the differences that are present in being male and female? A pursuit of biblical equality should not try to blur the lines between male and female or seek to form a genderless society, but a pursuit of biblical equality should level the playing field for both genders in order to allow for them to be the fullest expressions of themselves as male and female. It sounds great in theory. How do we go about this in practice? This question is one that I am extremely passionate about.

Over the last few years of journeying with a growing number of church leadership teams, and in experiencing the wonderful adventure of marriage, my husband, Julian, and I have discovered some possible ways of pursuing biblical equality that do not come at the expense of the diversity of gender, but end up putting that diversity on display in a beautiful way.

This chapter is an offering from what we have learnt together. The suggestions I make here are by no means a comprehensive list, but I trust that they might prove helpful for those who are looking for a way to start.

Equality in Church Teams
Permission vs. Pursuit

I have come to the conclusion that permission is insufficient. If we want to see equality in our churches, we will have to go further to an intentional *pursuit* of women. What I mean by this is that simply saying, 'Our women are now allowed to do anything that the men can do' is not enough to engage women to fully express all the gifts that are in them. Women have been the underdogs for many generations. Permission alone will not bring them out from that place. It is up to those who are in leadership and who have the advantage of experience and training to actively pursue those they see around them who are recognised to have gifts in seed form that can be nurtured and encouraged into maturity.

This takes an intentionality and a willingness to count the cost in the short term. For example, many churches currently are male-heavy in leadership. When those men want to train others or invite others into travelling opportunities with them, the most natural choice is to choose other men. Men training men feels natural and keeps traditional safety boundaries for those who are concerned to protect the morality of their teams (although these safety boundaries obviously do not take into account any issues of same-sex attraction). This way of doing things, however, will inevitably continue to sow and reap inequality in our leadership teams because women will consistently be at a disadvantage in training. In the short term, our teams may need to think of different ways of training. Some might end up having to count a greater cost to travel with a group of trainees so that women can be included. The point is, intentionality of pursuit is what is needed beyond simply saying that women are allowed to do whatever they feel God is leading them to. That places too heavy a load on women to take initiative in contexts where they often do not feel brave or equipped enough to do so. If we are serious about raising teams where both genders are treated equally, then our job as leaders is going to get more complicated in the short term in order to see a much healthier expression of church in the long term.

Assess Your Culture

I have lost count of the number of times women have spoken to me who are struggling in their roles in church leadership teams because whilst they are told they are welcome in that team and that their role is valuable, the underlying culture betrays something quite different.

There are many ways to make people feel unwelcome or insignificant. It is important for those who wish to pursue greater equality in their teams to assess the underlying culture represented in the room. What are the jokes like in your team? Think about whether they would make women feel included or excluded. Team leaders, how do you describe and defend the role of your women when you are questioned by other leaders? Are you committed to backing your women even when others treat them as somehow less than the men in the room? How does your team respond to emotion? Would women feel safe to get passionate about something in your team meeting without feeling like they would be assessed as 'overly emotional'?

The funny (well, sad) thing is that when men get passionate, people tend to see that as a good thing, but when women do the same, people tend to see that as emotional. Equally, when men take the lead, people tend to view that as leadership skill, whereas when women take the lead they are often viewed as bossy. Men who dominate a room are viewed as 'A-type leaders', whereas women who are dominating are viewed as controlling and difficult. My point isn't to say that all of these behaviours are healthy in leadership, but to point out a bias that often exists between how we view the same behaviour in the two genders. If we are able to recognise the existence of this bias, then we can start asking ourselves and our teams why this bias exists and what we can do to resolve it.

The problem is, if we do not change our team cultures to make them more inviting for women, one of two things is likely to happen:

1. Women will stop showing up. Perhaps they will simply stop coming to the meetings or ask for less responsibility so that they don't have to attend. Or perhaps they will attend but will just retreat into themselves and not speak up. You will lose out on the gifts these women have to offer.

2. Women will start adopting more and more of a masculine expression as they use their gifts in order to feel heard. We will end up with women who downplay their femininity in order to legitimise being in the room. This is not an issue of women simply refusing to wear make-up or choosing to no longer wearing high heels. This is a serious problem where women feel fearful to shine as *women*— whatever that looks like for them—in case that display of who they

are might make them assessed as less worthy to be listened to. If we feel uncomfortable about the secular agenda to erase the lines between genders, then we should feel uncomfortable with women feeling the need to adopt greater masculinity or downplay femininity in our church settings in order to feel that they can use their voice.

My aim in saying all of this is not that we create a culture where the men are frightened of offending the women and women end up being wrapped up in cotton wool out of respect for their sensitivities. Rather, what I am trying to argue for is that we work hard to create contexts where both men and women can feel the freedom to be the best expression of themselves without fear of being belittled or excluded. That is no small task. It will require creating a culture of honesty where your team is able to speak of what they experience in the culture that is already present. It will require really listening to the fears and concerns of women. It will require changing habits that we may not be conscious of in order to change the messages that we are sending with how we speak, the words we use, our body language, etc. Some of this may feel so unnatural in the beginning but will be well worth the effort if we create a culture in our churches in which both men and women will be able to come alive.

Platform vs. Influence

The conversation around equality in churches has sometimes been reduced to an issue of platform, where we're almost keeping count of how often women are allowed to be up on the stage in preaching or hosting meetings, rather than allowing the discussion into the much wider arena of who we are open to having genuine influence and authority in a leadership setting. The proof of equality in your church is not simply limited to how many times you have women preaching on your stage, but includes how much women are able to influence the back room leadership conversations. If women are excluded (whether explicitly or culturally) from exerting influence in leadership team settings, then I have to ask how much equality is actually at work in that context.

Now, before I am misunderstood, let me get one thing straight. I have no desire to see women included simply because they are women. My intention is to see women included because they are *gifted*. This means that I am not advocating for churches to fill up a quota of women preachers or women leaders simply so that the numbers reflect equality. In that way we end up dishonouring gifting at the expense of gender. However, if we genuinely make room for gifting, regardless of gender, we will find that over time our leadership teams, as well as our church platforms, see an increasing number of women flourishing there because the gifts of the Spirit have no gender bias. There are fantastic women gifted to lead just as there are fantastic men gifted to do so—do our teams reflect this?

Equality in Marriage

Whilst I have spent the last few months researching and writing this book, my husband, Julian, has taken on the lion's share of family life and home administration in order to facilitate my work in this season. In other seasons, there are times when he is preaching and I'm taking care of the children, and times when I'm preaching and he is taking care of the children. For us, we have made a decision to work hard to facilitate seasons of favour for each other where we back each other's gifts and make room for them to shine in a very practical way. We have made this decision out of a conviction that that is what the Trinity is like. In the beautiful dance of the Trinity—*perichoresis*—Father, Son, and Spirit move around one another, preferring one another, allowing one to represent the whole in different moments as there is need. I love that the Trinity works to consistently put the spotlight on each other. I believe the best marriages work like this, where the role of one is not to permanently serve the other, but the role of both is to serve each other in order to together change the world.

Because of this, Julian and I flesh out the practicalities of our marriage based on gifts and abilities rather than gender. He does not take all the 'leadership' roles, leaving me with all the 'serving' roles, in order to assert a leadership headship over me. Rather, we believe that we are called to mutually submit to each other, and the best way to do this is to submit to each other in each other's strengths and gifts. His submission is best expressed in servant love. My submission is best expressed as an outworking of honour and respect.

When we first got married, I was better at administration and finances than Julian, and so he submitted to my organisation of our finances and spending. Since having two babies, my capacity for numbers has taken a downward spiral, and I now gratefully submit to Julian's leadership in that regard. For each part of our lives we agree to follow whichever one of us is better to meet the need of the moment. I tend to take the lead in high-risk moments, being a bit more comfortable with risk-taking than Julian. He tends to take the lead in securing our family, being much better than me at taking the time for due diligence. Our marriage would not be well served if Julian was simply in charge of all things because he is a man. Equally, our marriage would not be well served if it were the other way around! There is a dance of preferring one another that we are learning to do according to gift and moment, and in those moments we see the wonderful, mysterious beauty of marriage on display. Of course, there are many moments when we fall short of the ideal picture I've painted above. But this is the picture we are pursuing and the one we see bringing the greatest blessing to our marriage relationship and to our family.

In 1 Corinthians 7, Paul talks of married couples making decisions, particularly about sexual intimacy, 'by agreement' (v. 5). Given that sexual intimacy reflects the very heartbeat of marriage unity, I believe this is a great model to follow for all marriage decisions. To journey together to come to an agreement. Of course, we will not always see eye to eye on everything, but that is when the reality of mutual submission is displayed in all its glory, where we make decisions in preference of what the other is seeing, and submit to whoever has the biggest strength in that area.

The reality is that what I have described above is probably reflected in many marriages where the spouses adhere to complementarian theology. The practical outworking of one spouse permanently being an authoritative head and the other being in permanent submission makes for an unhappy marriage if fully enforced in all aspects of life. I am not aware of many complementarians who would push headship to this meaning in the everyday reality of how they relate to their spouse. Happy marriages tend to have an element of mutual submission, regardless of our theological beliefs on paper.

A Few Sticking Points

To finish this chapter, I want to take the time to look at three concerns that are often raised at the practical implications of egalitarian theology. Firstly, some have raised concerns over the rising tide of militant feminism. Doesn't egalitarianism risk slipping into a secular feminist agenda? Secondly, some are concerned over the loss of the diversity of male and female expression if we push for complete equality in all spheres of life. Thirdly, some question whether adopting egalitarian theology will inevitably lead us onto a 'slippery slope' of adopting liberal ideology around sexuality. Though there is much that can be said on these questions (well beyond the scope of this book), I will offer a few thoughts on each.

Feminism

I am not a feminist. I know this statement may surprise some or offend others, so let me explain. I wholeheartedly believe that men and women are completely equal (in value, authority, and gifting) and that women should be allowed to flourish every bit as much as men. In this regard I suspect that my belief system echoes the heart of many who would identify as feminist, and in that case I can completely adhere to feminist thought. However, I am becoming increasingly aware that biblical egalitarianism and feminist ideology (particularly in its militant form) are on somewhat different trajectories because of the reality of very different starting points and different end goals. And so, whilst I sympathise with and would stand alongside the majority of those who call themselves feminists, I disagree with some fundamental roots of strict feminist ideology.

Unlike biblical egalitarianism, the starting point for feminism is not God or His Word, but the female experience.[1] Feminism is a system of thought built primarily around the experiences of women and the injustices that women have suffered. That the experiences of women are important and significant I have no doubt. It is the fact that they appear to be the core impetus to the ideology that is of concern. If we focus on the experiences and injustices women have suffered, then everything that has caused these or allowed these experiences becomes an evil that needs to be eradicated. The more militant arm of feminism seems to be on a trajectory to bulldoze any thought or person who does not affiliate themselves with the elevating of female experience. I would question where the gospel of mercy and grace fits in such a fervent push to resolve the injustices done to women at seemingly any cost. Such an ideology leads to beliefs that women are the only ones who have a right to dictate what they should do with their bodies. If they choose promiscuity, it is their legitimate choice. If they choose abortion, it is their legitimate choice. The outworking of such feminist thought gives rise to an idolatry of women's 'rights' in a way that is completely disconnected from the plans, purposes, and boundaries of God.

Furthermore, it is difficult to see where God fits in the picture with militant feminism. I am reticent of any worldview that is more focussed on Him fitting into our story than us fitting into His. Militant feminism seems to have defined its own trajectory outside of the trajectory of God and His kingdom. This sense of 'we can define ourselves' in feminism has vast implications, not least of which on the defining of gender and sexuality outside of biological parameters.[2] The problem is, of course, that we *cannot* define ourselves (not accurately, anyway). Without Jesus as our defining lens, our worldview will get increasingly skewed which I believe is exactly what is driving the feminist agenda in a dramatically different direction to biblical egalitarianism.

In many ways, militant feminism has set its course to stand against systems of hierarchy and distinction.[3] The difficulty, for the Christian, is that the Bible is filled with legitimate systems of hierarchy and distinction. There are distinctions between God and His creation. There are distinctions (at the very least, in biology) between male and female. There are distinctions between humanity and the rest of creation. There are distinctions between good and evil. The blurring of distinctions in a drive to end all hierarchy has a concerning trajectory towards the Godhead where even 'God and our view of God must be liberated.'[4]

Whilst the above almost certainly is not true of everyone who would claim to be a feminist, the full trajectory of strict feminist ideology is one that concerns me and is not one that I would align myself with.

I believe in equality between men and women. I believe that God created men and women with this inherent equality. But I believe that men and women fit into the beautiful, redemptive, unstoppable kingdom of God, and *that* is where both men and women can truly find themselves and express their equality legitimately. Anything else to this is simply a counterfeit.

To those who are then concerned by the rising tide of militant feminism, I would say I wholeheartedly agree with your concerns.

However, I would suggest that the *precipitant* of feminism is not biblical egalitarianism but, rather, the continuing oppression of women. If the church were to rise up and present a gospel of equality in its fullness, the vacuum that restrictive theology has contributed to would be filled with truth instead of allowing room for the counterfeit ideology of militant feminism to take hold.

Diversity

The second concern that is often raised is that of the loss of diversity of male and female expression. As we pursue equality in all contexts and open all roles to men and women, do we not risk losing what it means to be male and female? Are we not somehow blurring the lines and forcing humanity into some sort of androgynous way of life?

Whilst I understand the concern, research into the impact of egalitarian societies suggests the exact opposite of such an assumption. In societies where there is greatest equality between men and women, far from seeing a uniformity between men and women, a much greater diversity is seen.

Jordan Peterson talks of this paradox:

> You'll find the relevant studies—they've been done with tens of thousands of people—and what they've showed quite clearly is that in those societies where the most has been done to move the social world into a position of radical equality (and so that would roughly be the Scandinavian countries because they've done more of that than any other

country), the personality differences between men and women maximise, they don't minimise, they maximise ... In the countries where the most has been done to equalise the playing field between men and women, men and women get more different rather than more the same.[5]

He points out how paradoxical this might seem:

It's very strange because no one would have really believed that, right? You make society more the same and men and women get more different? It's like what's up with that? Well the answer seems to be is that there's fundamentally two sources of variability in personality ... you can categorise them as roughly genetic and roughly sociological. Well if you take out all of the sociological differences between the landscape in which men and women are raised then all you have left are the biological and genetic differences, so they maximise. Well that's exactly what's happened. And this actually matters. It really matters.[6]

Despite our fears, then, modern research seems to be telling us the exact opposite of what many complementarians have stated is a potential problem of egalitarian theology. As it turns out, recognising equality of value, authority, and opportunity in both men and women does not stunt the diversity between genders nor does it blur the lines of distinction. Equalising the playing field actually *increases* the differences seen between male and female.

Sexuality

Lastly, many complementarians harbour a concern that those who adhere to egalitarian theology have 'softened' the truths of Scripture, and hence any adoption of egalitarianism is likely to lead to a 'softening' of many other teachings in Scripture, not least of which in matters of sexuality and the endorsement of LGBTQ lifestyles.[7] Arguments for gender and sexuality are viewed with suspicion as cultural norms that are infringing on biblical truths and seeking to overthrow them.

A number of years ago, a friend warned me that my pursuit for greater freedom as a woman would inevitably lead me into a 'slippery slope' where I would set aside what Scripture teaches on homosexuality in favour of cultural standards. Adopting arguments for one would undoubtedly lead to adopting arguments for the other.

Despite the popularity of this viewpoint, however, there is good reason to conclude otherwise. Without making comment on the merit of either argument, a survey of the *basis* of each argument reveals that they are not as related as some suppose.

In recent years, the sexuality debate has become intermingled with identity where much weight has been placed on the fact that sexuality is a foundational determining factor of who we are. Thus, arguments often rely on the defining right of sexuality. For those who argue for gender equality, however, the crux of argument relies on something quite different. Where the discussion on the endorsement of LGBTQ lifestyles relies on sexuality as a defining force, the discussion on gender equality relies on *spirituality* as its defining force. Those who argue for gender equality argue that being 'in Christ' is the ultimate definer, not gender, or sexuality, or anything else for that matter. Hence, Kroeger notes, 'Some argue that if a church ordains women despite the few passages seeming to restrict women, then it ought also to ordain homosexuals. But this is to mix apples and oranges. First and foremost, women maintain that they are spiritual beings, made in the image of God ... In contrast, some homosexuals maintain that their sexuality defines their very essence.'[8]

Secondly, when we come to verses that refer to homosexual practice, they are consistent and unwavering throughout the Bible. In contrast, verses that are relevant to gender equality give a much greater tension of revelation within the breadth of the Bible and require us to wrestle with the question of how to reconcile all the verses into one coherent message. 'Though only a few biblical texts speak of homoerotic activity, all that do mention it express unqualified disapproval. Thus, on this issue, there is no synthetic problem for New Testament ethics. In this respect, the issue of homosexuality differs significantly from matters such as slavery or the subordination of women, concerning which the Bible contains internal tensions and counterposed witnesses. The biblical witness against homosexual practices is univocal.'[9]

Thirdly, whilst there are multiple 'exceptions' and standout examples of women who operated outside of what more restrictive passages on gender roles would suggest (e.g., Junia, Phoebe, Priscilla), these are notably lacking for any homosexual practice. 'The New Testament offers no accounts of homosexual Christians, tells no stories of same-sex lovers, ventures no metaphors that place a positive construal on homosexual relations.'[10]

Fourth, for those who believe biblical trajectory to be important (which would presumably include anyone who wishes to argue that the Bible is not pro-slavery), scriptures on homosexual practice and those on gender equality head in different directions. The former stays consistently negative. For gender roles, however, there is a progressive positive trajectory of increasing freedom and opportunity for women throughout Scripture.

Finally, when we come to look at the purpose of restrictive teaching on homosexuality and gender roles respectively, we encounter something different for each. For homosexuality, there is no mention in any of the verses that there is a temporal purpose attached to the restriction. In contrast, restrictive teachings on gender roles consistently highlight a purpose for that teaching.[11] First Timothy 2 highlights peaceability as its aim (something which was sorely lacking in the Ephesian context). First Peter 3:1 highlights its purpose as evangelistic, and Titus 2:5 states its teaching is so that 'the word of God may not be reviled.'

Each of the above points underlines how different the basis of argument for gender equality is from arguments that steer towards an endorsement of homosexual practice. My aim in pointing these out is not to give a conclusive view on the Bible's teaching on homosexuality—that is not the purpose of this book—but simply to bring enough of a comparison between the foundations of the two arguments to show that seeing these as two interlinked ideas is a mistake.

Hence, despite what some have feared, there is no inevitable adoption of a less conservative stance on sexuality as a result of egalitarian theology. Such a concern finds its footing in the assumption that egalitarianism is primarily influenced by secular culture and follows a similar reasoning to arguments for the endorsement of homosexual lifestyles. However, in this section I have sought to show that this is not a fair assessment and that conclusions on the one do not necessarily impact on conclusions on the other.

Interestingly, Scripture gives us much more reason to link the idea of slavery with that of gender equality. Both are rooted in recognising that our union with Christ is what ultimately defines us. Both slavery and gender equality follow the same positive trajectory pattern in Scripture with seeds of freedom being sown with greater momentum as we enter into the revelation of the new covenant. As with gender roles, teaching on slavery often points to a temporal purpose, most commonly the furthering of the gospel (see for example the teachings to slaves in 1 Timothy 6:1 and Titus 2:9–10).[12] Furthermore, there are notable standout examples for slavery (e.g., Onesimus) as there are for gender roles. All of these raise the question why many are comfortable with adopting a biblical trajectory stance when it comes to the issue of slavery, but are reticent to do so when it comes to gender equality.

Concluding Thoughts

This chapter has sought to address a few of the practicalities and implications of egalitarian theology. For those who are wanting suggestions of how to start implementing increasing equality both in church teams as well as in marriages, I hope some of my stories and suggestions will prove to be of some benefit. For those who have had some concerns about the implications of egalitarian theology in practice, I hope the last section in this chapter has at least provided some food for thought. Far from accelerating the decline of our generation, I believe egalitarian theology may well prove to be an antidote; opening the world's eyes to the beauty that God intended right from the beginning and empowering men and women to be all that He has made us to be in order to bring His kingdom into greater reality on the earth.

CONCLUSION

> In the nineteenth century, the central moral challenge was slavery. In the twentieth century, it was the battle against totalitarianism. We believe that in this century the paramount moral challenge will be the struggle for gender equality around the world.[1]

I had just preached my heart out at a conference hosted by a group of churches well known to me. This family of churches has gone on quite a journey with their views towards women, and in the last decade or so, doors to women have been opening increasingly so that today women are given room to preach on local and trans-local platforms. At the end of the meeting, a wonderful older lady who has been part of that group of churches for most of her life came to me with eyes brimming. The look on her face is still fresh in my mind despite the number of years that have passed since that moment. As tears fell down her face, she said to me, 'When I look at you, I can't help but think what might have been. But it's too late for me now.'

As she spoke, the privilege of what I get to walk in dawned on me, as did the weight of responsibility to make this freedom *count*. Not only is this book important to me for the sake of generations to come, but it has become important to me in order to honour generations that have passed; generations of men and women with Evangeline Booths and Heidi Bakers and Jackie Pullingers in seed form who never found themselves in environments that allowed them to be who they were made to be. Of course, we all have individual responsibility to pursue what God tells us with all our might, but our environment can be so pivotal to that pursuit, can't it? I am so grateful for the stakes in the ground that women like those mentioned above have put in place for women like me to follow. I just wonder how many others were destined to be world changers just like those women and yet never came to full fruition, sitting in pews hearing that they were somehow less than the male counterparts sitting beside them.

I believe we are living in a generation where the tide is turning on the issue of gender equality. Though the world has its own agenda and version of what it's pushing for, I believe that God is orchestrating a much more life-giving turning of the tide within the church and for the sake of the world, where men and women will rise up *together* to bring His kingdom on the earth.

In this book we have looked at some of the most debated scriptures that are at the centre of the battlefield for gender roles. We have also spent time addressing some themes which often find themselves involved in these discussions. I am not naive enough to think that I am 100 percent correct on everything I have said or that I have been able to provide conclusive proof on every point. However, what I have sought to do is to show that biblical egalitarianism is not a viewpoint only for those who hold the truths of the Bible more casually than others. This could not be further from the truth. The more I have read, the more I have encountered men and women who care deeply about the words they find in Scripture and have given themselves to pulling out the true meaning of the treasures they find within. I hope that I have built enough of a case to show that egalitarian theology stands on solid ground and there are very good reasons to believe that when God made male and female, He did so using an equal scale.

We have seen how in Eden both the man and woman were given the mandate to rule together. We have seen how Jesus was radical in how He released women to be so much more than the culture of His day thought appropriate. We have seen how Paul's discussions in Corinthians are not a good basis to limit gender roles and that it may well be that Paul was quoting Corinthian slogans that he disagreed with, in which case he was saying the exact opposite of what traditionalists have thought. We have seen that the context of the book of 1 Timothy is integral to its interpretation, and given Paul's use of peaceability to frame his ideas, his unusual terminology for authority, his careful grammar in 'I am not permitting', and that his interactions with women elsewhere was positive, it is highly unlikely that 1 Timothy 2 was his universal thesis on the behaviour of all Christian women. We have seen that 1 Timothy 3 is not a good basis of argument against women elders—and that many influential complementarian scholars would not use it to argue to this end. We have looked at Paul's teaching on marriage and seen how his teaching in Ephesians is built on an understanding of mutual submission, and that his teaching in 1 Corinthians 7 is built on an understanding of an equality of authority. We have seen how Paul wholeheartedly recommended and honoured women who were in public ministry and who undoubtedly held positions of significant authority, including apostleship. Furthermore, we have looked at discussions around the Trinity and assessed whether these discussions should have a bearing on our conclusions on gender. Suffice it to say, the breadth of reasoning for an egalitarian interpretation on gender roles is quite remarkable. Despite this, some maintain that egalitarianism stretches Scripture in order to reach its conclusions. Perhaps it is more true to say that egalitarianism stretches our traditional sensibilities instead?

I have recently been asked why I take all of this so seriously and why I speak so passionately on a topic that has been subject to different interpretations. I am astonished that people would need to ask such a question with the state of the world as it is. If full equality is what God always purposed, then complementarian theology will only serve to rob the destinies of Christian women as well as significantly hinder those of Christian men.

And its negative impact will not stop there. Although complementarians assert that they, like egalitarians, believe that men and women are equal, the world, alongside many Christians, is not buying the rhetoric of 'less authority and less opportunity still equates to equal value'. We can keep insisting that all we're talking about is a difference in roles, but scratching beneath the surface, what we're really talking about is an inherent difference in authority. A complementarian worldview cannot help, however subliminally and unwittingly, to communicate to the world that women are, on some level, less than men.

I believe this is contrary to what the church was designed to teach and model. A message of inequality is not a message the world needs any reinforcement of, given that women are recognised as the most oppressed people on the planet today. An essay written in 1990 asserted that globally 'more than 100 million women are missing.'[2] Since then it has been concluded that 'every year, at least another 2 million girls worldwide disappear because of gender discrimination.'[3] Studies show that 'girls in India from one to five years of age are 50 percent more likely to die than boys the same age. The best estimate is that a little Indian girl dies from discrimination every four minutes.'[4] The more statistics you read, the more heartbreaking they become. 'It appears that more girls have been killed in the last fifty years, precisely because they were girls, than men were killed in all the battles of the twentieth century. More girls are killed in this routine "gendercide" in any one decade than people were slaughtered in all the genocides of the twentieth century.'[5] And it goes on and on and on.

If the destinies of Christians are not enough to wake me up from apathy over the role of women in the church, these statistics certainly cause me to sit up and take notice. We are foolish if we do not believe that what we preach inside the church has the potential to radically impact the outside world. And so, for those who wonder why I may get 'overly emotional' on this issue, here is my response. There is simply too much at stake not to. Destinies are being robbed and the world is dying. Correction, the *female* world is dying. And it's time for the male and female church to rise up and be all that she was purposed to be in order to rebuild ancient ruins. I believe this is part of God's mandate on every Christian today.

It is time for us to honestly, humbly, and openly reassess what the church has declared to be God's intention towards women. There is too much at stake to simply 'tow the party line'. Each of us as believers in Christ has a responsibility to dig deep *for ourselves* and come to a conclusion in good conscience. What we cannot do is simply follow the current (which courses equally powerfully in conservative religion as it does in secular feminism) at the cost of the destiny of so many in the body and at the cost of the lives of so many in the world.

Two centuries ago, a man by the name of William Wilberforce had the audacity to defy a theology that the church had been defending with regards to slavery. Destinies and lives were being robbed and still the church insisted that they were following the purposes of God. Here we stand again at a crossroads having to decide whether our interpretation of Scripture is a true reflection of God's heart. For my daughter's sake, I hope that we will have the courage of Wilberforce.

NOTES

Introduction

1. Written by Nicholas D. Kristof and Sheryl WuDunn.

Chapter 1—From Eden to Eternity

1. Gilbert Bilezikian, *Beyond Sex Roles* (Kindle edition) (Grand Rapids, MI: Baker Academic, 2006), 19–20.

2. Bilezikian, *Beyond Sex Roles*, 24.

3. Richard S. Hess, 'Equality with and without Innocence: Genesis 1–3,' in *Discovering Biblical Equality, Complementarity without Hierarchy*, ed. Ronald W. Pierce, Rebecca Merrill Groothuis, Gordon D. Fee (Downers Grove, IL: Inter-Varsity Press, 2004), 84.

4. Linda L. Belleville, 'Women in Ministry: An Egalitarian Perspective,' in *Two Views on Women in Ministry*, ed. Stanley N. Gundry, James R. Beck (Grand Rapids, MI: Zondervan, 2005), 30.

5. For a more thorough argument through particularly points 1 and 3, see Bilezikian, *Beyond Sex Roles*, 159 (footnotes 10 and 11).

6. Belleville, 'Women in Ministry,' 30.

7. Craig L. Blomberg, 'A Response to Linda Belleville,' in *Two Views on Women in Ministry*, ed. Stanley N. Gundry, James R. Beck (Grand Rapids, MI: Zondervan, 2005), 115.

8. Belleville, 'Women in Ministry,' 27.

9. Craig S. Keener, 'A Response to Craig Blomberg,' in *Two Views on Women in Ministry*, ed. Stanley N. Gundry, James R. Beck (Grand Rapids, MI: Zondervan, 2005), 185–86.

10. Hess, 'Equality with and without Innocence,' 87–88.

Chapter 2—Jesus and Women

1. Leonard Swidler, 'Jesus Was a Feminist,' God's Word to Women, www.godswordtowomen.org/feminist.htm.

2. Swidler, 'Jesus Was a Feminist.'

3. Kenneth E. Bailey, *Jesus through Middle Eastern Eyes* (London: SPCK, 2008), 190.

4. Bailey, *Jesus through Middle Eastern Eyes*, 190.

5. David P. Gushee and Glen H. Stassen, *Kingdom Ethics: Following Jesus in Contemporary Context*, 2nd ed. (Kindle edition) (Grand Rapids, MI: Eerdmans, 2016), 237.

6. Kenneth E. Bailey, *Finding the Lost Cultural Keys to Luke 15* (Kindle edition) (St. Louis, MO: Concordia, 1992), loc. 266–91.

7. Aída Besançon Spencer, 'Jesus' Treatment of Women in the Gospels,' in *Discovering Biblical Equality, Complementarity without Hierarchy*, ed. Ronald W. Pierce, Rebecca Merrill Groothuis, Gordon D. Fee (Downers Grove, IL: Inter-Varsity Press, 2005), 133.

8. See, for example, James A. Borland, 'Women in the Life and Teachings of Jesus,' in *Recovering Biblical Manhood and Womanhood*, ed. John Piper, Wayne Grudem (Wheaton, IL: Crossway, 2006), 121–22.

9. Spencer, 'Jesus' Treatment of Women,' 136.

10. Spencer, 'Jesus' Treatment of Women,' 136.

11. Bailey, *Jesus through Middle Eastern Eyes*, 195.

12. Tom Wright, *Surprised by Scripture* (London: SPCK, 2014), 70.

13. Bailey, *Jesus through Middle Eastern Eyes*, 193.

14. Bailey, *Jesus through Middle Eastern Eyes*, 193.

15. R.J. Kernaghan, *Mark* (Downers Grove, IL: Inter-Varsity Press, 2007), 188.

16. Danielle Strickland, *The Liberating Truth* (Kindle edition) (Oxford: Monarch, 2011), loc. 1120.

17. Bailey, *Jesus through Middle Eastern Eyes*, 201.

18. Bailey, *Jesus through Middle Eastern Eyes*, 220.

19. Bailey, *Jesus through Middle Eastern Eyes*, 208.

20. Craig L. Blomberg, 'Women in Ministry: A Complementarian Perspective,' in *Two Views on Women in Ministry*, ed. Stanley N. Gundry, James R. Beck (Grand Rapids, MI: Zondervan, 2005), 143.

21. Gilbert Bilezikian, *Beyond Sex Roles* (Kindle edition) (Grand Rapids, MI: Baker Academic, 2006), 72.

22. Wright, *Surprised by Scripture*, 70.

23. Wright, *Surprised by Scripture*, 72.

Chapter 3—1 Corinthians 11: Hierarchy by Design?

1. Alan F. Johnson, *1 Corinthians* (Downers Grove, IL: Inter-Varsity Press, 2004), 180.

2. Lucy Peppiatt, *Women and Worship at Corinth* (Eugene, OR: Cascade Books, 2015), 5, 68–69.

3. Craig S. Keener, *1–2 Corinthians* (Kindle edition) (New York, NY: Cambridge University Press, 2005), loc. 1301.

4. Philip B. Payne, *Man and Woman, One in Christ* (Grand Rapids, MI: Zondervan, 2009), 118.

5. Payne, *Man and Woman*, 119.

6. Payne, *Man and Woman*, 129.

7. Payne, *Man and Woman*, 129.

8. See Chrysostom's extended discourse on this in Peppiatt, *Women and Worship at Corinth*, 88–91, and Payne, *Man and Woman*, 132–33.

9. Gordon D. Fee, 'Praying and Prophesying in the Assemblies: 1 Corinthians 11:2–16,' in *Discovering Biblical Equality, Complementarity without Hierarchy*, ed. Ronald W. Pierce, Rebecca Merrill Groothuis, Gordon D. Fee (Downers Grove, IL: Inter-Varsity Press, 2005), 151, citing *Ad Arcadiam et Marinam* 5.6.

10. Payne, *Man and Woman*, 117.

11. Fee, 'Praying and Prophesying,' 142.

12. Payne, *Man and Woman*, 142–43, 159.

13. Peppiatt, *Women and Worship at Corinth*, 45.

14. Peppiatt, *Women and Worship at Corinth*, 34.

15. Peppiatt, *Women and Worship at Corinth*, 34.

16. Peppiatt, *Women and Worship at Corinth*, 10.

17. Payne, *Man and Woman*, 172, citing Wallace, *Grammar* 486 no. 97.

18. Payne, *Man and Woman*, 172.

19. Peppiatt, *Women and Worship at Corinth*, 52.

20. Douglas A. Campbell, *The Deliverance of God: An Apocalyptic Rereading of Justification in Paul* (Grand Rapids, MI: Eerdmans, 2009), 536.

21. Campbell, *Deliverance of God*, 537.

22. Campbell, *Deliverance of God*, 540.

23. Peppiatt, *Women and Worship at Corinth*, 8.

24. Peppiatt, *Women and Worship at Corinth*, 59, citing Jerome Murphy-O'Connor, *Keys to Jerusalem* (Oxford: Oxford University Press, 2012), 131.

25. Peppiatt, *Women and Worship at Corinth*, 102, citing Thomas P. Shoemaker, 'Unveiling of Equality,' *Biblical Theology Bulletin: Journal of Bible and Culture* 17, no. 2 (1987): 61–62.

26. Peppiatt, *Women and Worship at Corinth*, 8.

27. Peppiatt, *Women and Worship at Corinth*, 61.

28. Fee, 'Praying and Prophesying,' 148.

Chapter 4—1 Corinthians 14: Women, Be Silent

1. Philip B. Payne, *Man and Woman, One in Christ* (Grand Rapids, MI: Zondervan, 2009), 218.

2. Payne, *Man and Woman*, 219, quoting from Claude Jenkins, 'Origen on 1 Corinthians IV,' *Journal of Theological Studies* 10 (1909): 40, line 37.

3. Craig S. Keener, 'Learning in the Assemblies: 1 Corinthians 14:34–35,' in *Discovering Biblical Equality, Complementarity without Hierarchy*, ed. Ronald W. Pierce, Rebecca Merrill Groothuis, Gordon D. Fee (Downers Grove, IL: Inter-Varsity Press, 2005), 161.

4. D.A. Carson, '"Silent in the Churches": On the Role of Women in 1 Corinthians 14:33b–36,' in *Recovering Biblical Manhood and Womanhood*, ed. John Piper, Wayne Grudem (Wheaton, IL: Crossway, 2006), 140.

5. Alan F. Johnson, *1 Corinthians* (Downers Grove, IL: Inter-Varsity Press, 2004), 270.

6. Payne, *Man and Woman*, 257.

7. Bruce Winter, '1 Corinthians,' in *New Bible Commentary*, ed. D.A. Carson, R.T. France, J.A. Motyer, G.J. Wenham (Nottingham: Inter-Varsity Press, 1953), 1182.

8. Linda L. Belleville, 'Women in Ministry: An Egalitarian Perspective,' in *Two Views on Women in Ministry*, ed. Stanley N. Gundry, James R. Beck (Grand Rapids, MI: Zondervan, 2005), 76–77.

9. Johnson, *1 Corinthians*, 270–71.

10. Payne, *Man and Woman*, 221.

11. Payne, *Man and Woman*, 221–22.

12. Carson, 'Silent in the Churches,' 145.

13. Payne, *Man and Woman*, 222.

14. Craig S. Keener, *1–2 Corinthians* (Kindle edition) (New York, NY: Cambridge University Press, 2005), loc. 1709.

15. Payne, *Man and Woman*, 222.

16. Carson, 'Silent in the Churches,' 152.

17. Payne, *Man and Woman*, 218.

18. Payne, *Man and Woman*, 219.

19. Lucy Peppiatt, *Women and Worship at Corinth* (Eugene, OR: Cascade Books, 2015), 13.

20. Payne, *Man and Woman*, 219.

21. Gilbert Bilezikian, *Beyond Sex Roles* (Kindle edition) (Grand Rapids, MI: Baker Academic, 2006), 111–12.

22. Bilezikian, *Beyond Sex Roles*, 159 (footnote 27).

23. Peppiatt, *Women and Worship at Corinth*, 8.

24. Bilezikian, *Beyond Sex Roles*, 113.

25. Peppiatt, *Women and Worship at Corinth*, 13.

26. Payne, *Man and Woman*, 225.

27. Belleville, 'Women in Ministry,' 95.

28. Johnson, *1 Corinthians*, 272.

29. There are a number of scholars, including Gordon Fee and Philip Payne, who are proponents of this view.

30. Payne, *Man and Woman*, 225, 235.

31. Payne, *Man and Woman*, 229.

32. Payne, *Man and Woman*, 230.

33. Payne, *Man and Woman*, 233.

34. Payne, *Man and Woman*, 233.

35. Payne, *Man and Woman*, 246.

36. Payne, *Man and Woman*, 252–53, quoting Antoinette Clark Wire, *The Corinthian Women Prophets*, 150.

37. Payne, *Man and Woman*, 251–52.

38. Payne, *Man and Woman*, 263.

Chapter 5—1 Timothy 2: Teaching and Authority

1. Douglas Moo, 'What Does It Mean Not to Teach or Have Authority over Men? 1 Timothy 2:11–15,' in *Recovering Biblical Manhood and Womanhood*, ed. John Piper, Wayne Grudem (Wheaton, IL: Crossway, 2006), 183.

2. Linda L. Belleville, 'Teaching and Usurping Authority: 1 Timothy 2:11–15,' in *Discovering Biblical Equality, Complementarity without Hierarchy*, ed. Ronald W. Pierce, Rebecca Merrill Groothuis, Gordon D. Fee (Downers Grove, IL: Inter-Varsity Press, 2005), 206.

3. Belleville, 'Teaching and Usurping Authority,' 219.

4. Steve Robbins, '1 Timothy 2:8–15: Paul and the "New Roman Women" at Ephesus,' September 2009, St. Johns Vineyard, www.sjvineyard.com/uploads/2/9/4/1/2941034/paul_and_the_new_roman_women.pdf.

5. There are those who use 1 Timothy 3:14–15—'I am writing these things to you so that, if I delay, you may know how one ought to behave in the household of God'—as evidence that the whole letter is written as a sort of 'manual' for church order. Philip Payne very helpfully and solidly refutes this idea in his book *Man and Woman, One in Christ* (Grand Rapids, MI: Zondervan, 2009), 305–10. What is not immediately obvious in the English is that 'you' in verses 14–15 are both singular, i.e., in reference to Timothy and not the community. Furthermore, whilst it is grammatically possible to translate *dei* in verse 15 to be inclusive of the wider community ('how *one* ought to'), given how Paul uses *dei* elsewhere in the New Testament, it is more plausible to keep Timothy the subject of the sentence rather than introducing a new subject (which the Greek does not do). In view of the grammatical structure of this sentence and Paul's usage with the same structure elsewhere, to translate *dei* as 'how one ought to' instead of 'how you (Timothy) ought to' here means we are arbitrarily choosing to make this the one exception of Paul's usage in the New Testament. To further underline his argument, Payne shows how every usage of 'these things' (seen in verse 14) in the letter addresses Timothy, not the whole congregation. Therefore, a more accurate translation here would read: 'I am writing these things to you [Timothy] so that if I delay you might know how

[you—Timothy] should conduct [your]self in the church.' The point being, Paul is writing this letter to help Timothy know what to do in this church context, not intending the letter as a manual of church order for all believers to follow.

6. Craig L. Blomberg, 'Women in Ministry: A Complementarian Perspective,' in *Two Views on Women in Ministry*, ed. Stanley N. Gundry, James R. Beck (Grand Rapids, MI: Zondervan, 2005), 165.

7. Moo, 'Authority over Men,' 189.

8. Payne, *Man and Woman*, 297.

9. Payne, *Man and Woman*, 319.

10. Blomberg, 'Women in Ministry,' 167.

11. Jamin Andrew Hübner, 'A New Case for Female Elders: An Analytical Reformed-Evangelical Approach,' 235, http://uir.unisa.ac.za/bitstream/ handle/10500/14128/thesis_h%FCbner_ja.pdf?sequence=1.

12. Despite general scholarly agreement on the reading of *hēsychia*, Douglas Moo argues that it should be translated 'silence' to come into contrast with verse 12's instruction on teaching (Moo, 'Authority over Men,' 183). Furthermore, he claims that 'ἡσυχία [*hēsychia*] is the only word in his [Paul's] known vocabulary which could clearly denote silence' (Douglas J. Moo, 'The Interpretation of 1 Timothy 2:11–15: A Rejoinder,' *Trinity Journal* 2 NS (1981): 199). However, his rendering ignores how the word is not simply used as a contrast to teaching, but is the framing thought throughout the whole of verses 11–12. Additionally, given Paul's common use of the verb *sigao* elsewhere in his letters and its associated noun *sigé*, which Paul's ministry partner Luke uses six times through Luke and Acts, Moo's assertion that Paul had no knowledge of another word denoting silence seems dubious. If Paul meant an absence of noise including speaking, *sigé* would be the obvious choice as it is the most specific option in the Greek vocabulary to give that meaning. It is unlikely that Paul did not know the noun associated with a verb that he used, a noun which his ministry partner Luke was obviously in knowledge of, a noun that was not rare. If he meant to say women should learn in silence, there was a clearer noun to use at his disposal that would have meant just that. Because of Paul's choice *not* to use the noun that would have most obviously meant silence, as well as taking into account the theme of the chapter and letter at large, and the use of *hēsychios* in verse 2 already in relation to being peaceable, for us to choose to interpret *hēsychia* as 'silence' in verse 11 betrays a desire to elevate the teaching of verse 12, despite good reasons otherwise.

13. Moo, 'Authority over Men,' 183.

14. Payne, *Man and Woman*, 314.

15. Hübner, 'New Case for Female Elders,' 234.

16. Payne, *Man and Woman*, 327.

17. Moo, 'Authority over Men,' 185.

18. Hübner, 'New Case for Female Elders,' 242.

19. Payne, *Man and Woman*, 373, citing Baldwin, *A Difficult Word*, WCFA 78–80; *Important Word*, WCA 45–51; and Schreiner, *Dialogue*, WCA 97, 101, 102, 104.

20. Hübner, 'New Case for Female Elders,' 245.

21. Andreas Köstenberger, 'Was I Wrong on 1 Timothy 2:12?,' www.biblicalfoundations.org/was-i-wrong-on-1-tim-212/.

22. Craig S. Keener, *Paul, Women and Wives* (Kindle edition) (Grand Rapids, MI: Baker Academic, 1992), loc. 2125.

23. Payne, *Man and Woman*, 320.

24. Moo, 'Authority over Men,' 185.

25. Belleville, 'Women in Ministry,' 59.

26. Moo, 'Authority over Men,' 189.

27. Moo, 'Authority over Men,' 190.

28. Payne, *Man and Woman*, 316.

29. Moo, 'Authority over Men,' 191.

30. Moo, 'Authority over Men,' 191.

31. Payne, *Man and Woman*, 301. Further still, Payne quotes Gordon Fee, 'Great Watershed,' 37, on this: 'There is no known instance in Greek where the word *phlyaroi* means "gossips"'.

Chapter 6—1 Timothy 3: A Question of Eldership

1. I use the word *eldership* here because that is the church leadership structure in my context, and because most scholars agree that the office of overseer/bishop described in 1 Timothy 3 and again in Titus 1 are probably synonymous terms with the office of eldership. 'There is general concurrence among scholars that *elder* and *bishop* (meaning "overseer") are equivalent terms on the basis of their interchangeable use in Acts 20:17 (cf. v. 18) and Titus 1:5 (cf. v. 7).' (Gilbert Bilezikian, *Beyond Sex Roles* (Kindle edition) (Grand Rapids, MI: Baker Academic, 2006), 142). Therefore, throughout this chapter, I will use *elder* as an interchangeable term with *overseer* or *bishop*.

2. Wayne Grudem, 'But What Should Women Do in the Church?,' *CBMW News* (November 1995), 1, cbmw.org/wp-content/uploads/2013/05/1-2.pdf.

3. See Belleville's argument in Linda L. Belleville, 'Women in Ministry: An Egalitarian Perspective,' in *Two Views on Women in Ministry*, ed. Stanley N. Gundry, James R. Beck (Grand Rapids, MI: Zondervan, 2005), 69.

4. Craig L. Blomberg, 'A Response to Linda Belleville,' in *Two Views on Women in Ministry*, ed. Stanley N. Gundry, James R. Beck (Grand Rapids, MI: Zondervan, 2005), 117.

5. Susan Foh, 'The Head of the Woman Is the Man,' in *Women in Ministry: Four Views* (Kindle edition), ed. Bonnidell Clouse, Robert G. Clouse (Downers Grove, IL: Inter-Varsity Press, 1989), loc. 1004.

6. Belleville, 'Women in Ministry,' 61.

7. D.A. Carson, '"Silent in the Churches": On the Role of Women in 1 Corinthians 14:33b–36,' in *Recovering Biblical Manhood and Womanhood*, ed. John Piper, Wayne Grudem (Wheaton, IL: Crossway, 2006), 148.

8. Tom Wright, *Paul for Everyone: The Pastoral Letters: 1 and 2 Timothy and Titus* (Kindle edition) (London: SPCK, 2003), loc. 577.

9. Douglas J. Moo, 'The Interpretation of 1 Timothy 2:11–15: A Rejoinder,' *Trinity Journal* 2 NS (1981): 211.

10. Thomas R. Schreiner, 'Philip Payne on Familiar Ground: A Review of Philip B. Payne, Man and Woman, One in Christ: An Exegetical and Theological Study of Paul's Letters,' *Journal for Biblical Manhood and Womanhood* 15, no. 1 (Spring 2010): 35.

11. Marg Mowczko, 'Paul's Qualifications for Church Leaders,' https://margmowczko.com/pauls-qualifications-for-church-leaders/.

12. Philip B. Payne, *Man and Woman, One in Christ* (Grand Rapids, MI: Zondervan, 2009), 447.

13. Payne, *Man and Woman*, 447.

14. Payne, *Man and Woman*, 452, citing Wayne Grudem, EF 263 n. 107.

15. Payne, *Man and Woman*, 452, citing Grudem, EF 263 n. 107.

16. For a full explanation of this, see Payne, *Man and Woman*, 450–52.

17. Payne, *Man and Woman*, 451.

18. Stanley J. Grenz, 'Biblical Priesthood and Women in Ministry,' in *Discovering Biblical Equality, Complementarity without Hierarchy*, ed. Ronald W. Pierce, Rebecca Merrill Groothuis, Gordon D. Fee (Downers Grove, IL: Inter-Varsity Press, 2005), 275.

19. Foh, 'Head of the Woman,' loc. 1036.

20. Grenz, 'Biblical Priesthood,' 276.

21. Jamin Andrew Hübner, 'A New Case for Female Elders: An Analytical Reformed-Evangelical Approach,' 322, http://uir.unisa.ac.za/bitstream /handle/10500/14128/thesis_h%FCbner_ja.pdf?sequence=1.

Chapter 7—Ephesians 5: Marriage

1. Timothy Gombis, *The Drama of Ephesians* (Kindle edition) (Downers Grove, IL: Inter-Varsity Press Academic, 2010), 19.

2. Watchman Nee, *Sit, Walk, Stand: The Process of Christian Maturity* (Kindle edition) (Fort Washington, PA: CLC, 2009), 64.

3. Philip B. Payne, *Man and Woman, One in Christ* (Grand Rapids, MI: Zondervan, 2009), 271.

4. Payne, *Man and Woman*, 271.

5. I. Howard Marshall, 'Mutual Love and Submission in Marriage: Colossians 3:18–19 and Ephesians 5:21–33,' in *Discovering Biblical Equality, Complementarity without Hierarchy*, ed. Ronald W. Pierce, Rebecca Merrill Groothuis, Gordon D. Fee (Downers Grove, IL: Inter-Varsity Press, 2005), 186.

6. Payne, *Man and Woman*, 278.

7. Payne, *Man and Woman*, 278.

8. Wayne Grudem, 'Notes,' in *Recovering Biblical Manhood and Womanhood*, ed. John Piper, Wayne Grudem (Wheaton, IL: Crossway, 2006), 493.

9. Grudem, 'Notes,' 493.

10. For a fuller argument on this, see Payne, *Man and Woman*, 282.

11. Grudem, 'Notes,' 493.

12. Payne, *Man and Woman*, 280.

13. Payne, *Man and Woman*, 279.

14. Payne, *Man and Woman*, 281.

15. George W. Knight III, 'Husbands and Wives as Analogues of Christ and the Church: Ephesians 5:21–33 and Colossians 3:18–19,' in *Recovering Biblical Manhood and Womanhood*, ed. John Piper, Wayne Grudem (Wheaton, IL: Crossway, 2006), 167.

16. Payne, *Man and Woman*, 278, 283.

17. Thomas R. Schreiner, 'A Response to Linda Belleville,' in *Two Views on Women in Ministry*, ed. Stanley N. Gundry, James R. Beck (Grand Rapids, MI: Zondervan, 2005), 106.

18. Gordon D. Fee, 'Praying and Prophesying in the Assemblies: 1 Corinthians 11:2–16,' in *Discovering Biblical Equality, Complementarity without Hierarchy*, ed. Ronald W. Pierce, Rebecca Merrill Groothuis, Gordon D. Fee (Downers Grove, IL: Inter-Varsity Press, 2005), 154.

19. Marshall, 'Mutual Love and Submission,' 198.

20. Jamin Andrew Hübner, 'A New Case for Female Elders: An Analytical Reformed-Evangelical Approach,' 370, http://uir.unisa.ac.za/bitstream/handle /10500/14128/thesis_h%FCbner_ja.pdf?sequence=1.

21. Gilbert Bilezikian, *Beyond Sex Roles* (Kindle edition) (Grand Rapids, MI: Baker Academic, 2006), 122.

22. Payne, *Man and Woman*, 119.

23. Hübner, 'New Case for Female Elders,' 369–70.

24. Hübner, 'New Case for Female Elders,' 367–68.

25. Bilezikian, *Beyond Sex Roles*, 97.

26. Payne, *Man and Woman*, 272–73.

27. Marshall, 'Mutual Love and Submission,' 202.

28. Marshall, 'Mutual Love and Submission,' 192.

29. Marshall, 'Mutual Love and Submission,' 199.

30. Bilezikian, *Beyond Sex Roles*, 121.

Chapter 8—Women in the New Testament

1. Craig S. Keener, *Paul, Women and Wives* (Kindle edition) (Grand Rapids, MI: Baker Academic, 1992), loc. 3564.

2. Gilbert Bilezikian, *Beyond Sex Roles* (Kindle edition) (Grand Rapids, MI: Baker Academic, 2006), 91.

3. See how this was a challenge for Timothy in his ministry (1 Tim. 4:12).

4. Craig L. Blomberg, 'Women in Ministry: A Complementarian Perspective,' in *Two Views on Women in Ministry*, ed. Stanley N. Gundry, James R. Beck (Grand Rapids, MI: Zondervan, 2005), 145.

5. Bilezikian, *Beyond Sex Roles*, 93.

6. Jamin Andrew Hübner, 'A New Case for Female Elders: An Analytical Reformed-Evangelical Approach,' 289, http://uir.unisa.ac.za/bitstream /handle/10500/14128/thesis_h%FCbner_ja.pdf?sequence=1.

7. Thomas R. Schreiner, 'A Response to Craig Blomberg,' in *Two Views on Women in Ministry*, ed. Stanley N. Gundry, James R. Beck (Grand Rapids, MI: Zondervan, 2005), 191.

8. Blomberg, 'Women in Ministry,' 152.

9. Blomberg, 'Women in Ministry,' 152.

10. Blomberg, 'Women in Ministry,' 153.

11. Blomberg, 'Women in Ministry,' 154.

12. Tom Wright, *Paul for Everyone: Galatians and Thessalonians* (Kindle edition) (London: SPCK, 2002), 41.

13. Bilezikian, *Beyond Sex Roles*, 94.

14. Blomberg, 'Women in Ministry,' 146.

15. Hübner, 'New Case for Female Elders,' 321.

16. Derek Morphew, *Different but Equal: Going Beyond the Complementarian/ Egalitarian Debate* (Kindle edition) (Bergvliet: Derek Morphew Publications, 2011), loc. 1894, citing E.E. Ellis, *Prophecy and Hermeneutic in Early Christianity*, 141.

17. Linda L. Belleville, 'Women in Ministry: An Egalitarian Perspective,' in *Two Views on Women in Ministry*, ed. Stanley N. Gundry, James R. Beck (Grand Rapids, MI: Zondervan, 2005), 54.

18. Craig S. Keener, 'Women in Ministry: Another Egalitarian Perspective,' in *Two Views on Women in Ministry*, ed. Stanley N. Gundry, James R. Beck (Grand Rapids, MI: Zondervan, 2005), 215.

19. Thomas R. Schreiner, 'Women in Ministry: Another Complementarian Perspective,' in *Two Views on Women in Ministry*, ed. Stanley N. Gundry, James R. Beck (Grand Rapids, MI: Zondervan, 2005), 280.

20. Blomberg, 'Women in Ministry,' 148.

21. Schreiner, 'Women in Ministry,' 281.

22. Belleville, 'Women in Ministry,' 61.

23. Schreiner, 'A Response to Craig Blomberg,' 191.

24. Craig S. Keener, *Paul, Women and Wives* (Kindle edition) (Grand Rapids, MI: Baker Academic, 1992), loc. 3603, citing Streeter, *Woman*, 63.

25. Blomberg, 'Women in Ministry,' 147.

26. Belleville, 'Women in Ministry,' 59.

27. Blomberg 'Women in Ministry,' 147.

28. Thomas R. Schreiner, 'The Valuable Ministries of Women in the Context of Male Leadership: A Survey of Old and New Testament Examples and Teaching,' in *Recovering Biblical Manhood and Womanhood*, ed. John Piper, Wayne Grudem (Wheaton, IL: Crossway, 2006), 221.

29. Belleville, 'Women in Ministry,' 39–40.

30. Belleville, 'Women in Ministry,' 41.

31. Schreiner, 'Women in Ministry,' 286.

32. Belleville, 'Women in Ministry,' 41.

33. Belleville, 'Women in Ministry,' 42.

34. Belleville, 'Women in Ministry,' 42.

35. Blomberg, 'Women in Ministry,' 149.

36. Thomas R. Schreiner, 'A Response to Linda Belleville,' in *Two Views on Women in Ministry*, ed. Stanley N. Gundry, James R. Beck (Grand Rapids, MI: Zondervan, 2005), 105.

37. Blomberg, 'Women in Ministry,' 149–50.

38. Keener, 'Response to Craig Blomberg,' 186.

39. Hübner, 'New Case for Female Elders,' 403.

40. Thomas R. Schreiner, 'The Valuable Ministries of Women in the Context of Male Leadership: A Survey of Old and New Testament Examples and Teaching,' in *Recovering Biblical Manhood and Womanhood*, 221.

41. Keener, 'Women in Ministry,' 214.

Chapter 9—Gender Equality and the Trinity

1. Wayne Grudem, *Bible Doctrine: Essential Teachings of the Christian Faith* (Leicester: Inter-Varsity Press, 1999), 116.

2. Grudem, *Bible Doctrine*, 121, 122.

3. Kevin Giles, 'The Nicene and Reformed Doctrine of the Trinity,' www.patheos .com/blogs/jesuscreed/2016/11/23/kevin-giles-the-ets-response-to-grudem-and -ware/.

4. Grudem, *Bible Doctrine*, 121.

5. Millard J. Erickson, *Who's Tampering with the Trinity? An Assessment of the Subordination Debate* (Kindle edition) (Grand Rapids, MI: Kregel, 2009), loc. 1465.

6. Giles, 'Doctrine of the Trinity.'

7. See Erickson, *Who's Tampering with the Trinity?*, loc. 1461–82.

8. Giles, 'Doctrine of the Trinity.'

9. Kevin Giles, 'The Subordination of Christ and the Subordination of Women,' in *Discovering Biblical Equality, Complementarity without Hierarchy*, ed. Ronald W. Pierce, Rebecca Merrill Groothuis, Gordon D. Fee (Downers Grove, IL: Inter-Varsity Press, 2005), 335.

10. Giles, 'Subordination of Christ,' 337.

11. Grudem, *Bible Doctrine,* 116.

12. Giles, 'Doctrine of the Trinity.'

13. Bruce A. Ware, *Father, Son & Holy Spirit: Relationships, Roles and Relevance* (Wheaton, IL: Crossway, 2005), 72.

14. Ware, *Father, Son & Holy Spirit*, 77.

15. Giles, 'Doctrine of the Trinity.'

16. Giles, 'Doctrine of the Trinity.'

17. Ware, *Father, Son & Holy Spirit*, 77.

18. For a more thorough review of these and other scriptures, see Erickson, *Who's Tampering with the Trinity?*, loc. 1239–1355.

19. Erickson, *Who's Tampering with the Trinity?*, loc. 1373.

20. Erickson, *Who's Tampering with the Trinity?*, loc. 1617, citing Augustine, *On the Trinity*, 2.5.9.

21. Gilbert Bilezikian, 'Hermeneutical Bungee-Jumping: Subordination in the Godhead,' *Journal of the Evangelical Theological Society* 40, no. 1 (March 1997): 59, www.etsjets.org/files/JETS-PDFs/40/40-1/40-1-pp057-068_JETS.pdf.

22. Bilezikian, 'Hermeneutical Bungee-Jumping,' 65.

23. Erickson, *Who's Tampering with the Trinity?*, loc. 1124, citing Wayne Grudem, *Evangelical Feminism*, 412.

24. Erickson, *Who's Tampering with the Trinity?*, loc. 1144, citing Grudem, *Evangelical Feminism*, 414.

25. Erickson, *Who's Tampering with the Trinity?*, loc. 1388, citing John Calvin, *Commentary on the Epistles of Paul the Apostle to the Corinthians*, 2:32–33.

26. Erickson, *Who's Tampering with the Trinity?*, loc. 1393, citing Charles Hodge, *An Exposition of the First Epistle to the Corinthians*, 333–34.

27. Erickson, *Who's Tampering with the Trinity?*, loc. 1589, citing Augustine, *On the Trinity*, 1.11.22–23.

28. Erickson, *Who's Tampering with the Trinity?*, loc. 1607, citing Augustine, *On the Trinity*, 1.7.14.

29. Bruce A. Ware, 'Equal in Essence, Distinct in Roles: Eternal Functional Authority and Submission among the Essentially Equal Divine Persons of the Godhead,' *Journal for Biblical Manhood and Womanhood* 13, no. 2 (Fall 2008): 52, citing Novatian, *A Treatise of Novatian concerning the Trinity*, 27 in *Ante-Nicene Fathers*, vol. 5, 638.

30. Ware, 'Equal in Essence,' 52.

31. Erickson, *Who's Tampering with the Trinity?*, loc. 1461.

32. Kevin Giles, 'The Subordination of Christ and the Subordination of Women,' in *Discovering Biblical Equality, Complementarity without Hierarchy*, 346, citing Charles Hodge, *Systematic Theology* (Edinburgh: T&T Clark, 1960), 1:464.

33. Bilezikian, 'Hermeneutical Bungee-Jumping,' 64, citing Robert Letham, 'The Man-Woman Debate: Theological Comment,' *Westminster Theological Journal* 52, no. 1 (1990): 68.

34. Erickson, *Who's Tampering with the Trinity?*, loc. 1764.

Chapter 10—Egalitarianism in Practice

1. Derek Morphew, *Different but Equal: Going Beyond the Complementarian/Egalitarian Debate* (Kindle edition) (Bergvliet: Derek Morphew Publications, 2011), loc. 766.

2. Morphew, *Different but Equal*, loc. 1041.

3. Morphew, *Different but Equal*, loc. 924.

4. Morphew, *Different but Equal*, loc. 945.

5. Jordan Peterson, 'Mayhem While We're Freezing and Starving,' 18 March 2017, talk given at University of Western Ontario, from 27:43, www.youtube.com /watch?v=fBsR7-SiLPY.

6. Peterson, 'Mayhem While We're Freezing,' from 29:30.

7. I am aware that the LGBTQ community represents a broad range of sexual expressions and preferences that I cannot possibly hope to cover in this section. For simplicity and brevity, I will focus on the arguments raised for

homosexuality as these tend to be the ones that are seen to reflect similar arguments in the gender debate. Please be aware that my focus is not intended to disregard a wider range of sexual orientations, but is simply intended to help keep this chapter engaged with the wider purposes of this book.

8. Catherine Clark Kroeger, 'Does Belief in Women's Equality Lead to an Acceptance of Homosexual Practice?,' *Priscilla Papers* 18, no. 2 (Spring 2004).

9. Richard B. Hays, *The Moral Vision of the New Testament: Community, Cross, New Creation, A Contemporary Introduction to New Testament Ethics* (New York, NY: HarperCollins, 1996), 389.

10. Hays, *Moral Vision of the New Testament*, 395.

11. William J. Webb, *Slaves, Women and Homosexuals* (Kindle edition) (Downers Grove, IL: Inter-Varsity Press, 2001), 107–9.

12. Webb, *Slaves, Women and Homosexuals*, 105–6.

Conclusion

1. Nicholas D. Kristof and Sheryl WuDunn, *Half the Sky: How to Change the World* (Kindle edition) (London: Hachette Digital, 2010), loc. 162.

2. Kristof and WuDunn, *Half the Sky*, loc. 129.

3. Kristof and WuDunn, *Half the Sky*, loc. 137.

4. Kristof and WuDunn, *Half the Sky*, loc. 142.

5. Kristof and WuDunn, *Half the Sky*, loc. 159.

BIBLIOGRAPHY

Bailey, Kenneth. E. *Finding the Lost Cultural Keys to Luke 15* (Kindle edition) (St. Louis, MO: Concordia, 1992).

Bailey, Kenneth. E. *Jesus through Middle Eastern Eyes* (London: SPCK, 2008).

Bailey, Kenneth. E. *Paul through Middle Eastern Eyes* (Kindle edition) (London: SPCK, 2011).

Belleville, Linda L. 'Teaching and Usurping Authority: 1 Timothy 2:11–15,' in *Discovering Biblical Equality, Complementarity without Hierarchy*, ed. Ronald W. Pierce, Rebecca Merrill Groothuis, Gordon D. Fee (Downers Grove, IL: Inter-Varsity Press, 2005).

Belleville, Linda L. 'Women in Ministry: An Egalitarian Perspective,' in *Two Views on Women in Ministry*, ed. Stanley N. Gundry, James R. Beck (Grand Rapids, MI: Zondervan, 2005).

Bilezikian, Gilbert. *Beyond Sex Roles* (Kindle edition) (Grand Rapids, MI: Baker Academic, 2006).

Bilezikian, Gilbert. 'Hermeneutical Bungee-Jumping: Subordination in the Godhead,' *Journal of the Evangelical Theological Society* 40, no. 1 (1997), 57–68, www.etsjets.org/files/JETS-PDFs/40/40-1/40-1-pp057-068_JETS.pdf.

Blomberg, Craig. L. 'A Response to Linda Belleville,' in *Two Views on Women in Ministry*, ed. Stanley N. Gundry, James R. Beck (Grand Rapids, MI: Zondervan, 2005).

Blomberg, Craig. L. 'Women in Ministry: A Complementarian Perspective,' in *Two Views on Women in Ministry*, ed. Stanley N. Gundry, James R. Beck (Grand Rapids, MI: Zondervan, 2005).

Borland, James A. 'Women in the Life and Teachings of Jesus,' in *Recovering Biblical Manhood and Womanhood*, ed. John Piper, Wayne Grudem (Wheaton, IL: Crossway, 2006).

Campbell, Douglas A. *The Deliverance of God: An Apocalyptic Rereading of Justification in Paul* (Grand Rapids, MI: Eerdmans, 2009).

Carson, D.A. '"Silent in the Churches": On the Role of Women in 1 Corinthians 14:33b–36,' in *Recovering Biblical Manhood and Womanhood*, ed. John Piper, Wayne Grudem (Wheaton, IL: Crossway, 2006).

Erickson, Millard J. *Who's Tampering with the Trinity? An Assessment of the Subordination Debate* (Kindle edition) (Grand Rapids, MI: Kregel, 2009).

Fee, Gordon D. 'Praying and Prophesying in the Assemblies: 1 Corinthians 11:2–16,' in *Discovering Biblical Equality, Complementarity without Hierarchy*, ed. Ronald W. Pierce, Rebecca Merrill Groothuis, Gordon D. Fee (Downers Grove, IL: Inter-Varsity Press, 2005).

Foh, Susan. 'The Head of the Woman is the Man,' in *Women in Ministry: Four Views* (Kindle edition), ed. Bonnidell Clouse, Robert G. Clouse (Downers Grove, IL: Inter-Varsity Press, 1989).

Giles, Kevin. 'The Nicene and Reformed Doctrine of the Trinity,' a paper given by Kevin Giles at the plenary forum on the Trinity at the Evangelical Theological Society annual conference, 15 November 2016 at San Antonia, www.patheos.com/blogs/jesuscreed/2016/11/23/kevin-giles-the-ets-response-to-grudem-and-ware/.

Giles, Kevin. 'The Subordination of Christ and the Subordination of Women,' in *Discovering Biblical Equality, Complementarity without Hierarchy*, ed. Ronald W. Pierce, Rebecca Merrill Groothuis, Gordon D. Fee (Downers Grove, IL: Inter-Varsity Press, 2005).

Gombis, Timothy. *The Drama of Ephesians* (Kindle edition) (Downers Grove, IL: Inter-Varsity Press Academic, 2010).

Grenz, Stanley. 'Biblical Priesthood and Women in Ministry,' in *Discovering Biblical Equality, Complementarity without Hierarchy*, ed. Ronald W. Pierce, Rebecca Merrill Groothuis, Gordon D. Fee (Downers Grove, IL: Inter-Varsity Press, 2005).

Grudem, Wayne. *Bible Doctrine: Essential Teachings of the Christian Faith* (Leicester: Inter-Varsity Press, 1999).

Grudem, Wayne. 'But What Should Women Do in the Church?,' *CBMW News* (November 1995), http://cbmw.org/wp-content/uploads/2013/05/1-2.pdf.

Grudem, Wayne. 'Notes,' in *Recovering Biblical Manhood and Womanhood*, ed. John Piper, Wayne Grudem (Wheaton, IL: Crossway, 2006).

Gushee, David P. and Stassen, Glen, H. *Kingdom Ethics: Following Jesus in Contemporary Context, Second edition* (Kindle edition) (Grand Rapids, MI: Eerdmans, 2016).

Hays, Richard B. *The Moral Vision of the New Testament: Community, Cross, New Creation, A Contemporary Introduction to New Testament Ethics* (New York, NY: HarperCollins, 1996).

Hess, Richard S. 'Equality with and without Innocence: Genesis 1–3,' in *Discovering Biblical Equality, Complementarity without Hierarchy*, ed. Ronald W. Pierce, Rebecca Merrill Groothuis, Gordon D. Fee (Downers Grove, IL: Inter-Varsity Press, 2005).

Hübner, Jamin Andrew. 'A New Case for Female Elders: An Analytical Reformed-Evangelical Approach,' http://uir.unisa.ac.za/bitstream/handle/10500/14128 /thesis_h%FCbner_ja.pdf?sequence=1.

Johnson, Alan F. *1 Corinthians* (Downers Grove, IL: Inter-Varsity Press, 2004).

Keener, Craig S. 'A Response to Craig Blomberg,' in *Two Views on Women in Ministry*, ed. Stanley N. Gundry, James R. Beck (Grand Rapids, MI: Zondervan, 2005).

Keener, Craig S. *1–2 Corinthians* (Kindle edition) (New York, NY: Cambridge University Press, 2005).

Keener, Craig S. 'Learning in the Assemblies: 1 Corinthians 14:34–35,' in *Discovering Biblical Equality, Complementarity without Hierarchy*, ed. Ronald W. Pierce, Rebecca Merrill Groothuis, Gordon D. Fee (Downers Grove, IL: Inter-Varsity Press, 2005).

Keener, Craig S. *Paul, Women and Wives* (Kindle edition) (Grand Rapids, MI: Baker Academic, 1992).

Keener, Craig S. 'Women in Ministry: Another Egalitarian Perspective,' in *Two Views on Women in Ministry*, ed. Stanley N. Gundry, James R. Beck (Grand Rapids, MI: Zondervan, 2005).

Kernaghan, R.J. *Mark* (Downers Grove, IL: Inter-Varsity Press, 2007).

Knight III, George W. 'Husbands and Wives as Analogues of Christ and the Church: Ephesians 5:21–33 and Colossians 3:18–19,' in *Recovering Biblical Manhood and Womanhood*, ed. John Piper, Wayne Grudem (Wheaton, IL Crossway, 2006).

Kristof, Nicholas D. and WuDunn, Sheryl. *Half the Sky: How to Change the World* (Kindle edition) (London: Hachette Digital, 2010).

Kroeger, Catherine Clark. 'Does Belief in Women's Equality Lead to an Acceptance of Homosexual Practice?,' *Priscilla Papers* 18, no. 2 (Spring 2004).

Köstenberger, Andreas. 'Was I Wrong on 1 Timothy 2:12?,' www.biblicalfoundations.org/was-i-wrong-on-1-tim-212/.

Marshall, I. Howard. 'Mutual Love and Submission in Marriage: Colossians 3:18–19 and Ephesians 5:21–33,' in *Discovering Biblical Equality, Complementarity without Hierarchy*, ed. Ronald W. Pierce, Rebecca Merrill Groothuis, Gordon D. Fee (Downers Grove, IL: Inter-Varsity Press, 2005).

Moo, Douglas J. 'The Interpretation of 1 Timothy 2:11–15: A Rejoinder,' *Trinity Journal* 2 NS (1981), 198–222.

Moo, Douglas J. 'What Does It Mean Not to Teach or Have Authority over Men? 1 Timothy 2:11–15,' in *Recovering Biblical Manhood and Womanhood*, ed. John Piper, Wayne Grudem (Wheaton, IL: Crossway, 2006).

Morphew, Derek. *Different but Equal: Going Beyond the Complementarian/Egalitarian Debate* (Kindle edition) (Bergvliet: Derek Morphew Publications, 2011).

Mowczko, Marg. 'Paul's Qualifications for Church Leaders,' https://margmowczko .com/pauls-qualifications-for-church-leaders/.

Nee, Watchman. *Sit, Walk, Stand: The Process of Christian Maturity* (Kindle edition) (Fort Washington, PA: CLC, 2009).

Payne, Philip B. *Man and Woman, One in Christ* (Grand Rapids, MI: Zondervan, 2009).

Peppiatt, Lucy. *Women and Worship at Corinth* (Eugene, OR: Cascade Books, 2015).

Peterson, Jordan. 'Mayhem While We're Freezing and Starving,' 18 March 2017, talk given at University of Western Ontario, www.youtube.com/watch?v =fBsR7-SiLPY.

Prior, David. *The Message of 1 Corinthians* (Nottingham: Inter-Varsity Press, 1985).

Robbins, Steve. '1 Timothy 2:8–15: Paul and the "New Roman Women" at Ephesus,' September 2009, St. Johns Vineyard, www.sjvineyard.com/uploads /2/9/4/1/2941034/paul_and_the_new_roman_women.pdf.

Schreiner, Thomas. R. 'A Response to Craig Blomberg,' in *Two Views on Women in Ministry*, ed. Stanley N. Gundry, James R. Beck (Grand Rapids, MI: Zondervan, 2005).

Schreiner, Thomas. R. 'A Response to Linda Belleville,' in *Two Views on Women in Ministry*, ed. Stanley N. Gundry, James R. Beck (Grand Rapids, MI: Zondervan, 2005).

Schreiner, Thomas. R. 'Philip Payne on Familiar Ground: A Review of Philip B. Payne, Man and Woman, One in Christ: An Exegetical and Theological Study of Paul's Letters,' *Journal for Biblical Manhood and Womanhood* 15, no. 1 (Spring 2010): 33–46.

Schreiner, Thomas. R. 'The Valuable Ministries of Women in the Context of Male Leadership: A Survey of Old and New Testament Examples and Teaching,' in *Recovering Biblical Manhood and Womanhood*, ed. John Piper, Wayne Grudem (Wheaton, IL: Crossway, 2006).

Schreiner, Thomas. R. 'Women in Ministry: Another Complementarian Perspective,' in *Two Views on Women in Ministry*, ed. Stanley N. Gundry, James R. Beck (Grand Rapids, MI: Zondervan, 2005).

Spencer, Aída Besançon. 'Jesus' Treatment of Women in the Gospels,' in *Discovering Biblical Equality, Complementarity without Hierarchy*, ed. Ronald W. Pierce, Rebecca Merrill Groothuis, Gordon D. Fee (Downers Grove, IL: Inter-Varsity Press, 2005).

Strickland, Danielle. *The Liberating Truth* (Kindle edition) (Oxford: Monarch, 2011).

Swidler, Leonard. 'Jesus Was a Feminist,' God's Word to Women, www.godswordtowomen.org/feminist.htm.

Ware, Bruce. A. 'Equal in Essence, Distinct in Roles: Eternal Functional Authority and Submission among the Essentially Equal Divine Persons of the Godhead,' *Journal for Biblical Manhood and Womanhood* 13, no. 2 (Fall 2008): 43–58.

Ware, Bruce. A. *Father, Son & Holy Spirit: Relationships, Roles and Relevance* (Wheaton, IL: Crossway, 2005).

Webb, William J. *Slaves, Women and Homosexuals* (Kindle edition) (Downers Grove, IL: Inter-Varsity Press, 2001).

Winter, Bruce. '1 Corinthians,' in *New Bible Commentary*, ed. D.A. Carson, R.T. France, J.A. Motyer, G.J. Wenham (Nottingham: Inter-Varsity Press, 1953).

Wright, Tom. *Paul for Everyone: Galatians and Thessalonians* (Kindle edition) (London: SPCK, 2002).

Wright, Tom. *Paul for Everyone: The Pastoral Letters: 1 and 2 Timothy and Titus* (Kindle edition) (London: SPCK, 2003).

Wright, Tom. *Surprised by Scripture* (London: SPCK, 2014).

BIBLE CREDITS